*The Politics
of the
FEMINIST
NOVEL*

**Recent Titles in
Contributions in Women's Studies**

The World of Women's Trade Unionism: Comparative Historical Essays
Norbert C. Soldon, editor

Traditionalism, Nationalism, and Feminism: Women Writers of Quebec
Paul Gilbert Lewis, editor

Only Mothers Know: Patterns of Infant Feeding
Dana Raphael and Flora Davis

"Give to the Winds Thy Fears": The Women's Temperance Crusade, 1873–1874
Jack S. Blocker Jr.

Film Feminisms: Theory and Practice
Mary C. Gentile

At the Very Least She Pays the Rent: Women and German Industrialization, 1871–1914
Barbara Franzoi

With Ears Opening Like Morning Glories: Eudora Welty and the Love of Storytelling
Carol S. Manning

Growing Up Female: Adolescent Girlhood in American Fiction
Barbara A. White

From Crime to Choice: The Transformation of Abortion in America
Nanette J. Davis

Silence and Narrative: The Early Novels of Gertrude Stein
Janis L. Doane

The Great American Housewife: From Helpmate to Wage Earner, 1776–1986
Annegret S. Ogden

The Ottoman Lady: A Social History From 1718 to 1918
Fanny Davis

Leading the Way: Amy Morris Homans and The Beginnings of Professional Education for Women
Betty Spears

The Politics of the FEMINIST NOVEL

Judi M. Roller

CONTRIBUTIONS IN WOMEN'S STUDIES,
NUMBER 63

GREENWOOD PRESS

NEW YORK
WESTPORT, CONNECTICUT
LONDON

64831

APR 2 7 1987

Library of Congress Cataloging-in-Publication Data

Roller, Judi M.
The politics of the feminist novel.

(Contributions in women's studies, ISSN 0147–104X ; no. 63)
Bibliography: p.
Includes index.
1. American fiction—Women authors—History and criticism. 2. Feminism in literature. 3. English fiction—Women authors—History and criticism.
4. American fiction—20th century—History and criticism. 5. English fiction—20th century—History and criticism. 6. Politics in literature. 7. Women in literature. 8. Sex role in literature. I. Title.
II. Series.
PS374.F45R65   1986   813'.009'9287   85-12718
ISBN 0-313-24663-7 (lib. bdg. : alk paper)
ISBN 0-313-25445-1 (pbk.)

Copyright © 1986 by Judi M. Roller

All rights reserved. No portion of this book may be reproduced, by any process or technique, without the express written consent of the publisher.

Library of Congress Catalog Card Number: 85-12718
ISBN: 0–313–24663–7
ISBN: 0-313-25445-1 (pbk.)
ISSN: 0147–104X

First published in 1986

Greenwood Press, Inc.
88 Post Road West
Westport, Connecticut 06881

Printed in the United States of America

The paper used in this book complies with the Permanent Paper Standard issued by the National Information Standards Organization (Z39.48–1984).

10 9 8 7 6 5 4 3 2 1

Copyright Acknowledgments

The publisher and author gratefully acknowledge permission to reprint excerpts from the following:

Simone de Beauvoir, *The Second Sex*, trans. and ed. H. M. Parshley. Copyright © 1953, reprinted 1974. Alfred A. Knopf, Inc.

Doris Lessing, *The Golden Notebook*. Copyright © 1962 by Doris Lessing. Reprinted by permission of SIMON & SCHUSTER, Inc. (U.S. rights.) Doris Lessing, *The Golden Notebook*, reprinted by permission of Michael Joseph. (World rights exclusive of the U.S.A.)

Mary McCarthy, *The Company She Keeps*. Reprinted by permission of the author and William Heinemann Ltd.

Louise Meriwether, *Daddy Was A Number Runner*, 1971 edition. Reprinted by permission of the author.

Judith Rossner, *Looking for Mr. Goodbar*. Reprinted by permission of SIMON & SCHUSTER, Inc.

From *The Man Who Loved Children* by Christina Stead. Copyright 1940, © 1968 by Christina Stead. Reprinted by permission of Holt, Rinehart and Winston, Publishers. (Open market territory exclusive of the British Commonwealth.)

Christina Stead, *The Man Who Loved Children*. Copyright © 1940, reprinted 1966. Martin Seeker & Warburg Limited. (British Commonwealth.)

Helen Yglesias, *How She Died*. Copyright © 1972 by Helen Yglesias. Reprinted by permission of Bernice Hoffman Agency.

Excerpts from SMALL CHANGES by Marge Piercy. Copyright © 1972, 1973 by Marge Piercy. Reprinted by permission of Doubleday & Company, Inc. (U.S., Canada, P.I., Open Market.) Reprinted with permission of Wallace & Shiel Agency, Inc. (Rights outside of the U.S. and Canada.)

Acknowledgment

The author also gratefully acknowledges a Wright State University College of Liberal Arts Research Grant, which helped make this volume possible.

For: Alice, Alice, Beth, Carl, Carol, Dave, Dossie, Eleanor, Frances, Genevieve, Jan, Jo, Karol, Kathy, Linda, Linda, Marian, Marilyn, Nancy, Nancy, Pat, Rachel, Ramona, Robin, Rosalee, Rosie, Sharon, Susan, Susan, Vicky, Virginia, Virginia, and Zola.

Contents

1. The Awakening 3
2. Authority and Autobiography 33
3. Fragmentation Versus Unity: The Shattered Novel 67
4. The Endings 101
5. Portrayals of Slavery and Freedom 137
6. Conclusion 181
Appendix: Critical Literature on the Political Novel 189
Bibliography 195
Index 203

*The Politics
of the
FEMINIST
NOVEL*

1
The Awakening

The argument that accurate character portrayals are a result of an author's greatness, not an outcome of his or her sex,[1] can lead to the conclusion that there is no need to focus on an author's sex. This viewpoint may have a certain validity, but one must add that many women agree with Isadora Wing that the women characters men create never represent anyone with whom the female reader can identify.[2] Differences in the development of female characters are only one of many disunities between novels written by male and female authors. These divergences result in part from women's separation from their societies and from a subsequently altered vision, a vision that argues against Simone de Beauvoir's statement that woman "cannot oppose positive truths and values of her own to those asserted and upheld by males; she can only deny them."[3] Not only can she assert them; she is doing so. Perhaps there are some benefits to be derived from having been separated from a dominant culture. Possibly it is because of this separation that de Beauvoir can observe of Stendhal's characters: "The so-called serious man is really futile, because he accepts ready-made justifications for his life; whereas a passionate and profound woman revises established values from moment to moment."[4] Perhaps, too, female authors can say of their societies as Lessing's Anna says of recent European history, "I wasn't part of it, and haven't had something destroyed in me."[5]

If one views the nation as an abstraction and sees its character as formed by the groups within it,[6] then it is possible that the same groups of people in different countries may exhibit many similarities as well as differences. For example, women everywhere live in more or less patriarchal societies; and women everywhere are more or less discriminated against. For this reason, female ideologies, such as feminism, may not be as culturally bound as other political beliefs, and it is likely that nationalistic influences may be of less importance in feminist novels than in other political works. Critics have suggested that in women's writings in general nationality may not be as important as it is elsewhere;[7] and, even further, that the human component to literature is more easily discussed by women nationally foreign to one another than by any woman with any man.[8] Because of this international quality in the experience of women, in the political attitudes they hold, and in feminism itself, studies of feminist novels need not be restricted only to those written by women sharing a common nationality nor even necessarily a common language. The American, British, Canadian, and Australian feminist novels included here do have a cohesion afforded by a joint language; but the authors' cultures also share a capitalistic economic system, a political heritage based upon the ideal of equal representation, and a similar patriarchal and hierarchical social system.

Perhaps the feminist novel has developed at least in part because "Neither the psychological nor the sociological novel is a form adequate to express the neo-feminist conception of woman, for she is not only a psyche, but a political being; not only a product and victim of her culture, but also a personal being who transcends it."[9] Whatever the reasons for the appearance of the feminist novel in the twentieth century, it has several characteristics that bind it together as a type of political novel. As one critic states, "feminist novels may perhaps be distinguished from androgynous novels in at least one way: in androgynous novels, the reader identifies with the male and female characters equally; in feminist novels, only with the female hero."[10] In fact, the central character or characters in a feminist novel must be female and must represent women generally as well as a woman specifically. In so drawing their characters, all the authors of feminist novels implicitly or explicitly portray women as a group oppressed. The best have somehow avoided attributing all meaning and importance either to the group alone or to the sole concerns of the private individual. They have dealt "with the disparity between the overwhelming problems of war, famine, poverty, and the tiny individual who [tries] to mirror them."[11] The implication is that human problems are collective as well as individual.

In addition, struggles between individuals, especially between individual men and women, illuminate or suggest the power relationships existing between groups. Such grapplings for control between characters can be called political battles when the characters function as representatives of men and women in general. The experiences of the women in the novels reviewed here do not support the genial notion that women really rule everything and that sex can buy power. Rather, in patriarchal societies where one group, men, controls another group, women, individual relationships between men and women are shown to be power-structured.

Further, the situations existing in these novels are presented as dependent, at least to some extent, upon economic, political, and social systems. The status of women with relation to these structures is that of a minority group. The relegation of a group to minority status does not depend upon its size or proportion of the population but upon its subordination. Similarly, a majority group need not be defined as a majority of a population but as a dominant social group equipped with the power to maintain its dominance. The stereotypes the majority group forms of various minority groups develop to fit its purposes and express its anxieties.[12] Because of the majority group's dominance and control over social, economic, and political institutions, the minorities are disadvantaged by those structures. This is the general view of the position of women implicitly or explicitly expressed in the feminist novel.

Frequently, the central character in the feminist novel is mad, but the character's personal madness is connected with public madness and does not stem solely from unique individual circumstances. In making this connection, the author manages to keep the reader from feeling separated from the character because of her insanity. If the mental illness is closely connected with society's illness and shown to be an expected and reasonable result of that public disease, then the mad character is explicable and the reader need not feel divorced from her.

Finally, the attitudes toward change and the ideas of progress inherent in these novels require for their fulfillment an economic, social, and political restructuring of society. All the novels suggest a need for basic change and restructuring in Western government, culture, and society, rather than simply reform or modification. They are not pragmatic strategy maps nor are they centered on the practical workings of government. They support Irving Howe's statement that Henry Adams' *Democracy* is not a political novel in the sense that *The Possessed* and *Felix Holt* are. That is, the former concerns itself basically with the procedures of government and with practical politics while the latter two focus on "classes in combat, voices threatening from the social depths, intellectuals yearning to reach 'the people.'"[13] The authors of these novels are not liberals. They do not cherish a belief in law and litigation as a route to fundamental change.[14] They neither value stability as a goal in itself nor show an interest in fighting off communism.[15] They do not place much value on property rights. They do not define equality as the equal right to take part in the contest for the advantages society offers the well-off.[16] In the political sphere, they see no usefulness or freedom proffered by the system of competing political parties and interest groups.[17] The value they do share with liberals is an interest in individuals and in human and civil rights. With one exception, these authors are not Communists, either. Rather, they present a different view, a combination of socialism, feminism, and humanism in search of a new kind of society. Some of them concentrate on the quality of life rather than on survival alone. Others focus on external necessity and on the control the material realm exercises over people's lives. Many of them do not consciously subscribe to any ideology. Nevertheless, they have all written feminist novels and appear to share the goal of a similar changed society. In fact, "The feminist demands are by no means unreasonable, but the hysterical reactions they have provoked attest to the fact that the changes they ask for would entail a radical revision in the way men and women think about each other and themselves."[18]

Novels which are included under these criteria are the following: Kate Chopin's *The Awakening* (1899), Virginia Woolf's *Orlando* (1928), Agnes Smedley's *Daughter of Earth* (1929), Christina Stead's *The Man Who Loved Children* (1940), Mary McCarthy's *The Company She Keeps* (1942), Lillian Smith's *Strange Fruit* (1944), Ann Petry's *The Street* (1946), Doris Lessing's *A Proper Marriage* (1954), Harriette Arnow's *The Dollmaker* (1958), Doris Lessing's *The Golden Notebook* (1962), Margaret Atwood's *The Edible Woman* (1969), Doris Lessing's *The Four-Gated City* (1969), Anne Roiphe's *Up the Sandbox!* (1970), Erica Jong's *Fear of Flying* (1971), Helen Yglesias' *How She Died* (1971), Louise Meriwether's *Daddy was a Number Runner* (1971), Marge Piercy's *Small Changes* (1972), Judith Rossner's *Looking for Mr. Goodbar* (1975), Marge Piercy's *Woman on the Edge of Time* (1976), Alice Walker's *Meridian* (1976), Marilyn French's *The Women's Room* (1977), Marilyn French's *The Bleeding Heart* (1980), Judith Rossner's *Emmeline* (1980), Marge Piercy's *Braided Lives* (1982), and Alice Walker's *The Color Purple* (1982).

Those novels that are feminist, like political novels in general, have an intellectual appeal and focus on ideas. Feminism itself is an ideology. When a literary work grows successfully out of feminism, however, it is difficult to isolate its various feminist aspects—its world view, values, goals, and tactics for social change.[19] There are identifiable implications but, rarely, stated goals and plans. These implications arise as often from stylistic elements as from situation and character. Certainly, the political attitudes and beliefs of an author are as likely to influence her style as her choice of subject and material. If the advent of socialism could and should profoundly modify American culture in form and style as well as in point of view,[20] then surely feminism can strongly affect the form and style of a novel as well as provide the basis of its thought. The formal elements of the feminist novel are central to its meanings because its stylistic features convey its ideology, its politics, and its values.

An understanding of the world view and values presented in the feminist novel can well begin with the example of *The Awakening*. As much as, if not more than any other feminist novel, *The Awakening* recalls a statement of Irving Howe's regarding the study of the political novel: "I had chosen to write about novels that seemed explicitly political in their reverberation, yet to my surprise and (at the time) uneasiness, I found that in all these books politics was not at the center of things."[21] In *The Awakening*, as in other feminist novels, human freedom seems to be what is at the center of things. The attainment of this freedom, it is implied in these novels, will be accompanied by the blessed disappearance of politics. Perhaps it is the evidence of this dislike for politics exemplified in *The Awakening* that causes some critics to label it neither feminist nor political. Of course, others apply to it either the first of these adjectives or both. Approaching *The Awakening* as a feminist novel reveals as much about it as looking upon it as a novel written by a southern wife and mother of six and prods speculation as to the interrelationships among Kate Chopin's thinking, writing, and biography.

Because *The Awakening* appears so much earlier than other feminist novels, it seems reasonable to examine it first, not solely because it is a forerunner but also because it exhibits and illuminates all of the central stylistic elements of the feminist novel. For example, Chopin's authorial stance and presence serve as a useful contrast to the approach usually chosen by authors of later feminist novels. The modern perplexity regarding the concepts of unity and fragmentation appears in *The Awakening* in Chopin's attack on societal imposition of human roles. Edna's unified life as a wife and mother is tied to her role-playing; with freedom comes fragmentation. *The Awakening* is not written in a fragmented form nor does Chopin make use of multiple narrators. It does deal, however, with the ideological themes of fragmentation and unity which are stylistically developed in later feminist novels. The ending of *The Awakening*, a crux in Chopin criticism generally, is also central to a discussion of the frequent escape and/or death endings encountered in the feminist novel. Finally, Chopin's use of imagery highlights later practices. Like other twentieth-century feminist novels, *The Awakening* is infused with a host of symbolic meanings. Edna's marriage, her children, and her own awakened sexuality are much more than the experiences of one woman's life.

As would be expected in an early representative of a genre, *The Awakening* is both similar to and different from later feminist novels. Kate Chopin shares her distrust of ideology and her dislike of authority[22] with later writers of feminist novels. The more contemporary authors often mirror this suspicion and hostility in the use of the first person or autobiography and in the avoidance of authorial intrusion and direction. Such stylistic features have a direct connection with woman's view of herself and with the feminist attitude toward authority, individualism, and ideology. Chopin, however, writes *The Awakening* using a third-person narrator, and she does allow herself to speak out.

One gains a negative impression of Mr. Pontellier, for example, not only from Edna but also from the narrator. The reader is told that he was a "rather" courteous husband "so long as" his wife was submissive. Once she is not, he becomes angry and "rude." At the same time, the narrator also informs us that Edna is becoming openly and honestly herself and is refusing to pretend to be a person she is not.[23] Although a certain pity is expressed for Leonce's resulting bewilderment, he is not described favorably. It is also the narrator, not Edna, who relates that he nags in "a monotonous, insistent way."[24] The narrator does not look upon his authoritarian approach toward his wife with approval. She informs us that an even more authoritarian patriarch, Edna's father, "had coerced his own wife into her grave."[25] The overall impression Chopin gives of Pontellier through narrative comments as well as through his effect on Edna is of a confused, obtuse, bourgeois man— one toward whom she, like Edna, feels some sympathy and concern but more exasperation.

Her observations concerning Edna, on the other hand, are generally compassionate and indulgent. Edna is elevated, for example, by being contrasted with the "mother-woman." These women are described by Chopin as chickens who flutter about with outstretched wings, hovering over their broods. In effect, she praises Edna by dissociating her from this group. She goes on to further satirize these women by juxtaposing the chicken comparison with the women's view of themselves as pious, angelic martyrs who idolize their children and husbands. They see themselves as winged angels rather than as clipped chickens.[26]

As much as Chopin may dislike ideologues and distrust authoritarianism, she chooses to write *The Awakening* in the third person and to permit herself as the author to comment on her characters. Many other authors of feminist novels reinforce their attack on authority with a matching authorial approach. In *The Awakening*, however, this seeming discordance actually mirrors the contradiction presented in the character of Edna herself. That is, despite the strong attack launched by this novel on authority and rules, it is still written in the third person and told by a narrator assuming the stance of authority. Similarly, Edna reveals her own personal contradictions. The awakened Edna appears before the reader as a free, exhilarating woman. She has "resolved never again to belong to another than herself."[27] She does not feel herself bound and fettered by anyone or by any of the thousands of constricting conventions society foists upon the individual. When she does not want to go to her sister's wedding, she does not go and feels no compunction to offer excuses. In fact, whereas earlier she had seemed listless to Dr. Mandelet, perhaps boring, she now reminds "him of some beautiful, sleek animal waking up in the sun."[28] All in all, Chopin presents her to the reader as an independent, free, interesting woman.

Yet, one finds that Edna is still almost completely dependent upon Robert, her lover, for her happiness. Although it is true that her relationship with Robert is different from that with her husband because she is drawn to Robert physically and emotionally, there is more than a suggestion that in many ways it is similar. Robert, as he is described by Mademoiselle Reisz, is quite ordinary, perhaps as traditional a man as Mr. Pontellier. Certainly he believes in marriage in the same way that

Mr. Pontellier does. Edna, as he sees it, belongs to Leonce, and only marriage would make her his own. He does not approach their relationship with Edna's passion and abandonment; quite the contrary, he tries to avoid Edna when their affinity for one another moves beyond the bounds of his Creole morality, and eventually he ends the relationship. Because of her dependence upon Robert, Edna is actually not nearly so free as she professes to be. She has not been able to incorporate fully within herself the essence of her awakening just as the author of it has not fully integrated her attack on authority with her narrative stance.

Of interest, too, is the tone of the narrative voice. In some ways, it seems the voice of a Dr. Mandelet, the voice of a cultured society. It recognizes the beauty of Edna's rebellion; it also condemns her sentimentality. Most important, it views the defeat of her revolt as inevitable, as part of the human condition. The narrator states, for example, that the light which shows the way also forbids it. She also describes Edna as a woman realizing her "position in the universe as a human being" and recognizing "her relations as an individual to the world within and about her."[29] At yet another point, the narrator comments that "The past was nothing to her [Edna]; offered no lesson which she was willing to heed. The future was a mystery which she never attempted to penetrate."[30] Through these comments and others, the suggestion is made that Edna's conflict, as society sees it, is simply part of being human.

Yet the characters, who themselves represent society, reveal the false aspects of this view and help to point out the political nature of Edna's struggle. At the same time, their actions help to condemn society. Madam Ratignolle, for example, uses society's strongest lever against Edna by insisting that she is bound by nature. Even Dr. Mandelet sees Madame Ratignolle's insistence on Edna's presence at her childbirth as cruel. Also, Dr. Mandelet, though presumably a voice of societal wisdom, immediately views Edna's rebellion as a result of Arobin's influence rather than as an awakening of her own. Robert reveals another paralytic aspect of society through his caution and fear, and he uses another of its weapons against Edna—the withdrawal of love and affection. Finally, Mr. Pontellier, another representative of society, denigrates her revolt by referring to her as having "some sort of notion in her head concerning the eternal rights of women."[31] Edna is defeated by societal forces represented by these characters. Edna's personal, internal conflicts are mirrored in the novel's representation of her struggle as partly political, partly the result of being human.

The distrust of authority expressed in *The Awakening* is developed in several other ways. Anti-authoritarianism ties in, for example, with the very center of this novel's feminism which resides in its attack on roles. In all feminist novels, the characters' attitudes toward roles are important because of the relationship of the unity roles proffer to the problem of modern psychic fragmentation. The conflict between fragmentation and unity is a major focal point in many of these novels. Possibly it is their animus against authoritarianism which causes these authors to agree with the statement that is is "not for us... to impose an external unity upon culture."[32] In their distrust of past unities and their dislike of present fragmentation, they seem to look forward to a future where the problem is resolved.

The author's attitude toward fragmentation frequently has a marked effect on the overall form of the novel. The fractured point of view and disjointed arrangement of chapters often mirrors the concern the author feels about the splintered nature of modern life. Ideology has other effects on the form of some of these novels. Some authors, for example, while fragmenting their novels, move back and forth between fantasy and reality. Their novels belie the statement that "realism is the only possible genre for radical fiction."[33]

Chopin does not experiment with a fragmented style, but she anticipates later authors with her contemporary assault on roles. It is precisely the confines of a role that Edna tries to escape after her rebirth. Chopin briefly sketches the role Edna has discontentedly been playing when the novel opens. At one point, Mr. Pontellier awakens her to send her out to do her duty in checking her son's temperature;[34] at another, he laments her sunburn while "looking at his wife as one looks at a valuable piece of personal property which has suffered some damage."[35] These experiences, representative of the life she has been living, cause "an indescribable oppression, which seemed to generate in some unfamiliar part of her consciousness" to fill "her whole being with a vague anguish."[36] It is revealed later, when Edna casts aside her "fictitious self," that it is the oppression of her real nature that has been causing her pain. It is made clear in *The Awakening* that Edna is not the only person who assumes a societally induced part; she only plays hers less well than others do. Adèle Ratignolle, for example, is "delicious in the rôle" in which Edna is miscast. Madame Ratignolle is quite amenable to the role of the "mother-woman"; she is also well aware that she is playing a role. Consequently, she is not afraid of Edna's rebellion; but she does fight it.

Robert, on the other hand, is markedly fearful. The reader is told that Robert's face grows a little white when Edna laughingly denies that anyone can give her away since no one owns her.[37] It is quite possible that Robert senses in Edna's attitude and statement what lies at the center of individual, personal radicalism—the refusal to participate in society's rituals and the determination to free the self from society's imposed roles. To reject society's rules regarding the conduct of one's life, the fulfillment of one's duties, and the ordering of one's commitments is to attack it at a fundamental level. Such an attack can form the beginning of political revolt when extended beyond the self.

There is also the suggestion in *The Awakening* that others besides Edna are aware of what she is discovering, perhaps more aware than she herself. Dr. Mandelet, for instance, early becomes cognizant of Edna's troubles. He has managed to deal with his own knowledge of the world by accepting its constrictions and wants to counsel Edna to do the same. There are hints that Madame Ratignolle also understands Edna, perhaps in part from difficulties of her own. Because she believes Edna and Edna's children would be best off if Edna returned to her earlier life, she seizes upon the future of her children as the one subject that might hold Edna. Mademoiselle Reisz understands Edna from yet another perspective. She has in many ways led the life Edna wants although she has also missed much. She fully realizes the hurdles in front of Edna; she suspects Edna's inability to surmount them; and she is aware of Edna's dependence upon Robert.

Most of the other characters in *The Awakening*, like Leonce and Robert, have become the embodiment of the roles they play—to the point that they simply cannot understand Edna. In refusing the specious unity the acceptance of a role would offer her, Edna makes a courageous stand. She is more alone than even those people who partially perceive the nature of her situation. Madame Ratignolle enjoys the role she plays. Dr. Mandelet has his work, his age, his experience, and also his gender to give him his bearing; and Mademoiselle Reisz has the firm base provided by a life narrowed to one thing— her music. Edna, on the other hand, has no supports. Alone, she confronts the confusion, fragmentation, and chaos of a free life and challenges society as well. At the same time, she carries the weight of her children's needs. She is not equal to the task as one discovers at the end of *The Awakening*.

Edna's personal weaknesses bear on the ending of the novel, an ending which foreshadows the conclusions of other feminist novels. The majority of these endings finalize in escape or death, either literal or figurative. Both types of endings make strong statements regarding society and the central heroine's character. Society is certainly condemned for causing Edna's death, but there are specific aspects of her personality and character that also contribute to her defeat. Her excessive reliance upon Robert is part of what makes her vulnerable. Despite her need for release and her desire for life and joy, essentially Edna's "fantasy of freedom depends on another human being."[38] When Dr. Mandelet first glimpses the change in Edna, he automatically assumes that it is the result of a man—Arobin.[39] A large part of Edna's problem is that she believes the change in her is partially due to a man—Robert Lebrun. Though she comes close to personal freedom when she moves into her own house, Edna can never completely break free because she never can become completely dependent upon her own life and her own resources for strength and support. Rather, she continues to depend upon her romanticism, upon a traditional love, upon another person. When that person deserts her, she cannot survive.

Through Robert, she expects satisfaction of her romantic as well as her passional longings.[40] Edna's fundamental romanticism never changes. Her romantic nature is revealed early in the novel when the narrator describes her feelings before her marriage with Pontellier: "As the devoted wife of a man who worshiped her, she felt she would take her place with a certain dignity in the world of reality, closing the portals forever behind her upon the realm of romance and dreams."[41] Her father's opposition to the marriage helps to encourage Edna also. Of course, Edna's view of herself and her husband is itself a thoroughly romantic notion and she never does close that door. Even at the very end, Edna still dreams romantic dreams: "The spurs of the cavalry officer clanged as he walked across the porch. There was the hum of bees, and the musky odor of pinks filled the air."[42]

The elements of her romanticism are revealed in many ways. Her imaginative nature and her tendency toward dreaminess are part of it as are her child-like impulsiveness and sudden shifts in mood. She also exhibits an intermittent sentimentality toward her children and Leonce. Her children, for example, are swooped up and then forgotten. When Leonce leaves, she exhibits similar feelings for:

As the day approached when he was to leave her for a comparatively long stay, she grew melting and affectionate, remembering his many acts of consideration and his repeated expressions of an ardent attachment. She was solicitous about his health and his welfare. She bustled around, looking after his clothing, thinking about heavy underwear, quite as Madame Ratignolle would have done under similar circumstances. She cried when he went away, calling him her dear, good friend, and she was quite certain she would grow lonely before very long and go to join him in New York.
But after all, a radiant peace settled upon her when she at last found herself alone. Even the children were gone.[43]

Edna also reveals at times an extravagant and unrealistic, idealized view of people, especially Robert, and of events, especially love and sex. These aspects of her nature, as well as her innocence and lack of experience, lead her to depend heavily on Robert for the realization of her desires. Her idealistic views and innocence also cause her to be shocked at the Creole's open discussion of sexuality while, at the same time, they enable her to seek the actuality with Robert. Edna's romanticism is closely related to a romanticism which revolts against rules and traditions and exalts the feelings and senses.

The voices of reality and realism intrude only occasionally until the end of the novel when they destroy her. Early in the novel, the reader is given a small picture of how reality affects Edna. While she is sitting in the dark beginning to awaken to a new knowledge of her life, mosquitos attack her and "the little stinging, buzzing imps succeeded in dispelling a mood which might have held her there in the darkness half a night longer."[44] Later, Mademoiselle Reisz assumes the voice of reality when she broaches with Edna her infatuation with Robert. Edna avoids confronting the essence of her feeling for Robert, and Mademoiselle Reisz remarks,"You are purposely misunderstanding me...."[45] At the end, it is reality which destroys Edna's romance. She realizes that her infatuation with Robert will someday end and that her reality will likely be a string of affairs, without love, without romance. Worse, these relationships will not be the result of her own passions but of someone else's desires, someone like Arobin. In effect, Edna, needing love and romance, faces the death of romanticism and sees only her reality as a person alone.

There are other aspects of Edna's character that demand consideration. For example, Edna is not presented as an extraordinary woman. To begin with, she falls in love with Robert, "a man of ordinary caliber,"[46] perhaps even shallow. Very early, for example, one finds that he "posed as an inconsolable" after the death of one of his beloved ladies.[47] He seems most often to be posing and playing. One finds that Mademoiselle Reisz, despite her fondness for Edna, recognizes her ordinariness. In effect, she thinks her thoroughly charming but mediocre.[48] She suspects that Edna does not possess a "brave soul,"[49] is not able to stand alone. The very things that make Edna so delightful, that draw Mademoiselle Reisz to her, her child-like impulsiveness, her romanticism, her dreams, are the very things that allow society to kill her and deny her her freedom. Paradoxically, they are also the very things that allow her to challenge social reality in the first place. She is, in fact, not as strong or as brave or as wise as she needs to be to defend herself. She feels about her life as she feels when in the sea. Just as, when swimming, "a certain ungovernable dread hung about her... unless there was a hand near by that might reach out and reassure her,"[50] so also, in her life, she always needs someone else's support for confidence. Swimming becomes a symbol of her life; when she awakens, she does the same as she does when she learns to swim. She grows "daring and reckless, overestimating her strength."[51] She grows much stronger as the novel progresses and so does her swimming; but, ultimately, when reality cannot be avoided, she is submerged.

In many ways, she is the opposite of Mademoiselle Reisz. The wisdom which Edna needs is to be found in Mademoiselle Reisz's music. It is because of this that "there was nothing which so quieted the turmoil of Edna's senses as a visit to Mademoiselle Reisz. It was then, in the presence of that personality which was offensive to her, that the woman, by her divine art, seemed to reach Edna's spirit and set it free."[52] Edna lacks the direction, the goal, the control that Mademoiselle Reisz exhibits in her music. Had she gained that, she might have been able, at least in part, to win her battle with society.

None of this, though, means that Edna deserves scorn. Her unexceptional abilities, her romanticism, her dependency upon Robert are not things for which she is to be blamed. They are only the things which prevent her from being strong enough and extraordinary enough to escape society's snare. It is organized society which is ultimately to be blamed for Edna's death. Only a few are capable of flying to personal freedom over society's obstacles; "the bird that would soar above the level plain of tradition and prejudice must have strong wings."[53] Edna, not being phenomenal, is not allowed to be free. She becomes a part of the "sad spectacle" of those who, bruised and exhausted, flutter back to earth.[54] This explicit political statement condemns society for Edna's death. It does not blame Edna for having human weaknesses nor does it suggest that perhaps, after all, it is just the way of the world that only the superior succeed.

Her death at the end is appropriate for this novel. Death is the only satisfactory resolution society allows Edna, given her personality and character. She has the options of the figurative deaths of life with Pontellier or life with no one or the literal death she chooses. She really does not have the independence and vision to make a life for herself alone over all the barriers the world puts in her way. Her awakening is not just to physical love but to life, her life, and, ultimately, to the realization that the world will not permit her to have it.

Additionally, her choice of suicide reemphasizes her weaknesses. Sylvia Plath states that "suicide is an assertion of power, of the strength—not the weakness—of the personality."[55] Such is not the message carried by the feminist novel. In Edna's case, suicide does allow her to assert herself in a sense; but it is also the only available escape for her, given her dependence on romanticism. It is, of course, an escape, and an unusual one in the feminist novel. Edna's giving in to it underscores her sense of hopelessness and the mixture of passivity and daring that forms her personality. Near the end, we are told that "she had abandoned herself to Fate, and awaited the consequences with indifference."[56] Yet we also find that she fancies suicide as a means of affirming and freeing herself. Because suicide is the sole escape the constricting world of the 1890s grants to a woman like Edna, the ending is quite fitting.

One might see a problem with the resolution in Chopin's handling of the children and Edna's relationship with them. Her portrayal of Edna's attitude toward them occasionally appears contradictory. On the one hand, Edna does not seem very interested in her children; she even seems unsuited for parenthood. We find, for example, that when they are gone for part of the summer, Edna

did not miss them except with an occasional intense longing. Their absence was a sort of relief, though she did not admit this, even to herself. It seemed to free her of a responsibility which she had blindly assumed and for which Fate had not fitted her.[57]

At another time, on her way home from having visited with them for a week, we learn that "All along the journey homeward their presence lingered with her like the memory of a delicious song. But by the time she had regained the city the song no longer echoed in her soul."[58] Throughout the novel she rarely thinks of her children. Her viewpoint is a harbinger of Lynda in Doris Lessing's *The Four-Gated City*, who responds to the child, Paul's, question, "Are you Francis's mother?" with the statement, "Yes. No. I suppose so. Not really. I'm not much good at being that kind of person. Some people aren't."[59] As is the case with Lessing and her character, Lynda, there seems no indication that Chopin blames or directs the reader to blame Edna for her loose attachment to her children. There exists a tacit assumption that not everyone is suited for parenthood. Generally, the male Ednas in literature fail to fall under the critical gauntlet for their "selfish" attitudes toward their children because it is "the man's practice, if not his stated belief, that where self-realization is concerned children shall not be an impediment."[60]

In the end, however, it is constantly the children Edna refers to. It is the children she cannot get away from although she has done so so easily throughout the novel. It is the children who matter, whom she cannot hurt. It might seem odd, too, that Madame Ratignolle should seize upon the issue of the children when trying to coerce Edna into staying. Although she herself is strongly attached to her children, there is nothing to suggest to her that Edna feels the same. Although Edna does not believe in the role of motherhood in the way that Madame Ratignolle does, she does love her children. She says, and the reader is to believe her, that she would die for the children. She also makes a concomitant statement, though, which is that she will not live for them. In other words, she will give up the unessential, her biological life, for them; but she adamantly refuses to give up the vital, which is her real life, herself, the person she knows herself to be and wants to be.

Of additional and primary importance is the symbolic function Edna's children serve by representing her imprisonment. Because they symbolize societal and marital impediments and obstacles, it is the children, ultimately, whom Edna cannot escape. This is why they are the trump card Madame Ratignolle plays when she urges Edna to think of them and abandon her folly. They are the prime representation of what Dr. Mandelet refers to when he speaks "of moral consequences, of arbitrary conditions which we create, and which we feel obliged to maintain at any cost."[61] It is the fact of Edna's motherhood that most causes society and the societal conscience in Edna to refuse to grant her her own life. Because she is a mother, she is not allowed to live as she wishes. Had she been a father, of course, few would find her guilty of "reprehensible selfishness."[62] The hold societal morality has on her is shown to be very strong indeed. There is no way finally for her to escape her children and society except by suicide. Neither Edna, Dr. Mandelet, nor Madame Ratignolle speaks of Raoul or Etienne personally; they speak generally of "the children" and of "mothers." In fact, neither of the boys is developed as an individual. They fundamentally stand for society's restrictions which Edna cannot surmount.

It is unusual in feminist novels for children to function as negative symbols, and it is through Chopin's use of metaphors and symbolism that the similarities and differences which exist between *The Awakening* and later feminist novels are revealed most fully. The symbolism in all these novels reveals a new view of society and a new host of values. What is presented is the "other's" vision of the world's arrangements and of the relationship between women and men. Like other authors of feminist novels, Chopin occasionally uses symbols in familiar ways; often, she does not. When writing within an established tradition, an author can often assume certain contexts will be taken for granted. If this were not so, one would be constantly explaining background.[63] Chopin did have the beginnings of a tradition of the feminist novel to rely upon when writing *The Awakening*. For example, feminist elements are present in *Jane Eyre, Pride and Prejudice*, and in Ellen Glasgow's novels. Mary Wollstonecraft drafted a perceptive treatise on feminism over one hundred years before *The Awakening* was written. Consequently, through the use of a developing pattern of symbolism, Chopin is able to present a background of ideas without constantly explaining herself.

There is a tacit statement made, for example, in the characteristics given to Edna as the central figure in *The Awakening*. As in many other feminist novels, the heroine of *The*

The Awakening

Awakening is an older, mature woman with children. Edna is not an adolescent taking a first, innocent plunge into life. Rather, she is an older woman who has lived her life, as the novel begins, as she had been expected to live it. In fact, she has reached the point in her emotional and intellectual life when she is just becoming a woman. Obviously, she physically became a woman many years earlier; but that stage is not the one usually focused on in the feminist novel. It is not the emergence of physical maturation but the formation of the spiritually mature woman that is at the center of the feminist novel. *The Awakening* presents a powerful condemnation of a society that makes life barren or impossible for the awakened, mature woman.

Edna is a living representation of another idea frequently developed in the feminist novel. Here, the ideal of success and the adoration of extraordinary talent and genius are discarded. In *The Awakening* Edna's talent as a painter is drawn as a minor one. Although Mademoiselle Reisz is most clearly and obviously a musician and a very good one, Edna is most certainly not an outstanding artist. She herself explains that she is "not a painter" and that "It isn't on account of painting that [she lets] things go."[64] Edna's ability is also downplayed by Chopin's presentation of her father's views on the subject. One hears that "he took the whole matter very seriously. If her talent had been ten-fold greater than it was, it would not have surprised him, convinced as he was that he had bequeathed to all of his daughters the germs of a masterful capability, which only depended upon their own efforts to be directed toward successful achievement."[65] Because Edna's father takes her painting seriously, the reader is directed not to, at least not in a sense of assuming it to be great. Obviously, if her talent could be ten times greater than it is, it is not of the highest order.

Chopin does not suggest, however, that Edna is to be denigrated for this. Instead, she proposes that Edna has a right to paint and to enjoy it even if she is not a great artist. She is pointing out that the average individual, as well as the extraordinary person, can have a capability for art and an appreciation of it and ought to be permitted to enjoy it. Edna is not exceptional in her talent, perhaps not even in her capacities for passion and life. The tragedy *The Awakening* presents is not the picture of society's destruction of a great talent and life but of society's refusal to let the average woman be free. According only average capability to Edna reveals another orientation of the feminist novel. Edna's father, for example, finds "successful achievement" important, at least in part because if his daughter succeeds, it reflects well on himself. *The Awakening*, however, does not elevate the importance of success in itself. The statement that the "idea of success has failed to engage the female imagination" can, with qualifications, be applied to certain characters in the feminist novel.[66] That aspect of success which implies superiority over others and failure if anything less than greatness is attained is scorned in the feminist novel. It is quite possible that this represents a reaction against competitiveness and materialism. In these novels work and creation are presented as joys, as lifelines to sanity, and as extremely important and meaningful even if unsuccessful by ordinary standards. It is most important that whatever capabilities the individual has should be allowed to flourish and bloom. How great the capacities are or whether the individual is completely "successful" in developing them is relatively unimportant. The feminist novel is aligned against the view of Zelda Fitzgerald's psychiatrists that "since she couldn't be 'great' as a dancer, a painter, a writer, it was damaging to try."[67] Rather, it is of the greatest aid for the human being to try; work and creation can provide the base of being and doing necessary for survival. Feminist novels support Anaïs Nin's response to a questioner who asked if she would advise all young people to write. She said, "I don't see why not, for even if they don't become great at least I think their lives would be enormously enriched. We don't have to look at everything as an achievement."[68] Similarly, we find it said of Edna that "being devoid of ambition, and striving not toward accomplishment she drew satisfaction from the work in itself."[69]

There is a problem involved here for Edna, however. In part because she has no goals and directions in her work and in her life, she is threatened. Edna does care about doing good work and destroys her painting of Madame Ratignolle because she thinks it is poorly done. On the other hand, she speaks cavalierly about "becoming an artist" and vows that she does not think of "any extraordinary flights." Although it is not important that she be "extraordinary," it is a lack in her that while she entertains impulsive flights, she has no sustained direction and control.

There are a number of representative elements besides her work in painting that Chopin uses to illustrate Edna's life and awakening. Marriage and sexuality, central facets of all feminist novels, come to typify the opposing forces fighting for Edna. Edna's marriage exemplifies the chains and restrictions holding her back from her desires, denying her her freedom, refusing her her life. The marriage is itself symbolized by another chain, her ring. The suggestion is made that the marriage cannot be destroyed, at least not by Edna because when "she stamped her heel upon it, striving to crush it, ... her small boot heel did not make an indenture, not a mark upon the little glittering circlet."[70] One finds that the marriage is indestructible in part because it is lifeless, because in Edna's relationship with her husband "no trace of passion or excessive and fictitious warmth colored her affection, thereby threatening its dissolution."[71] This somnolent marriage, in fact, is society's tool. It is one of the ways in which society binds Edna, restraining her even when she awakens. It is not Leonce she fights. She actually feels solicitous toward him at times and thinks of him as a "dear, good friend."[72] When he and her children are away and she feels a delicious, genuine relief, it has little to do with her need for freedom. It is not freedom from that individual person, her husband, that Edna needs. It is freedom from society's rules, duties, and regulations that she must have, freedom from its life-destroying routines.

Chopin makes use of other representative aspects of Edna's life to highlight the domesticity and confinement of marriage and society. As in the feminist novel generally, food and the preparation of meals are used to exemplify the servitude and drudgery of marriage. In *The Awakening* food, by itself, can provide a sensuous and highly pleasurable experience. When tied with marriage, though, it becomes one more trivial, routine task. The preparation, serving, and eating of meals becomes another monotonous chore, one more link in the marital chain of restrictions. Mr. Pontellier sets great store by properly prepared meals and frequently stalks off to "the club" when a meal is not to his liking. Edna, on the other hand, does "not mind a little scorched taste."[73] Eventually, after having been thoroughly depressed by her vision of the Ratignolles' marriage, Edna decides "a dinner of herbs" would be preferable to a "delicious repast" if the latter meant one had to live like the Ratignolles.[74]

Just before and after Edna goes out to live on her own, the harassment of meal planning is dispensed with. Edna plans a dinner, a fitting farewell, to celebrate her last night in her old house. Food is not really discussed, though. The appearance of the table, the guests' apparel and emotions, and the conversation are all drawn at length; but the food is fairly ignored except for the comment that the guests had "eaten well."[75] Without Mr. Pontellier, food and meals become a pleasant, enjoyable part of Edna's life. They are no longer part of the boredom and service of marriage. She cuts down on the amount of food to be ordered and places all the responsibility for meals upon the cook. The cook, apparently pleased to finally be free from control herself, blossoms into creativity.[76] When Edna is hungry and it is not mealtime, she simply rummages about until she finds some crackers, cheese, and beer.[77] There is no fuss, no constraint, no servitude. It is only later when Robert returns from Mexico that Edna reverts to the married habit. She sends Celestine "off in search of some added delicacy which she had not thought of for herself. And she recommended great care in dripping the coffee and having the omelet done to a proper turn."[78] In effect, Edna begins doing again what she eventually revolted against doing for Leonce. It seems likely that if her infatuation with Robert, like her romanticizing of her marriage, were to die off, the net result would be the same. Once again, Robert is connected with the things of Edna's past life and with her unforsaken romanticism.

Edna's real life, her awakened life, is symbolized by her newly discovered sexuality. It is outside of society where Edna must lead her essential life. Her renegade status is represented by her sexuality, which is not awakened in her marriage by her husband but outside of it by others. When "a certain light"[79] begins to dawn for Edna, when she begins to recognize her position in the universe, she begins to emerge as a real person from the societal cocoon and her sexuality emerges as well. She begins to awaken intellectually, emotionally, and physically all at once. An orderly, static, conservative society is threatened by this growth, by sexuality, and by the assertion of the need for individual autonomy.

Edna's sexuality and individuality and her awakened life in general are further elaborated upon by Chopin's symbolic use of birds and water. Several times, birds are used to represent the life Edna pursues. Early in the novel, Edna's death is prefigured when she imagines a man standing naked on a rock at the seashore, watching a bird flying away from him.[80] It is Edna's life the bird symbolizes. Edna becomes the standard representative of the human being, a man, not a woman. Edna wants to live as she imagines a man is allowed to live; so, when she pictures herself, it is as a man. The novel also makes the silent comment that men are not free, either. In fact, Edna wants to become the bird, leading the free life it possesses. Birds also are used to highlight Edna's weaknesses and her ultimate inability to overcome the obstacles society places in her path. Mademoiselle Reisz touches her shoulder blades to see if her wings are strong enough to carry her away from society's wrath. Evidently, they are not. One finds at the end, too, that Edna has become the "bird with a broken wing... reeling, fluttering, circling disabled down, down to the water."[81] She refuses to cluck and brood like a chicken and is not strong enough to lead the life of a swift.

Water and the sea are other very important symbolic elements in *The Awakening*. Edna's learning to swim and to enjoy the water in effect symbolizes the totality of her awakening to life. Before she "was like the little tottering, stumbling, clutching child." She bemoans the time she has "lost splashing about like a baby."[82] As she does come to life and learn how to swim, "she could have shouted for joy. She did shout for joy, as with a sweeping stroke or two she lifted her body to the surface of the water." Her new, impassioned life is a thing of great joy for Edna. She embraces it and her newly found sexuality, unlike Mademoiselle Reisz, who is afraid of the water and the sensual passion it represents. In order to live an independent and creative life, Mademoiselle Reisz has had to shun sexuality, something Edna refuses to do.

Edna lacks some of Mademoiselle Reisz's fortitude, however, and grows "daring and reckless, overestimating her strength." She wants "to swim far out, where no woman had swum before."[83] Edna wants all of the free life, including independence, sexuality, and friendship as well. Her romanticism, her lack of wisdom, and society's condemnation all combine to thwart her, however. It is true that "she had not gone any great distance—that is, what would have been a great distance for an experienced swimmer. But to her unaccustomed vision the stretch of water behind her assumed the aspect of a barrier which her unaided strength would never be able to overcome."[84] At the end, Edna is simply unable to live alone, without Robert. She is unable to face reality without romance. She is assuredly unwilling to compromise. The form and pattern of Edna's new life merge with the pattern of the novel which begins and ends with the sea and water and Edna's awakened sexuality. At the end Edna realizes that she would be alone in her new life and that she would be condemned to being misunderstood. She would be viewed as a Mrs. Highcamp by society. She cannot live without feeling a romantic attachment, without love. She cannot escape society; she cannot go back to her somnolent marriage. For Edna, because of society's rules, because of her own weaknesses, there is no ending but suicide in the sea where she first awakened.

All the aforementioned aspects of *The Awakening*, its antiauthoritarianism, its attack on roles, its ending, and its symbolism, are central to the feminist novel generally. *The Awakening* has been viewed from many other angles, however. Among the earlier mentioned critical discussions of this novel are several comparisons of Edna Pontellier and *The Awakening* with *Madame Bovary*. In many respects, though, the novels are quite different, primarily because one is thoroughly feminist and the other is not. For example, Edna's infidelity is really irrelevant to the meaning of *The Awakening* whereas Emma Bovary's would be pertinent to a discussion of *Madame Bovary*. Edna's affairs are not important to the novel; her awakening is. The affairs themselves are only symbolic of the awakening. Her relationships with Arobin and Robert symbolize her conflict between reality and romance, between what the world will permit her and what it will not. Chopin presents, in fact, a completely moral woman, one who has so completely incorporated society's strictures that in a battle between them and her own freedom, she is defeated and dies. She cannot completely enjoy a sexual relationship with Arobin because she does not "love" him. She cannot live without the man she does love— Robert. Finally, she cannot lead her own life because of her duties to her children and to society. Chopin's attitude toward her is far different from Flaubert's ambivalent feelings toward his heroine. Despite the viewpoint of society, *The Awakening* does not present the denial of sexuality and the self in a dead marriage as part of the human condition. Madame Ratignolle plays a role; Edna's demand for freedom is reality.

Chopin, too, has written a novel that is radical in the statement it makes about family life. In effect, it depicts marriage as a tomb, suitable for the dead but not for the living. It portrays marriage as another of society's traps, designed to confine, not to liberate. Its depiction of marriage illustrates, expands, and brings to life the statement that the absence of love "is implied in the very nature of the institution, the aim of which is to make the economic and sexual union of man and woman serve the interest of society, not assure their personal happiness."[85] In *The Awakening* Chopin draws the political story of many women.[86] Their political story is not told in congresses, in political campaigns, or in revolutions. It is told in their daily lives, in their marriages, in their awakenings.

It has been said of *The Awakening* that it is "a very odd book to have been written in America at the end of the nineteenth century."[87] In many ways, it really is not. If one looks back a century to Mary Wollstonecraft and after her to the feminist aspects of numerous novels, Kate Chopin's novel seems to have arrived on schedule. Actually, what more appropriate time could there have been for such a novel than the turn of the century! Feminism was hardly a new idea even then, and it certainly was part of the myriad of changes taking place in the 1880s and 1890s. In some ways, Edna herself seems a symbol of the shifts occurring as America moved into the twentieth century. Waking to her new life, she is enthusiastic and excited. Surely she shares the nineteenth century's view of rule as an affront and a challenge.[88] She tries to live her life—a life the twentieth century might allow a woman. But she retains her nineteenth-century romanticism and even its essential mores. When the ideals fostered by that romanticism and by those conventions are destroyed and when she cannot think her way into a new world, she dies. The end really does fit the novel, and the novel does fit the time. It is also a fitting prelude to the twentieth-century's feminist novels.

NOTES

1. Henry Hazlitt, "Literature versus Opinion," *The Writer and His Craft*, ed. Robert Morss Lovett (Ann Arbor: The University of Michigan Press, 1954), p. 46.
2. Erica Jong, *Fear of Flying* (New York: Holt, Rinehart and Winston, 1971), pp. 168–69.
3. Simone de Beauvoir, *The Second Sex*, ed. and trans. H. M. Parshley (1953; reprint, New York: Random House, 1974), p. 679.
4. Ibid., p. 277.
5. Doris Lessing, *The Golden Notebook* (New York: Simon and Schuster, Inc., 1962), p. 332.
6. Alfred Kazin, *On Native Grounds: An Interpretation of Modern American Prose Literature* (New York: Reynal and Hitchcock, 1942), p. 154.
7. Herbert Marder, *Feminism and Art: A Study of Virginia Woolf* (Chicago: The University of Chicago Press, 1968), p. 79.
8. Ellen Moers, *Literary Women* (Garden City, N.Y.: Doubleday and Co., Inc., 1976), p. 43.
9. Cheri Register, "American Feminist Literary Criticism: A Bibliographical Introduction," *Feminist Literary Criticism: Explorations in Theory*, ed. Josephine Donovan (Lexington: University Press of Kentucky, 1975), p. 18.
10. Carolyn G. Heilbrun, *Toward a Recognition of Androgyny* (New York: Alfred A. Knopf, 1973), p. 58.
11. Lessing, *The Golden Notebook*, p. xii.
12. Edgar Friedenberg, "The Image of the Adolescent Minority,"

The Awakening

The Radical Imagination, ed. Irving Howe (New York: The New American Library, Inc., 1955), p. 225.

13. Irving Howe, *Politics and the Novel* (New York: Horizon Press, Inc., 1957), p. 176.
14. Kenneth M. and Patricia Dolbeare, *American Ideologies: The Competing Political Beliefs of the 1970's* (Chicago: Rand McNally College Publishing Co., 1976), p. 72.
15. Ibid., p. 48.
16. Ibid., p. 45.
17. Ibid., pp. 40–41.
18. Martha Masinton and Charles G. Masinton, "Second-Class Citizenship: The Status of Women in Contemporary American Fiction," *What Manner of Woman: Essays on English and American Life and Literature*, ed. Marlene Springer (New York: New York University Press, 1977), p. 308.
19. Dolbeare, *American Ideologies*, p. 5.
20. Daniel Aaron, *Writers on the Left: Episodes in American Literary Communism* (New York: Harcourt, Brace and World, Inc., 1961), p. 252.
21. Irving Howe, "Arts and Letters: Literary Criticism and Literary Radicals," *American Scholar* 41 (Winter 1971): 114.
22. Margaret Culley, "The Context of *The Awakening*," *The Awakening*, by Kate Chopin (1899; reprint, New York: W. W. Norton and Co., Inc., 1976), p. 117.
23. Kate Chopin, *The Awakening* (1899; reprint, New York: W. W. Norton and Co., Inc., 1976), p. 57.
24. Ibid., p. 7.
25. Ibid., p. 71.
26. Ibid., p. 10.
27. Ibid., p. 80.
28. Ibid., p. 70.
29. Ibid., pp. 14–15.
30. Ibid., p. 46.
31. Ibid., p. 65.
32. Kazin, *On Native Grounds*, p. 518.
33. Richard Chase, "Radicalism in the American Novel," *Commentary* 26 (January 1957): 70.
34. Chopin, *The Awakening*, pp. 7–8.
35. Ibid., p. 4.
36. Ibid., p. 8.
37. Ibid., p. 107.
38. Patricia Meyer Spacks, *The Female Imagination* (New York: Alfred A. Knopf, 1975), p. 75.

39. Chopin, *The Awakening*, p. 71.
40. George M. Spangler, "Kate Chopin's *The Awakening*: A Partial Dissent," *Novel* 3 (Spring 1970): 250.
41. Chopin, *The Awakening*, p. 19.
42. Ibid., p. 114.
43. Ibid., pp. 71-72.
44. Ibid., p. 8.
45. Ibid., p. 81.
46. Ibid.
47. Ibid., p. 12.
48. Ibid., p. 81.
49. Ibid., p. 63.
50. Ibid., p. 70.
51. Ibid.
52. Ibid., p. 78.
53. Ibid., p. 82.
54. Ibid.
55. Elizabeth Hardwick, *Seduction and Betrayal: Women and Literature* (New York: Random House, 1974), p. 117.
56. Chopin, *The Awakening*, pp. 102-3.
57. Ibid., p. 20.
58. Ibid., p. 94.
59. Doris Lessing, *The Four-Gated City* (New York: Alfred A. Knopf, 1969), p. 177.
60. Hardwick, *Seduction and Betrayal*, p. 49.
61. Chopin, *The Awakening*, p. 110.
62. Spacks, *The Female Imagination*, p. 72.
63. Nathan Irvin Huggins, *Harlem Renaissance* (1971; reprint, New York: Oxford University Press, Inc., 1974), p. 234.
64. Chopin, *The Awakening*, p. 57.
65. Ibid., p. 68.
66. Spacks, *The Female Imagination*, p. 319.
67. Hardwick, *Seduction and Betrayal*, p. 96.
68. Anaïs Nin, *A Woman Speaks*, ed. Evelyn J. Hinz (London: W. H. Allen and Co., Ltd., 1978), p. 174.
69. Chopin, *The Awakening*, p. 73.
70. Ibid., p. 53.
71. Ibid., p. 20.
72. Ibid., pp. 71-72.
73. Ibid., p. 52.
74. Ibid., p. 56.
75. Ibid., p. 88

76. Ibid., pp. 72–73.
77. Ibid., p. 75.
78. Ibid., p. 98.
79. Ibid., pp. 14–15.
80. Ibid., pp. 26–27.
81. Ibid., p. 113.
82. Ibid., p. 28.
83. Ibid.
84. Ibid., p. 29.
85. de Beauvoir, *The Second Sex*, p. 485.
86. Florence Howe, "Feminism and Literature," *Images of Women in Fiction: Feminist Perspectives*, ed. Susan Koppelman Cornillon (Bowling Green, Ohio: Bowling Green University Popular Press, 1972), p. 273.
87. Edmund Wilson, *Patriotic Gore: Studies in the Literature of the American Civil War* (New York: Oxford University Press, 1962), p. 591.
88. Henry Steele Commager, *The American Mind: An Interpretation of American Thought and Character Since the 1880's* (New Haven, Conn.: Yale University Press, 1950), pp. 5–7.

2
Authority and Autobiography

For centuries critics have advanced descriptions of women's writings. Ellen Moers describes the most frequently presented characterization as one using such adjectives as "the spontaneous, the instinctive, the natural, the informal, the anti-classical, and the artless."[1] Whether or not these adjectives are indeed applicable to most women's writings is perhaps not as important as what this description implies about the speaker's attitude toward the subject. Such adjectives, attached to Romantic literature, indicate praise or at least neutrality. When they are applied to women's literature in general, they are often intended as, and are viewed as, negative criticism. An investigation of how and how well the stylistic approaches of an author work is surely much more valuable to the reader and critic than an attack upon or a paeon to the approaches themselves. An understanding of the possible usefulness of certain stylistic devices must precede an evaluation of group or individual successes or failures in using them. In other words, the correlation between a writer's choice of style and her subject, the mutual fitness of the two, is more important than the fact of the style itself.

The authorial stance adopted by women writers is one aspect of their writing that has received considerable criticism. For example, one finds Simone de Beauvoir judged for straining after "masculine authority" at the same time that Mary Ellmann is reproached for her evasiveness.² Instead of thus dictating what women ought to write or examining highly individualized styles, it is more instructive to investigate the writing patterns of groups of women writers. Here, one can find similarities which stem from a common intent. For example, in the feminist novel, as in modern literature generally, the author usually refrains from comment, direct or indirect, and avoids inserting herself into the novel, so one does not often feel the presence of the author. If it is true that "the greatest literary possibilities for women" lie "in the abandonment of authority as a rhetorical pose,"³ then these authors, in adopting this modern stance, are developing from it an important and congenial writing position for women authors. For the female author of a feminist novel particularly, the assumption of authority poses a special problem. There is a marked inconsistency involved in adopting an authoritative posture while at the same time attacking authoritarianism.

The withdrawn authorial pose is helpful in many feminist novels, but, of course, some of the novels exhibit it more consistently and more successfully than others. Novels in which the authors employ it with special advantage include *Orlando, The Golden Notebook, The Edible Woman, The Company She Keeps, How She Died*, and *Looking for Mr. Goodbar*. The structure of these novels is of special concern in large part because of their authors' silence. Anna makes numerous observations about the form of the modern novel in *The Golden Notebook*, but many of them are not substantiated by the form of the feminist novel. A look at some of Anna's opinions and the subsequent rejections made by the structure of feminist novels can help to illuminate the pattern of these novels, a pattern through which the author silently speaks. In effect, the construction of these novels serves as a medium for authorial comment.

The feminist novel does not provide examples to support Anna's observation in *The Golden Notebook* that at present the novel seems to be an outpost of journalism, something that one reads in order to find out what is going on, not in order to enter a philosophy.⁴ Rather, all these feminist novels do have a philosophy, even a political philosophy, although it is not one specifically elaborated upon by the author. Anna goes on at another point to declare that it is the real things—the small, unimportant, factual things—that are really important in the novel, not the author's analysis.[5] It is true that the same small, factual things are reiterated in all of Anna's notebooks, but the facts are not actually important in and of themselves. They are significant because they are the germs of thousands of different viewpoints. It is actually what is done with the facts that makes them meaningful. The authors of many feminist novels reconcile the facts and the philosophy, achieving a synthesis by having the facts comprise the spoken part of the novel and having the philosophy determine the novel's order, its structure, its progression. These small, factual statements might be seen, like the new criticism, as an "exercise in fragmentary perceptions rather than assumption of authority."[6] The new critic might appear to focus on individual instances, on the text in itself. In actuality, an ideology of exclusiveness underlies and binds all new criticism together. Similarly, the ideology of the feminist novel unites all the incidental facts presented in the novel. Each author's silently stated philosophy forms the cohesive force joining the novel's small facts together. One need not choose between fragmentation or authoritarianism, and the authors of these novels have avoided both.

The antonyms to the usual stylistic approach of the feminist novel are authorial intrusion and an authoritarian tone. These are particular dangers for an author using the third-person point of view. Speaking about oneself does not as easily lead to a judgmental tone as does speaking about someone else. Of course, a first-person narrator comments on other characters, but the reader weighs such judgments with full knowledge of the narrator's perspective. Perhaps it is for this reason that so many writers of feminist novels choose the autobiographical point of view. The first person can be an aid to the author who wants to avoid manipulating her readers and to avoid the editorializing, slanting, and sententiousness that can crop up when the third person is employed.[7] The author becomes the thing observed. The repeated use of autobiography or pseudo-autobiography in the feminist novel can suggest other connections with feminist ideology as well. For example, the use of autobiography serves to mirror the tension which exists in these novels between individualism and modern mass collectivism and between public and private experience. Writing in the first person may also be a form of female authorial rebellion against the novel written in the third person because the third-person format "allows—even encourages—just the self-effacing withdrawal that society fosters in women."[8] It could be as a result of all these factors that in nearly one-half of the novels considered here, the autobiographical approach is employed frequently or exclusively. These include *Daughter of Earth, The Golden Notebook, The Edible Woman, The Company She Keeps, Up the Sandbox!, Fear of Flying, How She Died, Memoirs of an Ex-Prom Queen, Daddy was a Number Runner, The Bleeding Heart, The Color Purple,* and *Braided Lives.*

Many charges have been made against the use of this technique. Autobiography has been described, for example, as a "beginning place" in the connection between feminism and literature.[9] Ordinarily, one leaves the starting place as one matures. Autobiography fits well also with the disparaging argument that women usually set their writing in the home or in their hometown because of their limited range of experience.[10] Kazin suggests in attacking autobiography that explicit autobiography loses the explicit intention at the base of art.[11] In an oblique condemnation of the first person, Claudette Chonez comments that French women writers tend toward sensation and personal confession and do not utilize their creative imaginations in the setting-up of their characters and social milieus.[12] Finally, Virginia Woolf observes appreciatively that "The impulse towards autobiography may be spent. She [the woman writer] may be beginning to use writing as an art, not as a method of self-expression."[13]

In actuality, in the feminist novel, autobiography is often inextricably connected with a high level of creativity and artistic achievement. The authors of these novels, like Margaret Sargent, were probably bothered by and "knew what it was to have a sense of artistic decorum that like a hoity-toity wife was continually showing one's poor biography the door."[14] However, most of them employ autobiography in spite of the animus against it and have managed to dispel the so-called dissonance between autobiography and literature. Their achievement even lends credence to Ludwig Lewisohn's conception of art as autobiography.[15] There is certainly a very strong connection between the life of a writer and the book s/he writes. Irving Howe suggests that this connection leads far less often to a re-creation of the events of a writer's past than to a re-creation of its atmospheres and emotional patterns.[16] Similarly, Anaïs Nin comments that women readers of her diary noted "that even though their fathers were not like my father and though they were not born in Europe—even though the facts were not quite the same, certainly the emotional reactions were."[17] Consequently, a novel may very well be autobiographical without being written in the first person. A novel may also be written in the first person and be a pseudo-autobiography because it presents neither the events nor even necessarily the emotions felt by an author. It is possible, however, to treat novels written in the first person as the narrators' autobiographies, especially if it is the effect of the autobiographical mode represented by first-person narration that is to be studied rather than the specific relationship between the authors' lives and their novels. Autobiography is appropriate for the ideology underlying the feminist novel and is often put to additional good use as an adjunct to the multiple point of view.

Autobiography is especially useful in an anti-authoritarian world like the one of the feminist novel because of its special tone. One can hardly be accused of authoritarianism when speaking about oneself. Even when the persona in one of these novels describes or comments upon other characters, one can scarcely attack her for being autocratic. After all, how else is the autobiography to proceed? Even when the central figure is wrong in her assessment, the reader's reaction is likely to be one of sympathy because s/he feels on close terms with the speaker. Just as the metaphorical isolation of a desolate setting may be necessary for the exercise of female authority,[18] so the isolated point of view represented by autobiography gives the speaker some authority without authoritarianism. Personal experience is one mode of learning through which a woman can gain expertise and declare herself an expert without arrogance.

Of course, Agnes Smedley does manage to sound dictatorial even in an autobiography; on the other hand, one reads *Looking for Mr. Goodbar* as though it were written in the first person when it is not. Usually, though, through the autobiography, the speaker tries to understand her own life and, consequently, her world. One watches Anna in *The Golden Notebook* as through a series of mirrors writing about writing about her life. Similarly, in *Fear of Flying*, Isadora sits down and leafs through all her notebooks and poems in an attempt to understand what has happened to her. One observes as well the growth of Celie and Nettie through their letters to one another in *The Color Purple*. In a sense, the characters in these novels hope "to achieve a personal reformation upon which a reformation of society might begin."[19] In their first-person struggles to redeem themselves from the world, they discover new values and meanings for themselves. In extrapolation, the world itself needs new goals and assessments as well.

The use of autobiography reinforces anti-authoritarianism in yet another way. Unless the speaking character is merely a stand-in for the author, there is no reason to assume that the autobiographical voice is one that speaks only wisdom and truth. Certainly, the Anna of *The Golden Notebook* and the Margaret of *The Company She Keeps* are keepers of enough private madness that their perceptions are not to be unthinkingly accepted as accurate. The variety of viewpoints presented in *The Golden Notebook* and *How She Died* constantly reminds the reader that the same events are presented very differently when the speaker changes. Through the use of the first person and a number of speakers, the author can underscore a prismatic view of the world.

The autobiographical approach fits very well with another preoccupation of the feminist novel, the war between subjectivity and objectivity. Ordinarily, one is exhorted to be objective. One hears, for example, from Bernard DeVoto that even literature should attempt to report life "objectively."[20] Similarly, Simone de Beauvoir states that "many problems appear to us to be more pressing than those which concern us in particular, and this detachment even allows us to hope that our attitude will be objective."[21] The writers of feminist novels do not strive for objectivity. Rather, they accept the subjectivity of all thought and writing and express this acceptance through their use of autobiography and through their disdain for authority. Doris Lessing dramatizes this suspicion of objectivity explicitly in *The Golden Notebook*. Anna remarks of her black notebook, for instance, that "it's full of nostalgia, every word loaded with it, although at the time I wrote it I thought I was being 'objective.' "[22] She ultimately sees that even the blue notebook, the factual, objective one, is false and embarrassing because of its emotionalism and fallacious, underlying assumptions.[23] In fact, the attempt at objectivity is doomed to deceit. Anna realizes that even if she tried to write down all the details of the first and last days of Paul and Ella's relationship, she "would still be instinctively isolating and emphasizing the factors that destroyed the affair."[24] Indeed, she would necessarily select and highlight those points which to her are most meaningful. She could not do otherwise. Dolores in *The Bleeding Heart* also attacks the ideal of objectivity but as a masculine construct when she comments on a man who should remove himself from an examining board because of bias, "but of course he won't. They [men] are so bloody sure they can keep things separate. So sure they're fair, objective."[25] In using autobiography and avoiding the tone of objective authority, the authors of these novels underscore the subjective nature of writing and thought.

This theme is handled very well in *The Company She Keeps*. Here Mary McCarthy uses all three vantage points, first, second, and third person. In so doing, she presents for the reader a picture of Margaret Sargent from all three different perspectives. The chapter on "The Genial Host" serves to some extent as a capsulation of Margaret's shifting self. Pflaumen, the genial host, decides who the guests he invites actually are. He turns them all into abstract, allegorical figures, and they accept it. They become the limited, circumscribed characters Pflaumen assigns to them when he gives them their "identity cards."[26] Pflaumen, were he a writer, would totally control his characters. From him one would never be given the multifaceted picture of Margaret presented in *The Company She Keeps*. In another chapter, "The Man in the Brooks Brothers Shirt," one gains an understanding of Margaret's lack of identity. The Brooks Brothers man actually directs their entire relationship. Everything Margaret does is only in reaction to something he has done or said. Margaret, in fact, looks to him, thinking that "perhaps at last she had found him, the one she kept looking for, the one who could tell her what she was really like."[27] She has no consistent self-image and no conception of her own being. It even occurs to her as a possibility that "her whole way of life had been assumed for purposes of ostentation";[28] everything she does is performed as a role with herself observing herself through the eyes of others. At times she feels the possibility for all things in herself; but she remains merely a mirror. As a result, one does not even learn her full name until the end of the novel; one does not need to know it since she is not defined by her name but by the company she keeps. Interestingly, this company never includes women friends. In turning to outside authority for self-definition, she cannot turn to women. They have no standing as experts. Further, it is difficult to form friendships when one does not have a being. Margaret's self-distrust and her shifting, insubstantial self are reflected by McCarthy's choice of constantly changing points of view. Thus, the autobiographical mode can enable an author to make a variety of statements concerning the main character's self-image.

On the other hand, autobiography occasionally seems to be fostered more by a very feminine, over-developed humility than by an authorial choice of effective style. One finds this most obviously in Agnes Smedley's *Daughter of Earth*. An attitude of humble submissiveness crops up frequently in this only partly fictionalized autobiography and jars with the revolutionary tone of the novel. This meekness merges with the very strong sense of guilt the central figure, Marie Rogers, feels about nearly everything. She feels guilty about her marriages because of her inability to love without fear. She feels guilty about not being able to help her brothers even though she realizes that capitalism fosters her brothers' situations. She feels guilty about going to a university at the same time that in factories "rows of girls sat at sewing machines making felt pennants to decorate the rooms of college and university students."[29] Marie does not always express this guilt directly. Smedley juxtaposes Helen's having sent Marie money for school and the fact of Helen's life as a prostitute and her work in the factory making pennants. It is clear that Helen may have made pennants for the very university Marie attends. Smedley makes it obvious that Marie has good reason to feel guilty. On the other hand, it is the repetition that unsettles the reader. Marie feels guilty about Helen, about her father, about her desire for success, even about Juan Diaz's raping her. The autobiography here allies as much with this sense of inferiority, with a humble reticence, as with the feminist import of the novel. The situations causing Marie's guilt are structured so that the reader feels the author shares much of this guilt. Marie decides to help her family members too late when they are either dead or in other ways beyond help. The author even indicates that, since Marie felt some desire for Diaz, she was a "passive participant"[30] in her own rape. This humility and overweening guilt are also attached to Marie's marked tendency to moralize on her own conduct and on that of others and to accept authoritarian dogma. Here is an impulse toward the use of autobiography which is perhaps not so much feminist as feminine.

The frequent use of autobiography in other feminist novels blends well, however, with the marked distrust of ideology evinced by their authors. As feminism distrusts ideology, so the feminist novel eschews formulated authorial proclamation. By avoiding the omniscient point of view and eschewing the stance of the ideologue, the authors underscore this mistrust. If one describes deductive literature as that which pronounces the human condition rather than examines it,[31] then one can generally label the feminist novel, which usually attempts the reverse, as inductive literature. Generalities grow from these novels, but the novels are not ordinarily formed by the generalities. In effect, the novel urges the reader not to "listen to the didactic statements of the author, but to the low, calling cries of the characters, as they wander in the dark woods of their destiny!"[32]

It is true in the feminist novel, as in other modern political novels, that the authors are more concerned with theory and ideology than past political authors were.[33] However, part of feminist ideology as it develops in these novels involves a suspicion of authority and distrust of ideology even to the extent that in delineating a promising sector of post-nuclear war society, Doris Lessing describes its chief positive characteristic as the absence of any "ideology, plan, constitution, or philosophy."[34] This hostility toward ideology is, of course, a hallmark of mid-twentieth century attitudes. It is unusual and paradoxical to find it as part of a political ideology. However, in displaying this apprehension, the feminist novel only recognizes those major developments in politics and philosophy which have occurred over the last decades.

For the feminist novel to exhibit a wary attitude toward ideology is also a reflection of the twentieth-century failure of world views and systems of belief. This skepticism is perfectly understandable at a time when most philosophies and ideologies have either been discredited or fragmented. One usually looks to the political left for progressive thought, but for many, Marxism now seems a gray, rigid, abstract doctrine.[35] For many, also, it has been badly multilated by the uses to which it has been put. It has been attacked for its failure to supply an ideological base for a sexual revolution[36] and has been described often as "finished as a force."[37] Likewise, to its own discredit, socialism has taken an authoritarian form almost everywhere.[38] The working class, a former bastion of left-wing hope, can hardly be described at present as "a whole committed to freedom."[39] Most recently, the 1960s counter-culture has been observed to be as sexist as any other element of society. Even writers presumably sympathetic to left-wing ideals, for example, Eugene Keller and Lewis Coser, when writing about the American family, observe with concern that the increasing numbers of married women in the workforce threaten "normal" patterns of living, leisure, and division of labor in households.[40] They also point out that because of the absence of fathers and their lack of authority in poor families, "pathological matrifocality" ensues.[41] Given this performance and the possibility that "in defense of an ideal, every group eventually substitutes itself for the ideal,"[42] the suspicious attitude toward ideologies revealed in the feminist novel is quite reasonable.

These novels certainly do not reject politics in the ordinary sense nor do they completely reject theories and ideology. They do recognize the limitations of all three, however. Margaret Sargent, in *The Company She Keeps*, tells us, "I'm not even political."[43] In the strict, narrow sense delineated by adherence to an ideology, she is not. The novel she appears in, though, does invest her life with a political meaning, by underlining it with the ideology of feminism while at the same time avoiding dogmatism and prescription. From Isadora Wing, one hears, too, that "any system was a strait jacket if you insisted on adhering to it so totally and humorlessly. I didn't believe in systems."[44] Feminism does not advance systems, either. Helen Yglesias, in *How She Died*, deals in depth with the moral and social problems caused by political systems. On the one hand, she presents Mary who is only strong when she is in control. She is a person who must make things happen.[45] This aspect of her personality causes her to be attracted to political organizing and theories. She eventually forms a theory of her own, one dealing with a design for community life, one that even Matt admires.[46] Even here, though, her main goal is to remove politics and the political from human life, to remove the power struggle from family arrangements.[47] On the other hand, Yglesias presents Jean who is, in many ways, Mary's opposite. Unlike Mary, she can float with events and allow them to happen around her. When Jean does try to control things, when she "meddles" as she puts it, the results are catastrophic. When she and Matt try to help Mary, even though they love her in their way, they cause her to be locked up in Bellevue and subjected to unnecessary and debilitating radical surgery. When, with Joanna, Jean and her children meddle with the sick birds they have found, they almost succeed in killing them.[48] Beneficial and malignant aspects of both approaches, Jean's and Mary's, are presented. Mary can make good things happen while Jean passively sits. On the other hand, interference can kill while the pulling back can allow life to continue or a quick death to ensue. All this tentativeness and even hostility toward systems and ideologies recalls Erica Jong's quotation from D. H. Lawrence that "the real trouble about women is that they must always go on trying to adapt themselves to men's theories of women."⁴⁹ The politics of the feminist novel attempts to avoid the straits of dogmatic political ideology.

At the same time that these novels reveal a suspicion of ideology, they recognize that it is impossible to escape it. Hence, they insist that all thought is subjective. They second Kate Millett's observation that a value-free discipline is probably inconceivable and would probably emerge as a monstrosity if it were possible.⁵⁰ A corollary in many of the novels is a corresponding elevation of feeling, intuition, and emotion. For example, the clearest sign of the beginning regeneration of Mr. _____ in *The Color Purple* is Celie's observation: "it do begin to look like he got a lot of feeling hind his face."⁵¹ Ultimately, Mr. _____ even regains his name—Albert. Feelings are, in effect, a sign of grace. On the other hand, in nearly every one of these novels, at least one male character represents the attempt at complete objectivity, pure reason, and totally controlled emotion. All the way up to Harley in *The Women's Room*, these figures invariably represent deformed humanity, beings only partly human. They also reveal that even the supposedly objective character has his own tightly held ideology.

In addition to its relation to subjectivist criticism, this recognition of the importance of feeling and emotion has an impact upon the feminist novel's relationship to contemporary fiction. Such fiction has been described generally as presenting a world in which there are no accepted norms of feeling or conduct. All that seems to remain is either courage or simply being.⁵² This is not the case in the feminist novel, possibly because it is political. Generally, except in *How She Died* where an examination of conduct is a thematic element, the feminist novel does have a base of codes posited as acceptable and unacceptable. Doris Lessing's *The Golden Notebook* reveals this morality quite clearly. The attitude presented through Anna is that next to essential human goodness, all intellectual and political stances are inadequate. In a revealing paragraph she comments upon her friends. Ideology has nothing to do with her evaluations of her friends' characters. She states:

Yet of that group, I will say simply, without further analysis, that George was a good person, and that Willi was not. That Maryrose and

Jimmy and Ted and Johnnie the pianist were good people, and that Paul and Stanley Lett were not. And furthermore, I'd bet that ten people picked at random off the street to meet them, or invited to sit in that party under the eucalyptus trees that night, would instantly agree with this classification—would, if I used the word *good*, simply like that, know what I meant.[53]

Here the import of the human being lies in the kindness, sensitivity, the basic goodness, of the individual, not in the ideology to which his or her thought may finally lead. For example, Johnnie, the pianist, and Stanley Lett are both working class and separated from the others because of it. Both have a world view formed by their economic status; yet, one is, as Anna says, "good" and the other is not. Similarly, George admires Willi's ideas and intellect, but George is a much better person than Willi. In this distrust of abstract formulae and programs, these novels insist that one must be willing to change sides with justice.[54] In fact, feminism as it is presented through these novels requires, for the most part, that one not be chained too tightly even to feminist ideology. In this respect, it is similar to the new liberalism in that it calls for improvisation and experimentation.[55] Both viewpoints recognize the reasons for the disrepute into which ideology and total planning have fallen.

Many of these novels even express a desire for the abolition of politics. Isadora Wing voices such a wish when she describes life as a fruitcake of joy. For her, when politics is no longer necessary, one can focus on the small pleasures of being alive. For *The Dollmaker*, Gertie, it is only the smell of cedar, the joy of her home, the pleasure of farming, the lives of her children, that she wishes to enjoy. Jean sums up the consensus at the end of *How She Died* when she describes the private joys of the individual and the "glorious surge of communal happiness" she felt at one time.[56] When these private and public loves can be combined and when people are free to enjoy their own small happinesses, then politics will no longer be necessary.

The rejection of authority, suspicion of ideology, and even dislike for politics expressed by the feminist novel is heightened still further by the main characters' reactions toward authority and, by extension, toward authoritarian political systems. If one views the twentieth century as being characterized by authoritarian modes of politics,[57] then the feminist novel deals with a central aspect of this century's political problems. The eventual outcome for the main characters in these novels often hinges in large part on their ultimate acceptance or rejection of authority. In most of these novels, this issue of power and authority is presented through male and female, husband and wife relationships. So, frequently, societal, political, and economic tyranny is symbolized by patriarchal authority. Those characters who manage to throw off the hold that authority has over their minds are usually granted a positive resolution at the end of their novels. Those who do not break free die, either literally or figuratively.

Among the group of characters who ultimately reject individual and societal authority over them, there exists a variety of experiences and resolutions. In three of the novels, the outcome for the main characters is joyous. Isadora, for example, at the end of *Fear of Flying*, has been released from her fear, is certain that she will survive, and finally is free of her need to be always joined with a man. Attaining freedom is especially triumphant for Isadora because of her previous constant fear of it, her desire to escape from it. For her, "the appeal of irresponsibility, or of responsibility defined by others"[58] is great. At one point, for example, she states, "I was nobody's baby now. Liberated. Utterly free. It was the most terrifying sensation I'd ever known in my life."[59] The two characters, though, who seem to gain nearly everything they desire, are Dorine in *Small Changes* and Celie in *The Color Purple*. Dorine throws off the old, suffocating behaviors trapping her in drudgery and is, at the end, establishing what looks like a fulfilling relationship with Phil, significant work for herself, and a balanced sharing of herself and taking from others. Celie stops writing to God, begins writing to her sister, Nettie, a woman, and eventually dares to sign her own name to her letters.

Mira in *The Women's Room* and Jean in *How She Died* both finally reject passivity, but the ultimate resolution for them is not so totally pleasant. Both, like Isadora Wing, must fight off the desire to capitulate and make things easier for themselves. Mira accepts living death with Norm for fifteen years in large part because of her fear of the outside world. Jean in her passivity fears to make a move. When she does, she often suffers guilt from the failures of her interventions. Both Mira and Jean succeed in freeing themselves but seemingly are forced to accept perpetual loneliness as a result. Mira is in some ways exiled at the end of *The Women's Room* and Jean, although not walled off geographically, is left without Matt or her friend, Mary.

For two others, Louie in *The Man Who Loved Children* and Beth in *Small Changes*, rejection of authority means flight. They throw off the authority of parents, husbands, and society and finally of man-made laws themselves. Louie helps her mother commit suicide, and Beth helps Wanda steal her children back. As a result, Beth is forced into hiding, at least for a time. Louie, unable to make her father see the truth and unwilling to become Henny, leaves to start her own life. Both achieve freedom but will not be able to be a part of society until society changes. The only characters who spurn authority and yet fail in freeing themselves are Francie in *Daddy was a Number Runner* and Edna in *The Awakening*. There is no way out for Francie at the end of her novel and no way out for Edna but death. The control exercised over Francie is economic force and that over Edna is social authority. It is not true for either of them that freedom is the absence of overt coercion.[60] Overt coercion is not only simpler to recognize than covert force, but the battle is more clearly defined.

Quite a few other characters fail to cast off authority and, consequently, fail generally. At the end of *The Company She Keeps*, Margaret Sargent remains unable to throw off the authority her husband has over her, primarily because she feels the same desire to escape from freedom that Isadora Wing experienced. She realizes that "the dictator is also the scapegoat; in assuming absolute authority, he assumes absolute guilt...."[61] The only freedom she does possess is the ability to see clearly; she at least does not delude herself. Not free herself, she is at least free of her husband's ideology. At the end, for example, "she thought, walking on, she could still detect her own frauds. At the end of the dream, her eyes were closed, but the inner eye had remained alert. She could still distinguish the Nazi prisoner from the English milord, even in the darkness of need."[62]

Gertie in *The Dollmaker* is unable to reject individual and societal control. The individuals who exert their authority over her are represented by her mother and her husband. Although a very strong person otherwise, she is never able to loosen the ropes her mother uses to hold her. The political, economic, and social systems which bind her and murder her children are centered in Detroit and its world of "adjustment." As alone as she is, she cannot fight the former, and as confused by strangeness and harangued as she is, she is unable to completely throw off the force of the latter. She is left supported solely by the knowledge of the beauty of the people she knows, the people in her neighborhood who are imprisoned with her.

Several other characters cannot escape from the authority of patriarchal and capitalist ideology. Lutie Johnson in *The Street* can never quite free herself from a conscience instilled in her from childhood. This conscience aids in causing her defeat which results primarily from an economic and political system that denies black women any chance at life or joy. Despite a rising anger and realization of injustice, she still in large part blames herself for her failure. She tells herself that "it was always the mother's fault when a kid got into trouble"[63] and so accuses herself for Bub's imprisonment. Similarly, she calls herself a murderer for killing Boots, thinking that "there wasn't any excuse for her. It hadn't even been self-defense."[64] Of course, self-defense was precisely what it was; she internalizes the judgment a white male court would make on her actions.

Miriam in *Small Changes* and Theresa in *Looking for Mr. Goodbar* also cannot shake off the inculcations of patriarchal ideology. For Miriam, it is "love" that she thinks she must have to be complete. So thoroughly has she blinded herself that she tries to convince herself even near the end of the novel—and her marriage—that Neil still loves her. She tries to reassure herself of his love by reminding herself that "she was a good woman, she had had his children, and they were beautiful. ..."[65] as though somehow those facts would make an impression on Neil. Theresa embodies all of patriarchy's strictures.

She even goes so far as to separate her personality completely in order to conform to society's views on female sexuality. Since sex is bad for women, she is only allowed to enjoy it as the solely sexual being, Terry, and then only with people like Tony who despise her. She cannot enjoy sex with James, partly because he loves her. As Miss Dunn, she is the good, asexual woman who teaches elementary school. As Theresa, she is herself, but because of the lies she has accepted, she can never begin to like herself or to accept her own sexuality. Her death is as much a suicide as a murder; she must kill her sexual side.

Finally, Smedley's Marie Rogers escapes only to the ideological confines of a strict Marxism. It might seem in some ways that she resembles Beth and Louie in that she denies capitalistic doctrine and eventually leaves the country which enslaves its people in poverty. In reality, though, she accepts Marxism so wholly and passively that she might be said only to have exchanged one set of chains for another. She submits totally to the authority of Marxist leaders; and, even at the end of the novel, she leaves primarily because she only sees herself hurting Anand, not because she is escaping to freedom.

This is one of the few novels in this group in which the author does not seem to recognize her own authoritarian tone or the passivity of her central character. She presents the Indian group with which Marie becomes associated as uniformly good. Juan Diaz, who appears to be a bad member, is eventually discovered to be a spy. Because he is a spy and is not really part of the group, the group remains thoroughly honorable. Smedley does not separate herself from the clichés and dogmatic statements Marie Rogers makes, either. There is no hint of irony or any awareness of contradiction on the author's part when Marie praises *The Call*, the socialist newspaper she works on, by stating: "The final message of the Communist leader contained a criticism of the Party, and yet we published the story."[66] She thinks it quite extraordinary that her paper would publish something it did not agree with, yet she literally demands the same of papers that are opposed to her views. In effect, she seeks praise for the Party for doing what she demands others do automatically and without hesitation. Smedley's writing degenerates into sentimentality and triteness at those times when Marxist dogma is foremost in her mind and when she turns to it in anger. During one riot, she describes the "blue, apelike arm" of the police and, on the other side, the "blinded and bleeding working men."[67] Similarly, while Marie Rogers is on a march in Washington, a woman she sees is described as "a symbol of the ruling class that was forcing us into the war, making our laws, owning our land and industries, forcing us to work for them for the right to live on the earth."[68]

The serious problems with *Daughter of Earth* occur when Smedley intentionally uses the novel to prove a point and for preachment. The contradictions between the Marxist doctrine of the 1930s and Smedley's feminism are never resolved. The autobiographical stance underscores the feminism of the novel, but at the same time Smedley is unable to resist soap-box oratory. Marie Rogers decries authoritarianism and femininity. At the same time, she accepts Marxist authority implicitly, rails at others for their failings, and is unable to recognize or divest herself of her own very feminine guilt and humility. It has been said that the greatest division in Marxist thought presently is over the perceived need for a rigidly authoritarian system at the beginning of a Marxist government.[69] If this totalitarian leaning had not been part of Marxism and, consequently, part of Smedley, *Daughter of Earth* might have succeeded better. Presumably, too, Smedley could have reached some accommodation between her Marxism and feminism. Then the conflicts between autobiography, authoritarianism, and authorial presence in this novel might have been resolved.

Similarly, in *Small Changes*, one frequently encounters passages and situations that appear forced to fit the author's ideology. The author seems to intrude, twisting the circumstances too much, setting up characters in order to knock them down. At one point Miriam, while talking to Beth, defends her marriage but is entirely unconvincing,[70] partly because of the author's manipulation. At another time, Miriam argues with Beth about living in a commune.[71] Both times, one is left feeling that the reader is being asked to believe that Beth is the fount of all wisdom, that marriages are bound to fail, and that any commune is more likely to succeed than a marriage. The author adheres so firmly and completely to her ideology that it gives the novel a strong authoritarian tone and a sense of impersonality in certain sections.

Of course, the authorial pose is not identical in all the novels reviewed here. Those novels in which the author does insert herself are generally less successful than the others, however. In some novels like *Strange Fruit* and *Looking For Mr. Goodbar*, there is only an occasional jarring appearance by the author. In *Strange Fruit*, for example, Smith enters at one point to comment that white women "knew of their men's lives only that which came into their homes. They did not want to know more."[72] The characters do not really show the reader that this is true; Smith simply asserts it. Similarly, Judith Rossner seems to appear as Evelyn in *Looking For Mr. Goodbar* to describe a consciousness-raising group which Theresa is being encouraged to join.[73] Theresa feels herself drawing close to Evelyn because Evelyn really does care about other women. On the other hand, Evelyn terrifies her because all the points Evelyn brings up in relation to the group strike specifically at Theresa's problems, problems Theresa views as uniquely her own. There is a shift in tone at this point as Evelyn's talk borders on the polemic. This interruption and the one in *Strange Fruit* are jolting only in part because they disrupt the consistency of authorial posture in the novels. Primarily, they are disturbing because they conflict with the basic philosophy underlying the novels. Obtrusive authorial comment is jarring to the reader when encountered in a novel based on anti-authoritarianism and egalitarianism. Of course, this problem occurs only very occasionally in these two novels, and it is true that "even the most artful of writers will give himself (and his morality) away in about every third sentence."[74]

In *The Street*, as well as in *Small Changes* and *Daughter of Earth*, the presence of the author is also noticeable. There are authorial exclamations in all three novels that sometimes extend into lengthy lectures. From Ann Petry, who comments on a situation in her novel, one hears that Henry Chandler's father "could afford to hire a Lutie Johnson so his wife could play bridge in the afternoon while Lutie Johnson looked after little Henry."[75] Here Lutie Johnson loses her standing as a character and becomes an example, a type. She becomes "a" Lutie Johnson, one the author is merely using as a representative. In *Small Changes*, after an extended description of a trapped turtle, Marge Piercy informs the reader that Beth "was the turtle going round and round the chicken wire."[76] It would have been impossible for the reader to miss the implication; the succeeding bald statement is unnecessary. Similarly, Agnes Smedley cannot resist stating that it was Knut's fate "to reap the bitter harvest that a harsh and distorted society had sown within me."[77] The reader does not need this interjection; Smedley clearly reveals Marie's problems throughout the novel. These occasional intrusions are annoying not solely because of their literary awkwardness, their aura of didacticism, and their dogmatism, but also because of their incompatibility with the ideologies of the feminist novel in general and of these novels specifically. In *The Street, Small Changes*, and *Daughter of Earth*, novels that decry authoritarianism, that despise roles and stereotypes, that attempt to dispel judgmental attitudes through their compassionate portrayal of their heroines' unpopular actions, authorial tirades are singularly inappropriate.

These novels call to mind Virginia Woolf's comments in *A Room of One's Own* on the problems women writers face in dealing with their anger. It is almost always anger that is expressed when these authors desert their usual pose and thrust themselves into their novels. The fury is certainly justifiable but more effectively used when controlled. These novels also recall Simone de Beauvoir's statement that "an unfavorable prejudice against one is only on very rare occasions a help in overcoming it. The initial inferiority complex ordinarily leads to a defense reaction in the form of an exaggerated affectation of authority."[78] It is certainly racial and sexual bias that goads these authors into their sometimes harsh interjections. It is far simpler to hew to a chosen course when one is not constantly fighting off attacks. For these authors, the sensed attacks lead to a didactic defense reaction. Certainly here the authoritarian pose has failed.

Despite their flaws, these novels do share many elements with the others, including a corollary to their anti-authoritarianism and rejection of authoritarian political systems which is a very marked strain of individualism. This individualist tenor does not have a reactionary base, however. The point in these novels is not that the separateness of the individual is of utmost importance or that the individual is more important than the group. The point is, rather, to avoid authoritarianism of any kind, to avoid the dictatorship of the group as well as of the individual, to save the person as well as the people. Although it is true that since socialism creates great concentrations of power, democracy must be pressed,[79] it is also true that all modern, industrial, corporate forms of government create great concentrations of power. Modern, urban, British and American societies generally consist of concentrated groups of power and people. In most feminist novels, there is a recognition that the individual may be eliminated as a result. A small minority of the novels, on the other hand, heavily press the importance of the mass. Most impressive are those few novels that attempt to reconcile the importance and claims of both individual and group. These novels, in recognizing the merits of both individualism and collectivism, point out an appropriate and important direction for the feminist novel.

Those feminist novels that stress individualism express it most often through an attack on roles and stereotypes and an emphasis on the importance of and need for individual self-determination. The writer's retreat from a dictatorial pose blends well with this concern of the feminist novel. These novels announce "the irrelevance of moralizing about what women should and should not do."[80] Most of them emphatically deny that there should be a set of prescriptive roles for either men or women. They insist on the right of individual choice. Like twentieth-century writers in general, most of these authors do not enter into judgments on their characters. There is a strong sense of ethics underlying the feminist novel, but there are no rules laid out for the leading of a male or female life. Although most modern fiction retreats from making proclamations about appropriate roles, it does not examine the foundations of the female model as the feminist novel does.

In three of these novels, the attempt to escape from confining roles and stereotypes highlights the central character's individual development. As Edna in *The Awakening* grows, the role she has been playing becomes more and more constricting.

The narrow roles permitted to women and the attendant stereotyping of women destroy the individual by forcing women to conform. Edna refuses to do so and is destroyed anyway. Chopin, in focusing on Edna's refusal to do as she is expected to do, centers the novel on Edna's individuality and on the conformism of many of the other characters.

Another character who ultimately must flee a role forced on her is Louie in *The Man Who Loved Children*. At the end of the novel, just before she escapes, Louie begins turning into Henny. Toward the end, when meals are served, like Henny, Louie "would take her own plate and go with it to sit on the front lawn, or down the orchard, and no matter how many messages were sent to her to come in and join the family, she would obstinately and even mutely sit there, self-righteous, proud, and contemptuous."[81] Similarly, at another time over dinner, Sam "insisted on Louie's being present this time and ignored the sullen, brutish face she put on, as she sat there mute in Henny's place...."[82] Of course, Louie is not just sitting in Henny's place; she is becoming Henny. Here Christina Stead does not simply attack the imposition of roles but illustrates how the assumption of a role annihilates the individual and turns the person who accepts it into a cipher. To the extent that the Pollit family represents the United States in microcosm, Louie and Henny symbolize the position of women. For this reason, they come to understand one another as Sam can understand neither of them. Sam cannot understand any woman. For this reason, Louie shouts at Sam, "What do you know about my mother? She was a woman."[83] In a final irony, too, the country the Pollits symbolize, the one that presumably exalts individualism, is the one Louie must flee in order to remain herself, to assert her individuality, and to avoid becoming trapped in the role assigned to her.

The Color Purple displays two women who possess their own individuality as the novel begins—Shug and Sofia—and two others who become themselves as the novel progresses—Celie and Mary Agnes. Mary Agnes' final declaration of independence comes when she insists upon being called by her real name and not by her nickname, "Squeak." Harpo responds, "Squeak, Mary Agnes, what difference do it make?" Mary Agnes retorts, "It make a lot, say Squeak. When I was Mary Agnes I could sing in public."[84] Squeak cannot, of course. All four of the women band together when Albert and Grady assert that they must conform so that they can "git a man." After this remark, Celie observes, "Shug look at me and us giggle. Then us laugh sure nuff. Then Squeak start to laugh. Then Sofia. All us laugh and laugh."[85] Stereotypes and enforced roles no longer confine any of these women.

In two other novels, the roles the characters play destroy their individuality, in one case for fifteen years and in the other for a lifetime. One, Mira in *The Women's Room*, loses herself for the fifteen years she lives with Norm. She rages at her children for a muddy footprint: "They did not understand, she knew that. The cleanliness and order were her life, they had cost her everything."[86] The numbed, lonely evenings she spends with her brandy and cigarettes and her silent, passive, divine adjustment are also a result of her having lost herself for fifteen years. Her terror when she begins attending graduate school at Harvard and hides in the women's room is the terror of being cut free with no sense of herself. It is only when she begins to develop into a person again that she can really come out of a small room or house into the world.

Unlike Mira, Theresa in *Looking for Mr. Goodbar* never does find herself. Alternately, she is Terry; she is Miss Dunn; she is Theresa. At the same time, she is none of these people. The real Theresa speaks through italicized words and terrifies and confuses the Theresa the world has made. The real Theresa is not allowed to have a life. If Theresa Dunn is mad, she is only mad in a way very acceptable to society. She accepts everything society tells her and incorporates it into her personality. The part of her that is capable of enjoying sex cannot be part of the same person who is a teacher or who is loved by James Morrisey. It is not James, of course, who rejects her sexuality but she who does so. She is not permitted to have women friends. She is not allowed to live, and she must be punished. So she obediently separates herself into all her different parts. When she begins to realize she has done this, she is murdered. Theresa is not an individual, is not herself. It is for this reason that at the end, when she starts to write a diary, she thinks, "What was there to say about her life?... Then, as though she needed to reassure herself that she had indeed had a life, she went to the phone and called Katherine."[87] Theresa is so terrified of looking at herself that she can never write. Her attempt at it contrasts markedly with Isadora Wing's total acceptance of herself as she reads her own diary. The reverse is Theresa's total acceptance of society's rules and strictures, which denies her the right to ever live as an independent individual.

In one other novel, *The Dollmaker*, the theme of the salvation of the individual is central. The code word for the modern force that would destroy the human being is "adjustment." Nearly everyone continually assures Gertie that she and her children must and will adjust. Gertie is not at all sure she wants to adjust. Early in the novel, when she first arrives in Detroit, a teacher at the school asks Gertie if she would leave a wooden basket she had made. She smiles and says in return, "I've left four youngens here. I oughtn't to mind leaven a old split basket."[88] For her, leaving her children all day, day after day, with strangers is very odd and unpleasant. Two of her children, Clytie and Enoch, adapt very quickly. They accept the values of the group and become part of it. Reuben and Cassie do not. They remain themselves while everyone hammers at Gertie to make them adjust. Reuben manages to survive by hating and eventually runs away. Gertie at this point decides that perhaps his running off was her fault because she had not forced him to adjust, and so she kills Callie Lou, the representation of Cassie's imagination. Through Gertie's attempt at adjustment, at fitting with the group, through her denial of her own individuality and Cassie's, comes death. Callie Lou and Cassie are both murdered by the attempt to adapt to a world that values machines and money above people, conformity above individualism, and facts above imagination. Adjustment in this world means gaining the ability to get along with an Adolf Hitler and, simultaneously, losing one's soul.

In at least two other novels, the group or mass forms the central focus of the novel; the emphasis is on the characteristics that members of a group share more than on their differences. In *Small Changes*, for example, the basis of the novel is the similarities in situation that the main characters share because they are women. Certainly there are marked personality differences between Miriam, Beth, Dorine, and Wanda. But what makes them coalesce as a group is the experiences they share because they are women. All of them have been hurt by men; all the marriages are bad; all have numerous obstacles placed in the way of their desires to work, to love, to be with their children. The only male and female relationship that eventually succeeds is between Phil and Dorine, and that occurs only after major personality changes on the part of both.

The problems with *Small Changes* as a novel are, to an extent, related to this emphatic stress on the characters as primarily members of a group. Some of the situations and characters seem developed just for the effect of reiteration. The repetition of bad marriages and thoroughly selfish, stony men occasionally lends a hostile, unthinking tone to the novel. The repeated poor outcomes of all of Miriam's choices become a litany. Certainly, Miriam's overwhelming need for protection and security creates many of her problems. Despite Miriam's dependence on love, however, she is portrayed as intelligent, energetic, and educated; yet everything she attempts ends in failure. There seems a relentless desire on the author's part to convince the reader that nothing will work out for Miriam until her personality changes. Similarly, the personality changes experienced by Dorine, Beth, and Phil create difficulties in the novel. The shifts are so major and so sudden that they appear to be a result of authorial manipulation and are not wholly believable. Ultimately, Dorine, Beth, Phil, and Wanda become the same personality. They think in so much the same way, say so much the same things, and face the world so similarly that they meld into one. This novel does attack roles, but it does not simultaneously advance the individual. In some ways, it exchanges the repression of a role for the repression of a single, fixed viewpoint and a single personality.

In *Daughter of Earth*, also, the mass rather than the individual is the central focal point. Although there is only one main character, Marie Rogers, her individuality is not the center of the novel. Rather, the importance of her life is as a depiction of the life of a daughter of a poverty-ridden family. It is as a representative of the poor, and of poor women particularly, that she is primarily presented. Through her life, the lives of other poor people and, later, of other radicals are illuminated. Further, her life represents the education of a Marxist although she always does carry her own individual, elemental feminism with her. Through her Marxist learning and her earliest and deepest experiences, class consciousness becomes the center of her thought. As a result, the ideology of the novel focuses on the mass as the central protagonist. For all its stress on the primacy of the group, however, this novel is paradoxically at its best when dealing with the individual. When Marie describes her mother's pride in her daughter's being a teacher, or when she relates her experiences with married women, or when she describes the young mothers with whom she is jailed, the novel is alive and has the effect on the reader Smedley wishes.

A third group of novels does not center specifically on either the individual or the mass but on the interactions of the two. Post–1960s Marcusian Marxism might share some similarities with this group as a result of its efforts to restore the individual within what has been seen as an abstract, cold, world-scale economic analysis. In these novels, the ideal of communal love is developed and, ultimately, is wedded to the alternative of personal, individual joy and happiness. Here, the mass is not presented as a solidified, nameless, faceless group. Instead, the central characters in the novels experience and grow into the joy of being a separate, and yet joined, part of a communal whole. There is a resemblance to the monkey-rope ties of brotherhood found during the squeezing of case by Ishmael in *Moby-Dick*. Gertie in *The Dollmaker* grows into the full sharing of this love at the end of the novel when she recognizes that all her neighbors are Christs and Judases. Even at the end when she has lost all her individual happiness, her hope, her children, and the symbolic block of wood, she finds them all again and is sustained by the connected love of her neighbors.

For Francie in *Daddy was a Number Runner* and Theresa in *Looking for Mr. Goodbar*, the end is different. Francie begins to feel the ties of community late in the novel when she is leaning on the windowsill and looking at the boys across the street in front of the drugstore. She finds that:

As I watched them they didn't seem so bad all of a sudden, just full
of fun, and I didn't want them to fall off the roof or cut each other or
be hauled off to jail but just to stay here, safe and sound forever,
laughing in front of the drugstore. I forgave them for making me hate
to walk past them while they shouted. . . .
I wanted to hug them all. We belonged to each other somehow. I'm
getting sick, I thought, as I shifted my elbows on the windowsill. I
must of caught some rare disease. But that sweet feeling hung on and
I loved all of Harlem gently and didn't want to be Puerto Rican or
anything else but my own rusty self.[89]

The ending is not the same for Francie, though, as for Gertie. Nothing can conquer the ugliness done to her world; at the end, Francie "tried to get again that nice feeling I had for all of Harlem a few weeks ago, but I couldn't. We was all poor and black and apt to stay that way, and that was that."[90]

Theresa in *Looking for Mr. Goodbar* never even gets the glimmering of an understanding of community. Her isolation is total. Having accepted and internalized all of society's rules for and attitudes toward women, she has been completely cut off from other women. This aspect of her loneliness can be traced through her reactions to Evelyn's suggestions that she come to her consciousness-raising group. Initially, all she can say is that the women's movement makes her uncomfortable and that she is uneasy in groups. Later, she is angry when Evelyn points out that Theresa only thinks of herself in relation to men, and she backs away because the women in the group sound "impressive" and "scary."[91] She begins to feel a "stirring of interest" anyway but retreats in terror when Evelyn mentions physical appearance. Theresa misses the point when Evelyn states that all women think they are deformed. She is unable to understand her connection with other women and assumes that her defect is unique. When she does finally go to a meeting and sees the shared love between the women, she is "at once moved and discomfited."[92] Finally, toward the novel's end, the group is one of the straws she grasps at, but Evelyn must check to see how the group feels about a new member. Theresa is never able to connect with the group she needs for communal support or with the individuals she needs for personal joy, although the novel envisions that support as a possibility.

In *How She Died* an attempt at resolution between the individual and the mass is finally made. During the demonstration, Jean, the complete individualist, begins to feel a communal bond. At one point:

> The triumphant, ritual wailing of the crowd, echoing and magnified in the tunnel, floated back to us. I did it too as we went through, my tongue beating against the roof of my mouth, something glorious freeing itself in the act, something getting out of me that I thought didn't exist or was totally imprisoned.[93]

Jean continues her growth throughout the novel and eventually begins to separate from Matt. As he talks about the importance of private joys, she tries to tell him about her feelings, explaining: " 'I went to a wild demonstration with Mary—when I acted as her guard, remember? I never felt that way before.' I stopped. How could I convey that glorious surge of communal happiness."[94] Matt is puzzled and returns to talking of personal joy to which Jean responds, " 'Maybe there's a way of putting them together,' I said. 'What?' he said. But I couldn't explain."[95] This joining together of the individual and the group provides an answer for the loneliness of Theresa, Mira, Miriam, and Edna. With this ideal as a reality, with communal happiness joined with the personal life, being alone can be experienced as solitude rather than loneliness. Solely private joys leave one alone to experience private hell as well; communal action alone negates the chance for a personal life, for solitude, for private joy. In the culmination of *How She Died*, Jean tries to weld the private and the public, the personal and the political. Just so, the authors of these feminist novels try to reveal the whole through the individual. As Doris Lessing says of the personal and general, "growing up is after all only the understanding that one's unique and incredible experience is what everyone shares."[96]

This close analogy drawn in the feminist novel between the private and the public, the personal and the political might reasonably lead one to expect the use of reportage, where the connection between the individual character in the novel and public events would be quite evident. This is not the case, however. Ordinarily, the modern political novelist is said to be attracted to journalism for several reasons. For the political writer especially, it permits breaking away from the absorption in the private consciousness representative of the twentieth century, and it also provides the immediacy of the event. This can be quite useful for such a writer. Of course, reportage and journalism also require placing stress on the event and may ultimately lead to the tyranny of the public over private experience. A journalistic style can contribute to the development of the attitude that nothing anyone could think or feel could be as important as the fact being reported.[97]

The feminist novels reviewed here do make reference to and connection with events and situations such as Vietnam, Kent State, Willow Run, World War II, and the Holocaust. But there is actually very little reportage as such except in sections of *The Golden Notebook*. Even here, though, it is used as an investigative technique rather than accepted as a legitimate form. Also, the emphasis is not put on the event in these novels but on the impression the event makes on the mind of the character. At times, too, the madness of various characters in the feminist novel is directly connected to events and occurrences in the modern world. One observes Anna in *The Golden Notebook*, for example, fragmenting as she papers her walls with newspaper clippings. Adele and Lily in *The Women's Room* and Theresa in *Looking for Mr. Goodbar* are trapped in the ideologies imposing non-life on women. The nameless heroine of *Up the Sandbox!* sees the deformity and madness of the world and her life reflected in the deformed children she fears.

None of this, though, reflects a total acceptance of the ideas behind reportage. In *The Golden Notebook* the relation of fact, event, and literature is of central importance and is examined closely. The real things, the same, small, simultaneously important and trivial, factual things in *The Golden Notebook* appear in all the notebooks. Ultimately, these facts and events by themselves are not significant; it is what one does with them that makes them meaningful. In *The Golden Notebook*, literature is not reportage or fact or life itself or nostalgia; "literature is analysis after the event."[98]

Also, although the allusions to current events in these novels do give a certain sense of immediacy, the novelists do not resort to reportage in order to dominate their novels. Rather, they attain an air of expertise and an assumption of authority through their use of autobiography. Otherwise, they keep themselves removed and unobtrusive. Perhaps the modern novelist's usual position of not knowing and not controlling is particularly congenial for the woman novelist in that women have been in a similar situation for so long. In any event, the reportorial style does not appear to be one that is proving useful in the feminist novel in the way that it has for Mailer or, earlier, for Dos Passos.

Evidently, what does seem to be useful is primarily autobiography and, secondarily, a very unobtrusive third-person point of view. These approaches, besides serving the functions earlier mentioned, also blend with the mistrust of ideology, suspicion of authority, and elevation of emotion so frequently evident in the feminist novel. They act further in highlighting the rejection of authoritarian political systems demonstrated in most of these novels and also by blending with their related strong strain of individualism. This individualism and the individuality of the characters in these novels is often presented by their casting aside the roles assigned to them.

It has been said that the neo-feminist novel tells the story of an education and that it is the task of the heroine to integrate herself.[99] Actually, it is, instead, the task of the heroine to discover all parts of herself and to reject the specious unity offered by ready-made roles. The characters in the feminist novel are not nineteenth-century figures secure in the verity of unity. Rather, they are modern characters awakening to the fullness of their personalities, the diversities of their desires, and the chaos and fragmentation of the twentieth century.

NOTES

1. Ellen Moers, *Literary Women* (Garden City, N.Y.: Doubleday and Co., Inc., 1976), p. 163.

2. Patricia Meyer Spacks, *The Female Imagination* (New York: Alfred A. Knopf, 1975), p. 28.
3. Ibid., p. 27.
4. Doris Lessing, *The Golden Notebook* (New York: Simon and Schuster, Inc., 1962), p. 60.
5. Ibid., p. 273.
6. Alfred Kazin, *On Native Grounds: An Interpretation of Modern American Prose Literature* (New York: Reynal and Hitchcock, 1942), p. 431.
7. Gordon Milne, *The American Political Novel* (Norman: University of Oklahoma Press, 1966), p. 101.
8. Sandra M. Gilbert and Susan Gubar, *The Madwoman in the Attic: The Woman Writer and the Nineteenth-Century Literary Imagination* (New Haven, Conn.: Yale University Press, 1979), p. 548.
9. Florence Howe, "Feminism and Literature," *Images of Women in Fiction: Feminist Perspectives*, ed. Susan Koppelman Cornillon (Bowling Green, Ohio: Bowling Green University Popular Press, 1972), p. 255.
10. Ellen Moers, "The Angry Young Women," *Harper's* 227 (December 1963): 89.
11. Kazin, *On Native Grounds*, p. 36.
12. Germaine Bree, *Women Writers in France: Variations on a Theme* (New Brunswick, N.J.: Rutgers University Press, 1973), p. 81.
13. Virginia Woolf, *A Room of One's Own* (New York: Harcourt, Brace and World, Inc., 1929), p. 83.
14. Mary McCarthy, *The Company She Keeps* (1942; reprint, New York: Harcourt, Brace and World, Inc., 1970), p. 264.
15. Kazin, *On Native Grounds*, p. 275.
16. Irving Howe, *Politics and the Novel* (New York: Horizon Press, Inc., 1957), p. 77.
17. Anaïs Nin, *A Woman Speaks*, ed. Evelyn J. Hinz (London: W. H. Allen and Co., Ltd., 1978), p. 163.
18. Moers, *Literary Women*, p. 230.
19. Elizabeth Hardwick, *Seduction and Betrayal: Women and Literature* (New York: Random House, 1974), p. 205.
20. Bernard DeVoto, *The Literary Fallacy* (Boston: Little, Brown and Co., 1944), p. 25.
21. Simone de Beauvoir, *The Second Sex*, ed. and trans. H. M. Parshley (1953; reprint, New York: Random House, 1974), p. xxxii.
22. Lessing, *The Golden Notebook*, p. 153.
23. Ibid., p. 468.
24. Ibid., p. 228.

25. Marilyn French, *The Bleeding Heart* (New York: Random House, 1980), p. 293.
26. McCarthy, *The Company She Keeps*, pp. 151–52.
27. Ibid., p. 101.
28. Ibid., p. 84.
29. Agnes Smedley, *Daughter of Earth* (1929; reprint, Old Westbury, N.Y.: The Feminist Press, 1973), p. 224.
30. Ibid., p. 297.
31. Richard Mitchell, "An Age of Issues and a Literature of Troubles," *Western Humanities Review* 17 (Autumn 1963): 353–54.
32. Erica Jong, *Fear of Flying* (New York: Holt, Rinehart and Winston, 1971), p. 335.
33. Milne, *The American Political Novel*, p. 105.
34. Doris Lessing, *The Four-Gated City* (New York: Alfred A. Knopf, 1969), pp. 599–600.
35. Kenneth M. and Patricia Dolbeare, *American Ideologies: The Competing Political Beliefs of the 1970's* (Chicago: Rand McNally College Publishing Co., 1976), p. 155.
36. Kate Millett, *Sexual Politics* (Garden City, N.Y.: Doubleday and Co., Inc., 1970), p. 169.
37. Lessing, *The Golden Notebook*, p. xi.
38. Dolbeare, *American Ideologies*, p. 134.
39. Ignazio Silone, "The Choice of Comrades," *The Radical Imagination*, ed. Irving Howe (New York: The New American Library, Inc., 1955), p. 16.
40. Eugene Keller, "Social Priorities, Economic Policy, and the State," *The Seventies: Problems and Proposals*, eds. Irving Howe and Michael Harrington (New York: Harper and Row, Publishers, 1972), pp. 108–9.
41. Lewis Coser, "What do the Poor Need? Money," *The Seventies: Problems and Proposals*, eds. Irving Howe and Michael Harrington (New York: Harper and Row, Publishers, 1972), p. 364.
42. Silone, "The Choice of Comrades," p. 17.
43. McCarthy, *The Company She Keeps*, p. 194.
44. Jong, *Fear of Flying*, p. 141.
45. Helen Yglesias, *How She Died* (Boston: Houghton Mifflin Co., 1972), p. 29.
46. Ibid., pp. 206–7.
47. Ibid., pp. 88–89.
48. Ibid., pp. 317–21.
49. Jong, *Fear of Flying*, p. 319.
50. Millett, *Sexual Politics*, p. 220.

51. Alice Walker, *The Color Purple* (New York: Simon and Schuster, Inc., 1982), p. 239.
52. Ihab Hassan, *Radical Innocence: Studies in the Contemporary American Novel* (Princeton, N.J.: Princeton University Press, 1961), pp. 115–17.
53. Lessing, *The Golden Notebook*, p. 109.
54. Silone, "The Choice of Comrades," p. 19.
55. Chester E. Eisinger, *Fiction of the Forties* (Chicago: University of Chicago Press, 1963), p. 118.
56. Yglesias, *How She Died*, p. 337.
57. Irving Howe, "What's the Trouble?" *The Seventies: Problems and Proposals*, eds. Irving Howe and Michael Harrington (New York: Harper and Row, Publishers, 1972), pp. 57–58.
58. Spacks, *The Female Imagination*, p. 77.
59. Jong, *Fear of Flying*, p. 295.
60. Dolbeare, *American Ideologies*, p. 58.
61. McCarthy, *The Company She Keeps*, p. 282.
62. Ibid., pp. 303–4.
63. Ann Petry, *The Street* (Boston: Houghton Mifflin Co., 1946), p. 405.
64. Ibid., p. 434.
65. Marge Piercy, *Small Changes* (1972; reprint, Greenwich, Conn.: Fawcett Publications, Inc., 1974), p. 536.
66. Smedley, *Daughter of Earth*, p. 345.
67. Ibid., p. 210.
68. Ibid., p. 251.
69. Dolbeare, *American Ideologies*, p. 199.
70. Piercy, *Small Changes*, pp. 332–34.
71. Ibid., p. 350.
72. Lillian Smith, *Strange Fruit* (New York: Reynal and Hitchcock, Publishers, 1944), p. 263.
73. Judith Rossner, *Looking for Mr. Goodbar* (New York: Simon and Schuster, Inc., 1975), pp. 241–43.
74. Joseph Conrad, "Author's Note," *Chance* (Garden City, N.Y.: Doubleday, Page and Co., 1925), p. xii.
75. Petry, *The Street*, p. 29.
76. Piercy, *Small Changes*, p. 39.
77. Smedley, *Daughter of Earth*, p. 200.
78. de Beauvoir, *The Second Sex*, p. 780.
79. Erazim V. Kohak, "Being Young in a Postindustrial Society," *The Seventies: Problems and Proposals*, eds. Irving Howe and Michael Harrington (New York: Harper and Row, Publishers, 1972), pp. 165–66.

80. Spacks, *The Female Imagination*, p. 107.
81. Christina Stead, *The Man Who Loved Children* (1940; reprint, New York: Holt, Rinehart and Winston, 1966), p. 482.
82. Ibid., 485.
83. Ibid., p. 488.
84. Walker, *The Color Purple*, p. 183.
85. Ibid., p. 182.
86. Marilyn French, *The Women's Room* (New York: Harcourt, Brace Jovanovich, 1977), p. 230.
87. Rossner, *Looking for Mr. Goodbar*, p. 273.
88. Harriette Arnow, *The Dollmaker* (New York: Macmillan Co., 1958), pp. 184–85.
89. Louise Meriwether, *Daddy was a Number Runner* (New York: Prentice-Hall, Inc., 1971), pp. 183–84.
90. Ibid., p. 188.
91. Rossner, *Looking for Mr. Goodbar*, pp. 242–43.
92. Ibid., p. 247.
93. Yglesias, *How She Died*, p. 176.
94. Ibid., p. 337.
95. Ibid.
96. Lessing, *The Golden Notebook*, p. xiii.
97. Howe, *Politics and the Novel*, pp. 207–8.
98. Lessing, *The Golden Notebook*, p. 228.
99. Ellen Morgan, "Humanbecoming: Form and Focus in the Neo-Feminist Novel," *Images of Women in Fiction: Feminist Perspectives*, ed. Susan Koppelman Cornillon (Bowling Green, Ohio: Bowling Green University Popular Press, 1972), p. 183.

3
Fragmentation Versus Unity: The Shattered Novel

Implicit within the view that the 1890s represents a turning point, a watershed in American history, is a characterization of America in the nineteenth century as agrarian, domestic, and self-confident in its uniqueness, and in the twentieth as primarily industrial, urban, and international. The essence of America today is change—abrupt change in population, economics, institutions, and technology.[1] It is sharply divided from the old world which is generally distinguished by its bounded unities. The new world is unbounded, complex, chaotic, fragmented.

In reflecting this kind of a world, the modern novelist focuses on a corresponding fragmentation of experience and relativity of values.[2] When the feminist novel confronts the antonyms of fragmentation and unity, its concern is centered specifically on the fragmentation of the female personality and the specious unity offered to the woman by man-made female roles. The female character attempts to bind herself together by becoming a reflecting mirror for the male or by adopting rigid roles. By jettisoning various parts of herself, she hopes to find unity. The ramifications of this adoption of roles are evident in the feminist novel. As the female characters lose parts of themselves in trying to narrow their personalities, so they lose themselves entirely when they mold themselves into a role. The character who successfully plays a role eventually becomes it and never discovers who she really is. By extrapolation, real wholeness in the modern world implies an acceptance of disorder and a concomitant rejection of both the deceptive unity offered by roles and the destruction of the personality implicit in separation and fragmentation.

This theme of fragmentation and unity in the feminist novel is surrounded by a complex of ideas which are often expressed stylistically. For example, the multiple point of view frequently reflects the fragmentation of an individual female character or of woman generally into many characters. This focus on the split in a character's individual, personal life mirrors a chaotic, complex, impersonal, political world. The fracturing of the female character also reveals the schizophrenia of the modern culture's views of women and the battle in women themselves between the old ways and the revolutionary spirit, between one's ambitions and desires and a restrictive social structure.[3] The pattern developed by fragmenting the novel itself assists, too, in expressing the theme of fragmentation. The novels are sometimes split into sections focused on different characters or on different parts of the same person or, as in *The Golden Notebook*, on different stories. Here the pattern of the novel, not its progression, is essential to its meaning; giving such a shape to a novel allows the female author to dispense with the necessity of writing and conversing linearly. This fragmented form often aids as well in presenting the passive and floating quality of the female characters' lives, lives which do not progress but simply continue. In other words, "in their form, women's lives tend to be like the stories that they tell: they show less a pattern of linear development towards some clear goal than one of repetitive, cumulative, cyclical structure."[4]

The multiple point of view often used in the feminist novel serves several functions in addition to those already mentioned. This stylistic feature is helpful to an author because it permits her to elucidate points of view by separating them.[5] The authors of *Small Changes* and *Looking for Mr. Goodbar* make good use of this advantage. More important, in some feminist novels, there is a connection between this approach and the usefulness of autobiography. In a novel using the first person and the multiple point of view, all the characters who speak have an equal voice in the matters dealt with in the novel; and all have, at least initially, the equal authority of the autobiographical mode. They stand or fall by the merits of their viewpoints rather than by the judgment of an omniscient author or of a single character. What is most central to the feminist novel, though, is that the fragmented point of view delineates the splitting of the modern female personality. It mirrors the disjunction, fragmentation, and separation of personality one finds in the modern world. It reflects the frustration of women's needs in a world where unity is achieved only by imposed limitation. Women may have work or love, not both; solitude or relationship, not both; community or singleness, not both.[6] For these reasons, the fragmented point of view is singularly appropriate for the feminist novel. It is particularly well used in *How She Died, The Golden Notebook, Up the Sandbox!, Small Changes*, and *The Company She Keeps*.

In *How She Died*, for example, Yglesias effectively uses the device of "twinning" by providing opposing viewpoints that begin to blend toward the end of the novel. In Mary and Jean one finds two opposites, the "supermoral" and "amoral," as Matt phrases it.[7] Mary represents the political, driving, active woman who wants to create, to lead, to change life. Jean, on the other hand, epitomizes the apolitical, withdrawn, passive woman primarily interested in romantic love and seemingly unable to control even her own life.

These characters serve as foils to one another initially. As the novel progresses, the reader and the characters find that neither character possesses merely one set of characteristics. Mary recognizes early that there are two parts to herself.[8] For Jean this understanding takes longer but by the time of the political demonstration, Jean, too, realizes that she is more than unified passivity. As Mary dies, Jean begins to grow. She develops a political awareness; she comes to long for more meaning than a single love can give; she desires the community of many loves rather than the solitude and singleness of one. Ultimately, she leaves Matt and strikes out on her own, reborn and strengthened by Mary. Mary is enriched by her relationship with Jean also. She eventually makes peace with her weakness, her approaching death, her enforced passivity. She learns to accept as well as to act. She enjoys, too, the desire for a physical relationship with Jean. The two at the moment of their kiss become one. Jean thinks:

> I stayed at her mouth past the recoil of horror at entering the body of her death and went on to a response of love throughout my body and down my limbs that melted me. Afterward I stood at her bedside in a daze of disbelief, understanding nothing, and myself least of all. Mary was asleep.[9]

Jean and Mary no longer represent the schizophrenia of two separate antonyms, distorted in their false unities. As Mary learns patience and acceptance, Jean learns to act and to demand. They both grow even as one dies.

Both Mary and Jean cast off the necessity for limiting themselves in order to keep control. At one point Terry, Jean's son, explains that one must keep control or go crazy.[10] Both Mary and Jean do lose the control they once had established by narrowing and focusing their personalities. However, they do not go crazy. Instead, they develop fuller, more encompassing, more rewarding lives even as death approaches for Mary. In contrast, the need to control and to remain unified stays with Matt always. He separates parts of his life, hoping in this way to achieve and maintain command over the various fragments. In his work he is able to do so, and this gives him great satisfaction.[11] With the other parts of his life, he is not so successful. He is never able to deal with Mary's death, and by the end of the novel, he can no longer even understand Jean. Giving up the desire for unity at any cost and also the rigidity of a limited, fixed personality allows Jean and Mary to blossom; for Matt there is only sterility.

In other feminist novels the split represented by Mary and Jean is developed through only one character. In Roiphe's *Up the Sandbox!*, for example, the one central character, Margaret Reynolds, is split into two. She is two separate people, both deformed, both unreal. She lives two roles, neither of which gives any real satisfaction. In her "real" life, she is a passive, frightened, isolated wife and mother. Her world is so narrow, so limited that it hardly supports even a bare existence. In her Walter Mitty daydreams, she is always a stick-figure political radical. Her daydream lives are unreal, narrow, exaggerated, and extremely pompous and affected. The novel itself is split into two; each chapter alternately represents one or the other of Margaret's two lives. The reader moves from chapter to chapter, bouncing back and forth between a destroyed, passive personality who feels inferior before everyone and an egotistical, haughty character who is awed by her own superiority. The novel's structure reveals that the chapters titled "in" a week represent Margaret's real life while those titled "out of" a week express her daydreams. The deformity she fears in unborn children represents the deformity and ugliness she sees in the twisted personalities allowed to her and to the world surrounding her.

In two other novels, *Fear of Flying* and *A Proper Marriage*, the thematic element of the split character is carried throughout, although the fictional structure itself is more conventional. Isadora Wing in *Fear of Flying*, though not at all as deformed as Margaret Reynolds, is similar in that there are two parts of her struggling for dominance. Her need for security, sameness, comfort, battles against her need for life, for change, for growth.[12] This same struggle is suggested in Lessing's *A Proper Marriage*. In this novel, much of modern life is characterized by the drive for security and safety. In their terror of change, upheaval, life, the characters hunger for security and, with its realization, find boredom instead. Because of their lack of values, there is no adventure for these characters except in violence and no life and pleasure except in cruelty.[13] Both Martha Quest and Isadora Wing find, however, that with security comes only death. The fear of a life of lies and stupefaction eventually overcomes the fear of freedom for both characters. Isadora returns to her beginning with Bennett while Martha leaves Douglas and starts out anew on her own. These novels suggest that there is no contest when the conflict is between unity, security, and safety on the one hand and growth and life on the other.

In *The Golden Notebook*, the theme of fragmentation is so central to the novel that the multiple point of view seems the only suitable structure for it. Anna is a multifaceted person and often discusses her many roles and personalities, including those of Janet's mother and Michael's mistress.[14] These personalities must be split from one another. So, it is perfectly reasonable that for Anna's notebooks, "a title appeared, as if Anna had, almost automatically, divided herself into four...."[15] She, too, separates things, including herself, out of fear of chaos. For her, as for Mary and Jean, rigid form and tight separation end when she is healed and, instead, there is "formlessness with the end of fragmentation."[16] The multiple point of view mirrors Anna's compartmentalization of herself. When she is whole, she need not sectionalize either her life or her novels.

In three other novels, there are two or more characters who provide a variety of points of view. In *Small Changes*, several different women provide views from their own vantage points. Here the different characters present the outlooks of a variety of women. The only problem with this method in *Small Changes* is that Piercy, toward the end, attempts to push all the characters into one correct viewpoint. They lose their distinctiveness and become too similar to one another to be believable. This heavy-handed insistence on one true viewpoint mars a novel which begins with a variety of characters and views, destroying the potential prismatic effect of the varied viewpoint.

In *The Color Purple* the two narrators, Celie and Nettie, both use the autobiographical form. The reader observes enormous differences in the two lives, but the net result of both characters' growth is the same. One, Celie, learns and changes through her interactions with the people she knows—Shug, Mary Agnes, Sofia, Harpo, and Albert. Nettie, on the other hand, gains her education through reading, traveling, and teaching Corrine and Samuel. Both Nettie and Celie come together at the end of the novel, however. By the time of their family reunion on July 4th, the reader finds that both Celie and Nettie have become strong and independent enough to make their own decisions, have come to a recognition of the impacts of sexism and racism on their lives, and have succeeded in pulling their family back together. The emphasis rests on the similar effects of political structures and atmospheres on their lives, effects so strong that they overwhelm the differences—differences that from another viewpoint might appear quite significant.

The use of multiple viewpoints in *The Company She Keeps* aids in expressing one of the ideas central to the novel. Margaret Sargent is defined by the company she keeps, not because she is attracted to people like herself, but because she is not a person in her own right. She does not have a self, an inner being she can look at and define. Rather, she changes shape depending upon the men with whom she is involved. The separate chapters are named after the men then prominent in her life. She does not really see herself but only herself in relation to others, in relation and reaction to the men around her. The various parts of the novel do not belong to her but to the men they are named after. Similarly, her shifting, insubstantial self does not belong to her but to the men around her. She depends upon them for explanation and definition, as when, in describing her imagined picture of her psychiatrist's life, she suddenly wonders: "Supposing she were wrong? He would not tell her. She would never know. It was like doing an algebra problem and finding that the answers were missing from the back of the book. She felt the ground give way beneath her."[17] At the end of the novel, she finally realizes the essence of her problem and is at least able to cling to the knowledge that she is not blind.

Some of the authors considered here, besides splitting their central characters and their points of view, also fragment their novels. Since novels permit the imposition of a pattern on life,[18] the view that modern life is primarily characterized by fragmentation suggests a corresponding fragmentation of the novel. As various structural features of the novel can determine or provide a chart of its meaning,[19] so the fragmented feminist novel welds structure and idea well enough to provide an elucidation of the statement "that the very form of a literary work, considered apart from its content so far as that is possible, is in itself an idea."[20] As stated in Lessing's *A Proper Marriage*, everything has to be given a form, placed, in effect, understood, before it can be forgotten.[21]

A prime example of fragmented form is Lessing's *The Golden Notebook*, the essence of which draws from the ideas of form, order, fragmentation, and unity. In many ways Lessing is concerned in *The Golden Notebook* with the same things that bothered D. H. Lawrence when he described America as being possessed by a "powerful disintegrative influence."[22] For Lessing, though, it is not America alone but the entire modern world which is menaced by the shape of destruction and disbelief. This force is born of chaos and fragmentation. It is the reason why, when Anna opens the casket containing that precious object, art, she finds "instead of a beautiful thing, which I thought would be there, there was a mass a fragments, and pieces. Not a whole thing, broken into fragments, but bits and pieces from everywhere, all over the world...."[23] The modern world and nearly everyone in it is paralyzed by this force, which is why nearly everyone wants to be an artist. One can create art and believe in it; art provides a means of defeating the shape of disbelief, destruction, and division.[24]

The splitting of the modern world, its sectioning off into nations, is mirrored by what happens to its inhabitants and to the shape of the novel. Anna and her novel are split into six parts, the five notebooks and the included novel, "Free Women," which itself is split internally by the notebooks. These various notebooks reveal the varieties of truth and falsehood found in politics and the intellect, in feeling and the emotions, in imagination and fiction, in detail and fact.[25] Toward the end of the novel, the yellow notebook of fiction and the blue notebook of fact begin to blend, and, ultimately, in "The Golden Notebook," Anna's and Saul's personalities begin to merge. The other notebooks end as Anna's parts begin to live with one another again. *The Golden Notebook* is not permitted to terminate with the success of "The Golden Notebook," however, but only with the partial defeat represented by the end of "Free Women."

The endless splittings-off which Lessing describes in *The Golden Notebook* are not just Anna's but the world's. The world and the individual in this novel are so closely connected that their union might be said to exemplify the idea that ontogeny recapitulates phylogeny. As there is minimally a period of infancy, a period of intellectual development, a Marxist phase, and a period of insanity in the development of each society, so also are there corresponding developments in the life of the individual. There is birth, growth, rise, decline, and death for each as there might also be for humanity generally. These connections are not linear. The dominant tendency of each period, for example, the insanity of the modern world, has the heaviest impact on that age's inhabitants. For this reason, the characters in *The Golden Notebook* are most affected by and can least easily escape from insanity, disbelief, and the principle of joy in destruction and evil. These tendencies most fully describe the modern world as it is presented in *The Golden Notebook*. These different phases and developments also contribute to the fragmentation of the novel, and it is only as they are dealt with that a culmination can be reached.

In other feminist novels, the use of the fragmented form provides a map to a different world. In *Small Changes* and *The Company She Keeps*, for example, the fragmented novel, with its lack of progression, aids in the depiction of lives primarily characterized by passivity and floating. There is a pattern to the lives of the characters, but there is no active progression. Neither the novel nor the character proceeds forward step by step. At one point in *Small Changes*, Miriam comments that "Dorine and I have practically changed places.... It's strange, Beth. As if our lives had no inner shape."[26] In many ways her observation is true, especially about her own life. Miriam, in particular, becomes enveloped by the men surrounding her. Her personality changes when she is with Jackson, with Phil, with Neil. They direct her moods and her actions; the impetus does not come from within herself. Dorine, for a large part of the novel, is characterized solely by her passivity. It is only after she does take the positive step of moving out of the apartment shared by Phil, Jackson, and Miriam that she begins to manage her own life. Beth has some measure of control; but even for her, there are long periods of floundering. The novel itself is split into "The Book of Beth," "The Book of Miriam," and "Both in Turn." In the separate books, one becomes familiar with the characters' separate outlooks and with the ways in which their lives intersect. The chopping of the novel into separate books and then into separate sections and separate viewpoints develops the sectioning, passivity, and suspended quality of the characters' lives.

The splitting of *The Company She Keeps* is perfectly in tune with the life and character of Margaret Sargent. The atmosphere, the ambience, the direction of each chapter is not set by Margaret Sargent. Separate parts of her being are brought forward and intensified, as they are called out by the men in her life, which is why most of the chapters are titled after the men they focus upon. For example, Chapter Three bears the heading "The Man in the Brooks Brothers Shirt" and Chapter Four, dealing with Pflaumen, is entitled "The Genial Host." In most chapters, Margaret's entrance is delayed; one is often not aware that she is the same heroine who appeared elsewhere in the novel until near the end. Pflaumen is, in many ways, a microcosm of the shape of her life because he attempts to define everyone, not only Margaret. Jim, too, is similar to Margaret in some ways. The reason that Jim is a "walking Gallup Poll"[27] is not because he embodies the central attitudes of the average American but because he imbibes those attitudes and makes them part of himself as soon as he sees them becoming dominant in the culture. He, too, is always playing roles and adapting himself to whatever is requested of him. He, too, is always primarily aware of how he will be seen by others and arranges himself with that in mind. Eventually, Jim is unable to write because he no longer believes anything, is anything. He has simply become a mirror. Margaret is superior to him, and to the others, because she has a clear view of herself. She knows that she is playing roles, that she is not a whole person, that she is fragmented and out of control. She asks, finally, "Preserve me in disunity."[28] The techniques of multiple viewpoints; of multiple use of first, second, and third person; and of fragmentation suit this novel admirably because they intensify Margaret's fragmentation.

The fragmentation of *Up the Sandbox!* heightens the fragmentation of the heroine's personality. She is split into two completely antithetical people. In the linear, chronological part of the novel, she is the epitome of housewifery. Passive, quiet, unmoving, she cleans, cooks, and cares for her children with her life going on only in her thoughts. In the interspersed fragments, she leads her fantasies of revolution, derring-do, and brilliance. She is and does all the things that cannot even be thought of in her real life. She needs to keep this part of her personality alive in order to survive. Ultimately, the active, demanding part of her personality is taken over and killed by her third pregnancy. The housewife part of her is pleased to find that she is pregnant again. In effect, it settles her life for her, removes all other options, makes things very simple. "Out of Week Six" is the same as "In Week Six." There is no longer any escape for her. The door has closed, and she no longer even daydreams. Herein lies the danger of fragmentation: that in order to escape it, one destroys an essential part of the self.

In *How She Died*, the ordering of the novel combines with the development of the characters. Initially, the twin figures with opposing personalities, Mary and Jean, alternate as the narrators of each chapter. About a third of the way through, Jean takes over all the chapters. From then on, as Mary weakens and dies, Jean grows and takes over the novel. Mary's being is reborn in Jean, and, finally, Jean goes on as a fusion of the two personalities. The overall structure of the novel ties in with the presentation of the main characters and the development of their lives and Mary's death.

The theme of fragmentation which is expressed stylistically through the multiple point of view and through the fragmentation of characters is further developed through the lives and experiences of the characters. The division in modern culture represented by the persistence of the old ways and of a restrictive social structure and the simultaneous emergence of the revolutionary spirit in women's ambitions and desires[29] is presented through these characters. At the same time that these novels attack fragmentation and its concomitant destruction of the personality, they also issue a powerful condemnation of imposed unity. The unity to be found in the path ordinarily assigned to women is presented in these novels as a specious unity, a unity attained by narrowing and limiting the personality, the intellect, the emotions, the vision. In fact, "if society encourages women finally to retreat within, guarding precious private heritages, it thus fosters a straitened maturity, involving the giving up of external claims."[30] This sort of maturity involves, too, the commitment of the self to other people, but only to a few other people, to one's family and immediate neighbors. In this way, one can find unity through the "complicated repression involved in giving up one's life to the service of others."[31] In this narrowing, one can escape from multiplicity, but one will most likely continue to be uncomfortable because "one is unconsciously holding something back, and gradually the repression becomes an effort."[32] On the other hand, it is uncomfortable, too, to experience the "sudden splitting off of consciousness... when from being the natural inheritor of [a] civilisation [one] becomes, on the contrary, outside of it, alien and critical."[33] The former state provides a possible end to confusion, uncertainty, unsteadiness at the same time that it deadens and destroys. The latter is enlivening, but at the same time, it opens the door to the terrifying prospects of fragmentation, struggle, and freedom.

Feminist novels recognize other dangers that can reside in the longing for unity. De Man's calling this desire a "nostalgia for some sort of lost unity or ideal form of consciousness"[34] recalls Doris Lessing's references to "lying nostalgia." When nostalgia takes over, one begins to long for a marvelous time past which, while it was being lived, was scarcely that. The consideration of this wish for individual, personal unity leads De Man to observe that "an organicist ideology tends to go hand in hand with retrograde political yearnings...."[35] If, indeed, the impetus for totality and a whole, coherent cultural pattern is essentially conservative,[36] then the individual's hunger for wholeness may also be a backward-looking impulse. When the illusion of wholeness must be created as in the dinner party in *To The Lighthouse,* then one can suspect that at least part of the driving force behind it is fear. Multiplicity, uncertainty, and the threats of fragmentation appear to be corollaries of freedom. The challenge to use oneself and one's life fully against the temptation to settle for something partial[37] remains a central issue for the characters in these novels who seem trapped between the enticements offered by beguiling unities and the terrors of fragmentation.

Doris Lessing's novels concentrate on the issue of fragmentation and unity. She states in the introduction to *The Golden Notebook* that "we must not divide things off, must not compartmentalize."[38] There is an unceasing abjuration in this novel to avoid fragmentation. Lessing is also aware, however, that one can, in avoiding fragmentation, retreat into limiting and narrowing oneself. To simultaneously escape fragmentation and an imprisoning narrowness, one must, of necessity, face conflict, doubt, danger. As Anna says:

the essence of living now, fully, not blocking off to what goes on, is conflict. In fact, I've reached the stage where I look at people and say— he or she, they are whole at all because they've chosen to block off at this stage or that. People stay sane by blocking off, by limiting themselves.[39]

To stay open is to invite turmoil, though not necessarily insanity. True wholeness and unity may be impossible to attain and undesirable as well, but to retain all of one's personality and being and to refuse to separate and isolate the intellect, the emotions, the body, and the mind is an essential first step toward living fully. Simone de Beauvoir expresses this viewpoint when she states that "the psychic life is not a mosaic, it is a single whole in every one of its aspects and we must respect that unity."[40] It is true that de Beauvoir urges a unity Lessing does not believe in, but they do agree on the necessity for fighting the modern tendency toward disintegration of the self. From a slightly different perspective, Anaïs Nin seconds Lessing and de Beauvoir when she states, "We think everything is either-or, black or white; we are caught between them and we lose all our energy in the conflicts. My answer, later on in maturity, was to do them all. Not to exclude any, not to make a choice."[41] Jane Eyre makes a similar decision when she decides not to settle solely for the fire of Rochester or the ice of St. John Rivers, not solely for passion or solely for work. She does not limit herself to one thing, a marriage with St. John, for instance," a marriage reflecting, once again, her absolute exclusion from the life of wholeness toward which her pilgrimage [had] been directed."[42]

To see and accept parts of life other than those one already knows and understands is also necessary to achieve community with others. Individual and community fragmentation are closely connected. When the world becomes whole in *The Golden*

Notebook, the boundaries marking off countries on the world globe disappear, and the variety of colors run together.[43] In *The Golden Notebook* and in *A Proper Marriage*, the fragmentation of the modern individual, or modern life, and of the modern world is presented in many ways. Many of the characters' personal and political lives are disconnected; they can make neither work.[44] In the personal life of Lessing's characters, sexuality and sexual relationships give a valuable index to the state of the personality. Simone de Beauvoir observes that it is more difficult for the female than for the male "to dissociate sex and sentiment, ... since in feminine adolescence the two are most profoundly associated."[45] For Doris Lessing, it is impossible to separate the two because doing so means fragmenting the character and the personality. It means splitting up the human being into various parts and eliminating, at one time or another, aspects of the human personality. It is for this reason that Ella feels irritation and annoyance "when her husband attempted to rouse her by physical manipulation against her emotions. The end of that was frigidity."[46] So it is, too, for the heroine of French's *The Bleeding Heart*, who thinks after the end of one of her husband's rages, "So another one was over and forgotten. Except by her body. Forever after that, whenever he approached her, her body flinched a little."[47] It is a lie to separate the feelings and sexuality, and for those who manage to, there is only falsehood and loss. The refusal to do so entails frustration and conflict, but it also brings truth and preserves the integrity of the individual. It is for these reasons that Martha Quest does not want to divide herself into pieces, that she feels fury when Douglas tries to stimulate her physically when her feelings are against him.[48] Physical feelings are an invaluable register of truth. As Dolores comments in *The Bleeding Heart*, "On the other hand, she had learned over the years of her life to trust her body. It was the only thing that always told you the truth. The mind lied; the body did not."[49]

For the male, it is easier to separate himself into parts and, consequently, more difficult to remain a whole person. The men in *The Golden Notebook* are not only split themselves but also want their lovers to be. Paul Tanner, for example, picks up several different personalities and wants Ella to be serious with each one, a response which would split her.[50] He adopts various false personalities because of his fear of emotion, and they divide him further. These deceptive fronts are designed to hurt Ella and her son when their warmth and feelings pull him too close to them.[51] In effect, Paul is so splintered that he needs women to mirror various parts of himself. His wife, Muriel, represents his stable, sensible side. Ella realizes this at one point:

She was silent, thinking: If he really likes living like that, or at least, needs it, it would explain why he's always dissatisfied with me. The other side of the sober respectable little wife is the smart, gay, sexy mistress. Perhaps he really would like it if I were unfaithful to him and wore tarty clothes. Well I won't. This is what I am, and if he doesn't like it he can lump it.[52]

Ella must finally be disposed of because she is a real person and remains so, refusing to assume a false personality that can make love with his false personality. Ella speaks to the male world represented by Paul Tanner as Gloria Anzaldúa speaks to the white world when she comments, "Who, me confused? Ambivalent? Not so. Only your labels split me."[53] Just as Paul actually wants the Ella he condemns, not the real one, so, too, does Saul want the jealous Anna, the one he rails at for being jealous. His making love with Jane Bond is calculated so that Anna will know that he has. Then when Anna becomes jealous, he is able to respond warmly to her.[54] He can be loving to her when she is miserable.

There are several different aspects to this fragmentation as it is presented by Lessing. Tommy speaks to one of them when he states, "People like Anna or Molly and that lot, they're not just one thing, but several things.... But you'll never be different, father."[55] Part of what is revealed here is that Anna has not resigned herself to the specious unity provided by narrowing and limiting the self. Indeed, she is split into many different parts, but she does not destroy them. During her insanity she flies apart, but she does not murder parts of herself. All the parts are still there at the end, waiting to be pulled back together. She retains all of herself although she feels the conflicts that come from the force of disintegration. She does not narrow herself solely to the job that she does, to being a mother, or to her relationship with a man. Tommy's father, Richard, does do that. He limits himself to one fragment, the economic businessman. He has wholeness only because he will always be the same, because he is only one small part of what a human being can be. Saul, though fragmented, is still better off than Richard because Saul cannot manage to kill off all the parts of himself. Anna's problems are reflected in her search for wholeness. She cannot reconcile all of herself, either. Joining the Communist Party is part of her search for completeness, but, of course, it, too, cannot offer a holistic solution. Like Anna, Martha Quest finds it a falsehood that one's personal problems are an unimportant background to one's real responsibilities. The personal and political must be recognized as being joined together, as being reflective of one another, if a full life is to be lived.

For Doris Lessing, this fragmentation, this splitting, is representative of the major ills of the twentieth century. The chaos, anarchy, and splitting off of the world's peoples are illustrated by the fragmentation of the individual personality. The modern world is so complex, so divided, so out of control that Anna ultimately comes to a stage where she can only cut out newspaper articles and paste them to her wall and then sit and stare at them. She can no longer function and deal with the world or order it. She can only sit passively and stare at it "like Thomas Wolfe, who was reduced to making lists of all those things and scenes in the world he tried vainly to bind together."[56]

Other characters in *The Golden Notebook* fall into other insane states as a result of their attempts to deal with a world characterized by violence, destruction, and loss. Tommy, for example, ultimately succumbs to the principle of anarchy and fragmentation. He remains skeptical when Anna insists that it is necessary to continue striving for human progress. He nods with a "sort of malicious triumph" when Anna betrays her own words by the "small self-accusatory smile on her face."[57] As in *A Proper Marriage*, the nihilism, loss of faith, and embracing of evil characteristic of the twentieth century make enthusiasms and idealism seem ridiculous.[58] Unable to pull himself away from the modern tendencies, Tommy finally turns into what he tried to kill himself to escape.[59]

Other characters are constantly tempted by and occasionally fall into the failure and escape of passivity and self-limitation. Martha Quest describes this temptation as a "familiar lassitude."[60] It comes from the feeling that she cannot do anything to change anything anyway; that there is no meaning, no purpose, no pattern to life; that nothing really matters. At times, though she resists it, she almost feels as though she wants another baby.[61] For her, this would be the easiest course. Her life would be nailed down, finished, over. She would have no more decisions to make. She would have given up and accepted the unity of intentional self-limitation. Of course, then, for her, her life really would not matter anymore.

For Lessing's male characters, the escape is found in war and cruelty. For example, Doug's boring and meaningless life is not unusual.[62] In a world where ideals are scoffed at, where one's best talents and thoughts are not only not needed but not wanted, where enthusiasm and love are made to seem ridiculous, boring and meaningless lives predominate. In a world where these qualities are absent, war and violence provide adventure. A feeling of nostalgia for a lost unity can be sated in the illusion of common purpose provided by war. When Victor comments on war to Dolores in *The Bleeding Heart* by stating, "It brings men together, you know?" she thinks, "Yes. Too bad you need a war to do it. Need a war to cry for each other. To love each other."[63] Cruelty and violence can also make one feel alive by jolting one out of boredom. Further, the destruction stemming from war and cruelty can provide a malicious satisfaction in that the annihilation of the outside world parallels the wreckage of the self. The viewpoint of the feminist novel toward violence is far removed from Norman Mailer's presentation of it as the saving assertion of the self. Just as a revolutionary situation can fuse the political and private life into one burning existence,[64] so, too, can war furnish a deceptive purpose and unity for a meaningless, divided world. This purposelessness, chaos, division is the "dark, impersonal destructive force that [works] at the roots of life and that [expresses] itself in war and cruelty and violence."[65]

In *The Edible Woman*, nearly all the characters, like Tommy's father in *The Golden Notebook*, are strongly tempted to retreat to the unity of the single fragment. Len, the reader finds, is repulsed by birth and nature. They bring out his fear of confusion and untidiness; he prefers that everything be orderly and programmed.[66] Duncan, too, would prefer things in black and white, not in the colors of growth and vegetation. Marion has her own terrors, her images of people feeding off each other, of birth and death.[67] These fears of the chaos of modern life can be met by a retreat into narrow rigidity. Ainsley, for example, has her practical rules for life including the dictum that "everyone should get married."[68] These rules allow her to avoid the difficulties involved in thinking and decision-making. Marion, for her part, feels strongly at one point that she wants to get married and let Peter make the decisions.[69] She really does want to assume the role of wife, let go of the rest of her personality, and, in the bargain, escape from the terrifying freedom which promises conflict and confusion. Eventually, the remembrance of seeing herself, small and oval, mirrored in Peter's eyes,[70] merely a reflection of a person, is more frightening. The limiting, narrowing, and cataloguing of the individual takes place at Marion's place of work, too. Here, pregnancy is seen as an act of disloyalty to Seymour Surveys.[71] An employee is just an employee and nothing more. Conrad's "job sense" does not fit in this world. In the world of the edible woman, the pressure to narrow the self, to limit one's life, to retreat, is almost overwhelming and drives Marion to insanity for a while as it did Anna in *The Golden Notebook*.

In other novels the enticements of false unity are described differently. Mira in *The Women's Room*, for example, consciously limits and narrows herself and her life after her near rape and subsequent marriage. She confines herself to her house and to the ordering of it. Indeed, she becomes entombed like a living dead person in a vast vault. Her being becomes restricted to a life centered on lemon furniture polish. The order of the house and its cleanliness become of paramount importance to her. As is true for Len in *The Edible Woman*, the compulsive need for order and a programmed life subsumes Mira. In true wholeness, there is formlessness[72] because the minute separation and labeling of fragmentation is gone. The limitation of the self provides only a seeming whole, the apparent unity of a single fragment.

In Agnes Smedley's *Daughter of Earth*, there is also a recognition of the struggle for wholeness against fragmentation. Early in the novel, the heroine states, "I shall gather up these fragments of my life and make a crazy-quilt of them. Or a mosaic of interesting pattern—unity in diversity."[73] She, too, wants to find wholeness and looks for it in the Communist Party. But for her, though politics encompasses much of her life, there remain the enigmas of love and joy and peace. The various fragments of her life remain unreconciled. These feminist novels encourage the recognition that "nothing is 'simply one thing.' There must be room in one's scheme of reality for the whole of experience."[74]

While many of these novels depict their characters circumscribing their lives and themselves, others focus more specifically on the escape provided by ready-made roles and its inherent dangers. Through a role, the character assumes a character or function that may, in fact, have no connection at all with her own character or personality. The character who limits herself at least still owns a part of herself. The character who becomes thoroughly adept at the assumption of roles loses herself entirely. Of the novels dealing with this aspect of fragmentation, some center specifically on how role adoption ties in with the lives of women and others on how it mirrors the political realities of our time.

In one of the former, *The Awakening*, the reader sees that Edna's early married life is held together by her attempt to adopt the role of Mrs. Pontellier. Later, when she decides instead to be Edna, her family disintegrates. Its cohesion depends upon her playing the role of wife; by extrapolation, the family in general, as it is ordinarily constituted, depends upon the wife's obliterating her personality, her needs, her desires, for the wants of the family. On the surface, it would not seem that "casting aside that fictitious self which we assume like a garment with which to appear before the world"[75] should cause such outrage. In fact, if the wife should do so, it destroys the conventional family. For the married woman, the playing of a role is to be her life. If she succeeds completely in adopting it, her own self will be perfectly erased; she will become the role so that she no longer feels any conflicts. She herself will no longer exist. For Edna, either accepting or rejecting the role condemns her to death.

In *Orlando* the reader is shown how a role can easily take over the personality of the player. Simply because s/he is wearing female clothes, Orlando begins to exhibit female behaviors, to act in typically feminine ways.[76] Revealed quite clearly is the belief that it is the outside environment which makes men act masculine and women act feminine. The restrictions of Orlando's dress and the narrowing of her possibilities are what make her act feminine. The power of such outside influences on Orlando recalls the experiences of George Sand when she adopts male dress in order to "deprovincialize" herself and to become "informed about the ideas and the arts" of her time. After donning male clothes and boots, she exclaims that:

"With those little iron-shod heels, I was solid on the pavement. I flew from one end of Paris to the other. It seemed to me that I could go round the world. And then, my clothes feared nothing. I ran out in every kind of weather, I came home at every sort of hour, I sat in the pit at the theater. No one paid attention to me, and no one guessed at my disguise."[77]

As a woman, of course, in women's clothes, she would no longer feel that she could fly, let alone go round the world. Further, the implication is that as a woman, she would very likely be condemned to provinciality and ignorance. Something very similar happens to Orlando in her androgynous state. Such is the power of the role of woman over women's lives; even mere clothes can change the personality.

In *Looking for Mr. Goodbar*, the role demanded of modern women is presented as one unavoidably leading to schizophrenia. Theresa's fragmentation stems directly from the split role required of women, and in this novel, the sexual aspect of the role is central. Her Catholic background intensifies her difficulties and makes her eventual madness almost inescapable. Theresa's entire outlook is inherited from a traditional family view of women and daughters and from an initial sexual relationship which only serves to strengthen her earlier experiences.

Her mother laughs at Theresa when she states that she plans to go to college because, of course, she is only a girl. She is inferior to her older sister who is more beautiful and more outgoing than she because these traits are those that really matter in a girl. Theresa dares to get sick at the same time that her brother dies; her brother, because he is a son, is the center of the family. She always feels guilty for having drawn attention to herself when he was so much more important than she. Her first sexual encounter with Engle only reinforces the views of herself and the attitudes toward the world which her family instilled. When she and Engle first have sex, he hurts her physically, but she cannot say anything because it is her duty to be hurt. She learns that he becomes very hostile toward her when she feels sexually aroused and alive. Her view of herself is totally destroyed when he sends her away; she becomes "an empty whole."[78]

Theresa, because she is not as important as a man, because her sister is more beautiful than she, because she has the hideous blemish of a scar, because she does not measure up, naturally condemns herself. She knows that her parents cannot possibly love her because she is worthless and ugly. She thinks James must be blind or crazy or both for describing her as "charming and interesting."[79] She cannot believe she is liked. When she says she does not like children who are sick, she means she does not like herself. Although Theresa's characteristics are exaggerated somewhat because of her madness, this novel presents her view of herself as one bound to be fostered by society's view of women and the role it expects them to play. She is supposed to see her appearance and her compliance as her most important qualities. All women have a blemish which they will magnify into hideous dimensions as they try to measure up to the ideal of beauty set for them. All will view themselves as worthless when they cannot neatly separate themselves and adopt the roles prepared for them.

Theresa loses herself and falls into deeper masochism. Anonymous sex becomes a good thing because she is not forced to recognize her own being, something she finds painful because she thinks herself so miserable a person. Her masochism can be seen in her having "acquiesced in her own rape";[80] the rape does not matter since she is so worthless. Actually, she has no self; she buries herself and then has no real will. At one point, when contemplating the act of refusing to have sex, "she tried to remember how she had refused someone in the past and then realized that she couldn't remember because she'd never actually done it."[81] A person with no being cannot agree or disagree; she simply, passively, acquiesces.

Theresa consents to all male demands on her, but she does not have any women friends. Because she accepts society's view of women and of herself, she does not think of women as important and does not know how to relate to them. All she can really feel toward Katherine is jealousy of a more beautiful woman. She cannot really feel close to Katherine even though Katherine, too, has many problems of her own. When Evelyn asks her to join her consciousness-raising group, Theresa "knew that however interesting some of the ideas were to her, she wouldn't be able to sit around with a bunch of women and talk about them."[82] Eventually, even Theresa realizes "that not since her high school days had she had a really close girlfriend. Someone she could talk to easily, not just in time of crisis."[83] She is isolated from the company of other women and limited to men, who are her problem.

While Terry or Miss Dunn, her alternate personalities, control most of Theresa's life, Theresa sinks away. Terry simply cannot understand James. For one thing, he talks "as though the truth mattered."[84] Terry does not understand truth, honesty, or a real person. She only understands anonymous people and the most superficial of relationships. Because sex seems ugly to her, it must be anonymous and disconnected from love. It is one of the reasons Theresa connects James with her own brother. Theresa and James' love must be like a brother's and sister's love; there can be no love connected with sex. She can only open up with people she has no real relationship with. Otherwise, they might get to know her, and she would be forced to be real. As she says, she can talk more with Victor than with James because "it was precisely that fact, that she hadn't seen him and wouldn't, that she didn't know him and couldn't, that had enabled her to relax and open up to him."[85] He cannot hurt her.

It is not true that Terry cannot enjoy sex with James because he is clumsy. She cannot feel sexually aroused with him because he likes her, because he is kind and human. At one time, half-asleep, she responds to him; but all sexual feeling vanished "at the moment she realized it was James in the chair with her."[86] It is precisely because he loves her and she loves him that she cannot enjoy him. Since sex is bad, it must be separated from love and respect. As Theresa says, *"I'd probably like you better if you could walk out on me. Or at least smack my face."*[87] In fact, she cannot be sexually attracted to a good person. She must be hurt, abused, abased, to feel sexual. She thinks, "Something there was that couldn't really be interested in a man who liked powerful, intelligent women. Something there was that wanted a man from Marlboro Country. Smart only in the way he subordinated his girls."[88] That something is society's insistence that sex is filthy and that because women symbolize sex, they should be abased and abused. As a consequence, Theresa, too, must be worthless. Therefore, anyone, like James, who cares for her, must be mad. For Theresa, there is no way to integrate her personality, to resurrect her real being. She realizes, "She was more herself, the real Theresa, in some ways with James, than she'd ever been with anyone."[89] But being her real self is too painful, too terrifying, to endure. There is no way, finally, for Theresa to live.

Rossner does not portray only women as being invaded by fragmentation, by roles, and foreign personalities. Gary White, the murderer, is, if anything, more disabled than Theresa. He can only enjoy himself sexually with a woman if the relationship involves force because he cannot admit the homosexual part of his nature. In fact, murder does not really bother him; homosexuality does. For example, "In contrast to his readiness to relate much of what happened with Theresa, Gary *gagged* as he described, at the urging of the police, the wig, tiara, white satin gown and silver platform sandals George had provided for him."[90] Finally, he cannot really have any relationship with a woman as Theresa cannot with a man. He thinks of himself as a victim of Theresa's and assumes that anyone in the same circumstances he was in would have killed her. Such is the result of the acceptance of stereotypes, of male and female roles on the lives of women and men. Certainly, Gary and Theresa are extremes, but only as an intensification of the norm.

In some other novels where the theme of fragmentation and unity centers on role-playing, the emphasis rests on the role-player's loss of inner guidance. The character who only follows a role loses the authority and direction of her own thoughts and feelings. In *Small Changes*, for example, Sonia learns to distrust her own feelings. Her family, when Sonia tells them she is ill, "told Sonia she was a drag, always complaining. They tuned out, till she could not believe in the legitimacy of her feelings."[91] Having played the role of Jewish mother for so long, she has lost any sense of what she, Sonia, really thinks and believes and feels, and so she must rely on the authority of others to interpret her to herself.

In this respect she is similar to Margaret Sargent in *The Company She Keeps*. From the beginning, Margaret interprets all of her own actions as though she were an actress playing a role, which, of course, she is. The capitalization of "How Her Husband Would Take It,"[92] when she is thinking about telling him of her affair, serves as a magnification of her role and the way she appears to those around her. It gives the effect of an old movie in which scenes are introduced by phrases flashed onto the screen. Margaret is always separating herself from herself and standing apart watching how well she performs her role. Her real interest in herself is in how she looks to others. Unfortunately, she eventually loses control over herself as a result. There really is not a Margaret at all. She changes from the child she had been into a witty sophisticate, then, when she marries, into Aunt Clara, and then into an adulterer, never really knowing which one she is. Finally, "she came at last to the place where she wondered whether the false self was not the true one. What if she were an imposter?"[93]

The form of the novel helps to illuminate Margaret's wavering, ghostly self. Each section appears as though it is a different part of her life which does not fit with the others or belong to her. Indeed, Pflaumen's chapter is almost a condensation of the entire novel. Everyone turns into what Pflaumen invites him or her to be. For Margaret, that is not unusual.

Ultimately, Margaret comes to realize the true dangers of her position. Like Theresa in *Looking for Mr. Goodbar*, she never says "no." She is acquiescent, passive, agreeable to the Nazi. In losing herself, she loses direction, guidance, inner balance. She can only rely on outside authority to direct her. She can only hope that she can continue to recognize what she is doing, even if she cannot stop herself from doing it. She hopes that the parts of herself, true and false, can at least survive, even if they are disconnected.

For Doris Lessing, the implications of role-playing are even more sinister. In *The Golden Notebook*, role-playing is an expected result of fragmentation. If the personality is split into various parts, one only has the option of playing various roles fitting the parts since there is never a whole person behind each section. One finds oneself playing the role that fits the part of the self one is momentarily using. When Anna joins the Communist Party, for example, she finds that various people must act in certain ways toward her because she is now typed. She, in return, must inexorably respond as she has been categorized. In the space of one day, she must assume three different political roles. It begins when she

> had lunch with John, the first time since I joined the Party. Began talking as I do with my ex-party friends, frank acknowledgement of what is going on in Soviet Union. John went into automatic defence of the Soviet Union, very irritating. Yet this evening had dinner with Joyce, *New Statesman* circles, and she started to attack Soviet Union. Instantly I found myself doing the automatic-defense-of-Soviet-Union act, which I can't stand when other people do it. She went on; I went on. For her, she was in the presence of a communist so she started on certain clichés. I returned them.[94]

Later, her third role is called for when Michael stops in and begins "speaking in his role of East European exile, ex-revolutionary, toughened by real political experience, to me in my role as 'political innocent.' And I replied in that role, producing all sorts of liberal inanities. Fascinating—the roles we play, the way we play parts."[95] What is most important in this exchange is that Anna is not herself. She is playing roles that have nothing real to say about her; she is simply doing what is expected of her and becoming what the other person's role leaves out. She is losing Anna.

She sees this happening to others, too. She receives letters from three acquaintances of hers at similar times, and she remarks to Molly:

"The point is, these letters were interchangeable. Discounting handwriting, of course.... You couldn't possibly have said, this letter was written by Tom, or that one by Len.... Well, surely the thought follows—what stereotype am I? What anonymous whole am I part of?"[96]

What has happened is that as the personality has fragmented, it has been replaced by roles. The horror for the individual is that her personality, her center is gone. Anna finds a more general threat involved in this process when she remarks, "If a person can be invaded by a personality who isn't theirs, why can't people—I mean people in the mass—be invaded by alien personalities."[97] It is not only the individual but also the modern world which is disintegrating.

In *A Proper Marriage*, one finds similar circumstances. At one point, it is observed that "Mrs. Quest did not really believe in any of this, she was simply playing a role laid down for her."[98] In this way she is like Douglas when he watches himself to see how he appears or like the White Zambesian leaders when they indulge in self-pity. None of them really believes in anything; they simply adopt roles. It is this lack of belief, of being, that threatens the modern world. Anna recognizes it in herself when she uses the word "comrade" and then "stopped, hearing how I used the word, as we all do now, with an ironical nostalgia. I was thinking that it was first cousin to the jeering voice of the projectionist—it was an aspect of disbelief and destruction."[99]

This kind of world is similar to the world in *1984* in that individuality is obsolete and personality a crime. In this world, the self no longer holds any value at all.[100] Role-playing in Lessing's novels thus becomes a symptom of an underlying disease and is politically charged.

These novels, in their attacks on fragmentation, eschew both the adoption of roles and the deceptive unity offered by simplification and narrowing of the personality. Some, in using sexual mores to symbolize fragmentation, describe pornography as a separation of the sexual being and the human being; in effect, pornography, through this separation, demands the destruction of the personality. Other novels focus on the limiting of the self as it is called for by most political ideologies. For example, it may be true that the dialectical approach sees everything as being interconnected, nothing existing in isolation, only in terms of its relationship to or with everything else. This ideology may today theoretically call for a total integration of structures, events, beliefs, and personal lives.[101] As it is presented in Doris Lessing's novels, however, it is an isolated ideology which calls for the elimination of the personal life. In her novels, it represents a falling away from the whole of humanism,[102] a feminist humanism. It demands that everything be rigidified and simplified into a construct. In her novels, though, real wholeness demands some acceptance of chaos and disorder.

These novels insist that male and female not be separated and fragmented. They illustrate the statement that one must "urge a dissemination to members of each sex of those socially desirable traits previously confined to one or the other while eliminating the bellicosity or excessive passivity useless in either."[103] They support the integration of male and female principles. As Orlando finds, s/he is the same person as a woman or a man;[104] everything is partly something else.[105] The various colors of her character and personality are all swirled together without lines being drawn between them.

Some novels focus intensely on the need for understanding that one's public and private lives are connected. They expand on the observation that feminism insists that socialism has no real sense of the need to make politics intensely personal, to connect sexuality and the family with the problem and process of change.[106] More generally, they show that the modern world separates the public-political and private-sexual lives.[107] These novels argue that the public and private worlds are inseparably connected and that to try to fragment them is folly and worse. Doris Lessing's insistence on the connection between public and private madnesses intensifies this view. This stress on the linkage between the political and private life seems so strange to some that it has been said of *Daughter of Earth*: "This expressed unity of the personal and political might well have made Agnes Smedley's books inaccessible...."[108]

The cry made by these novels against fragmentation is joined, however, with an understanding that its elimination will not bring wholeness and totality. As a result of the separation between actual experience and one's desire for totality, any attempt at a total understanding of our being will contrast to experience which is fragmentary, particular, and unfulfilled. Consequently, the individual will be frustrated by his or her own ability to acquire universal dimensions. To the novelist, this is particularly evident since the novel remains rooted in the particularity of experience.[109] At least, though, in refusing to split off or jettison parts of the self, in refusing to let the personality be destroyed, one can retain all of oneself even though confusion and disorder remain part of the whole. Margaret Sargent's plea at the end of *The Company She Keeps* illustrates that even in her extremity, she has retained the self.[110] In *The Golden Notebook*, too, the impossibility of totality and wholeness is recognized. In this novel, "the condition that makes ultimate freedom impossible is the human condition, the same for men and women."[111]

Nonetheless, Anna and Saul, along with such characters as Jean in *How She Died*, James in *Looking for Mr. Goodbar*, and Iso in *The Women's Room* come closer to completeness and the defeat of fragmentation than any other figures in the feminist novel. They acknowledge disorder and chaos without giving in to them. They realize the futile nature of the struggle for complete wholeness and dispense with such specious substitutes as role-playing and limitation of the personality. They accept all parts of themselves even though those parts do not form a completely coherent whole. Ultimately, because of these characteristics, they are not afraid—of themselves, of other people, of living. They become involved, and they commit themselves. They stand in most notable contrast to those characters who have bought unity at the price of their humanity: Richard in *The Golden Notebook*, Len in *The Edible Woman*, and Harley in *The Women's Room*. For them, the need for unity, the escape from chaos and disorder and freedom is worth the narrowness of their lives, the limitation of their beings, the unified totalitarianism of the single viewpoint.

In short, at the same time that the feminist novel argues against the fragmentation of the individual personality and of the world community, it recognizes the dangers of demanding a unity not possible. The assumption of roles is an acceptance of fragmentation in the modern world. It allows one to divide oneself into the parts appropriate for various roles. The narrowing of the self also superficially banishes fragmentation; in reality, it is a denial of the whole being. The feminist novel does not make the error of joining with the "mania" for unified totality which has been called characteristic of our time.[112] This yearning for totality may, in fact, lead to a desire for totalitarianism and stem from a fear of diversity, chaos, even freedom. The acceptance of wholeness, of the complete human personality, of the communities of the world implies also a facing of disorder, anarchy, confusion. As Annette Kolodny comments on Kate Millett, "... in some lives, if truth be told, chaos is not always reduced to order, but may exist simultaneously with it."[113] If, indeed, unity is lost with the nineteenth century, the multiplicity of the twentieth also has its virtues and rewards.[114] At least one critic has observed that multiplicity has not had a baneful but rather a beneficent effect upon creativity. It has forced writers to make their own choices. They cannot bend to official dogma since they do not have the security of a unified world view. They must accept the dreadful freedom of multiplicity.[115] The feminist novel sides more with plurality than with unifying interpretations. In the rejection of fragmentation and limitation of the self, one accepts the wholeness and concomitant disorder of the self and the world. In part, the feminist novel breathes life into Simone de Beauvoir's description of "The Other—she is... [the] diversity that destroys unity..."[116] at the same time that she accepts wholeness. In effect, to live in the twentieth century without being torn apart by it requires that one embrace freedom and agree to face its terrors as well.

NOTES

1. Henry Steele Commager, *The American Mind: An Interpretation of American Thought and Character Since the 1880's* (New Haven, Conn.: Yale University Press, 1950), p. 41.
2. Herbert Marder, *Feminism and Art: A Study of Virginia Woolf* (Chicago: The University of Chicago Press, 1968), p. 59.
3. Kate Millett, *Sexual Politics* (Garden City, N.J.: Doubleday and Co., Inc., 1970), p. 144.
4. Suzanne Juhasz, "Towards a Theory of Form in Feminist Autobiography: Kate Millett's *Flying* and *Sita*; Maxine Hong Kingston's *The Woman Warrior*," *Women's Autobiography: Essays in Criticism*, ed. Estelle C. Jelinek (Bloomington: Indiana University Press, 1980), p. 223.
5. Patricia Meyer Spacks, *The Female Imagination* (New York: Alfred A. Knopf, 1975), p. 32.
6. Ibid., p. 320.
7. Helen Yglesias, *How She Died* (Boston: Houghton Mifflin Co., 1972), pp. 118–19.
8. Ibid., p. 91.
9. Ibid., p. 326.
10. Ibid., pp. 146–47.
11. Ibid., pp. 102–3.
12. Erica Jong, *Fear of Flying* (New York: Holt, Rinehart, and Winston, 1971), p. 80.
13. Doris Lessing, *A Proper Marriage* (New York: The New American Library, Inc., 1954), pp. 282–83.
14. Doris Lessing, *The Golden Notebook* (New York: Simon and Schuster, Inc., 1962), p. 36.
15. Ibid., p. 55.
16. Ibid., p. vii.
17. Mary McCarthy, *The Company She Keeps* (1942; reprint, New York: Harcourt, Brace and World, Inc., 1970), pp. 253–54.
18. Sam Bluefarb, *The Escape Motif in the American Novel: Mark Twain to Richard Wright* (Columbus: Ohio State University Press, 1972), p. 52.
19. Irving Howe, *Politics and the Novel* (New York: Horizon Press, Inc., 1957), p. 207.

20. Lionel Trilling, "Contemporary American Literature in Its Relation to Ideas," *American Quarterly* 1 (Fall 1949): 196–97.
21. Lessing, *A Proper Marriage*, p. 141.
22. Alfred Kazin, *On Native Grounds: An Interpretation of Modern American Prose Literature* (New York: Reynal and Hitchcock, 1942), p. 373.
23. Lessing, *The Golden Notebook*, pp. 252–53.
24. Ibid., p. 236.
25. Spacks, *The Female Imagination*, p. 310.
26. Marge Piercy, *Small Changes* (1972; reprint, Greenwich, Conn.: Fawcett Publications, Inc., 1974), p. 434.
27. McCarthy, *The Company She Keeps*, p. 173.
28. Ibid., p. 304.
29. Millett, *Sexual Politics*, p. 144.
30. Spacks, *The Female Imagination*, p. 271.
31. Ibid., p. 93.
32. Virginia Woolf, *A Room of One's Own* (New York: Harcourt, Brace and World, Inc., 1929), p. 101.
33. Ibid.
34. Paul De Man, "Georg Lukacs' *Theory of the Novel*," *Modern Language Notes* 81 (December 1966): 529.
35. Ibid., p. 29.
36. Chester E. Eisinger, *Fiction of the Forties* (Chicago: University of Chicago Press, 1963), p. 178.
37. Spacks, *The Female Imagination*, p. 43.
38. Lessing, *The Golden Notebook*, p. x.
39. Ibid., p. 469.
40. Simone de Beauvoir, *The Second Sex*, ed. and trans. H. M. Parshley (1953; reprint, New York: Random House, 1974), pp. 49–50.
41. Anaïs Nin, *A Woman Speaks*, ed. Evelyn J. Hinz (London: W. H. Allen and Co., Ltd., 1978), p. 16.
42. Sandra M. Gilbert and Susan Gubar, *The Madwoman in the Attic: The Woman Writer and the Nineteenth-Century Literary Imagination* (New Haven, Conn.: Yale University Press, 1979), p. 366.
43. Lessing, *The Golden Notebook*, p. 299.
44. Selma R. Burkom, " 'Only Connect': Form and Content in the Works of Doris Lessing," *Critique: Studies in Modern Fiction* 11, no. 1 (1963): 53–54.
45. de Beauvoir, *The Second Sex*, p. 765.
46. Lessing, *The Golden Notebook*, p. 321.
47. Marilyn French, *The Bleeding Heart* (New York: Random House, 1980), p. 60.

48. Lessing, *A Proper Marriage*, pp. 340–41.
49. French, *The Bleeding Heart*, p. 58.
50. Lessing, *The Golden Notebook*, p. 209.
51. Ibid., p. 206.
52. Ibid., p. 223.
53. Gloria Anzaldúa, "La Prieta," *This Bridge Called My Back: Writings by Radical Women of Color*, eds. Cherríe Moraga and Gloria Anzaldúa (Watertown, Mass.: Persephone Press, Inc., 1981), p. 205.
54. Lessing, *The Golden Notebook*, p. 570.
55. Ibid., p. 36.
56. Kazin, *On Native Grounds*, pp. 497–98.
57. Lessing, *The Golden Notebook*, p. 276.
58. Lessing, *A Proper Marriage*, p. 313.
59. Lessing, *The Golden Notebook*, p. 659.
60. Lessing, *A Proper Marriage*, p. 11.
61. Ibid., p. 117.
62. Ibid., p. 251.
63. French, *The Bleeding Heart*, p. 30.
64. Daniel Aaron, *Writers on the Left: Episodes in American Literary Communism* (New York: Harcourt, Brace and World, Inc., 1961), p. 311.
65. Lessing, *The Golden Notebook*, p. 188.
66. Margaret Atwood, *The Edible Woman* (Boston: Little, Brown and Co., 1969), pp. 157–59.
67. Ibid., p. 144.
68. Ibid., p. 102.
69. Ibid., p. 90.
70. Ibid., p. 83.
71. Ibid., p. 24.
72. Lessing, *The Golden Notebook*, p. vii.
73. Agnes Smedley, *Daughter of Earth* (1929; reprint, Old Westbury, N.Y.: The Feminist Press, 1973), p. 8.
74. Marder, *Feminism and Art*, p. 145.
75. Kate Chopin, *The Awakening* (1899; reprint, New York: W. W. Norton and Co., Inc., 1976), p. 57.
76. Virginia Woolf, *Orlando: A Biography* (New York: Harcourt, Brace and Co., 1928), p. 187.
77. Ellen Moers, *Literary Women* (Garden City, N.Y.: Doubleday and Co., Inc., 1976), p. 9. From George Sand, *Histoire de ma Vie, 1876*, Chapters 13 and 14.
78. Judith Rossner, *Looking for Mr. Goodbar* (New York: Simon and Schuster, Inc., 1975), p. 81.
79. Ibid., p. 198.

80. Ibid., p. 141.
81. Ibid., p. 130.
82. Ibid., p. 243.
83. Ibid., p. 240.
84. Ibid., pp. 202–3.
85. Ibid., p. 189.
86. Ibid., p. 208.
87. Ibid., p. 201.
88. Ibid., p. 178.
89. Ibid., p. 219.
90. Ibid., p. 11.
91. Piercy, *Small Changes*, p. 124.
92. McCarthy, *The Company She Keeps*, p. 10.
93. Ibid., p. 29.
94. Lessing, *The Golden Notebook*, p. 157.
95. Ibid.
96. Ibid., p. 49.
97. Ibid., p. 623.
98. Lessing, *A Proper Marriage*, p. 378.
99. Lessing, *The Golden Notebook*, p. 623.
100. Howe, *Politics and the Novel*, p. 237.
101. Kenneth M. and Patricia Dolbeare, *American Ideologies: The Competing Political Beliefs of the 1970's* (Chicago: Rand McNally College Publishing Co., 1976), p. 194.
102. Burkom, "'Only Connect,'" p. 53.
103. Millett, *Sexual Politics*, p. 211.
104. Woolf, *Orlando*, p. 138.
105. Ibid., p. 323.
106. Dolbeare, *American Ideologies*, p. 185.
107. Howe, *Politics and the Novel*, p. 186.
108. Paul Lauter, "Afterword," *Daughter of Earth*, by Agnes Smedley (1929; reprint, Old Westbury, N.Y.: The Feminist Press, 1973), p. 425.
109. De Man, "Georg Lukacs' *Theory of the Novel*," pp. 530–31.
110. McCarthy, *The Company She Keeps*, p. 304.
111. Spacks, *The Female Imagination*, p. 311.
112. Howe, *Politics and the Novel*, p. 51.
113. Annette Kolodny, "The Lady's Not for Spurning: Kate Millett and the Critics," *Women's Autobiography: Essays in Criticism*, ed. Estelle C. Jelinek (Bloomington: Indiana University Press, 1980), p. 255.
114. Commager, *The American Mind*, p. 48.
115. Eisinger, *Fiction of the Forties*, p. 13.
116. de Beauvoir, *The Second Sex*, p. 90.

4
The Endings

The terrors of the twentieth century, its chaos, its fragmentation, and its ever-increasing dehumanization, are reflected as an aura of hopelessness in its novels. The twentieth-century political novel, in particular, is becoming increasingly more despairing as the century moves on.[1] Even the most hopeful of such novels can cling only to a small fragment of resistance or meaning for a possibility of salvation. The endings to these novels underscore this general tone of desperation. In the twentieth-century novel ending in escape, for example, there is no deliverance. The twentieth-century escape is one resulting from desperation and hopelessness. Escape is not an act of hope, optimism, and self-reliance as it often was in the nineteenth-century novel.[2] One can look, for example, at Huck Finn, Thoreau, and Theron Ware in *The Damnation of Theron Ware* and see successful escapes. They are not all equally optimistic, of course. Thoreau's escape to Walden Pond and Theron Ware's escape from an ugly way of living and being are relatively total. Huck's is much more ambiguous. When his flight is compared with the mutilated and futile attempts made by Bigger Thomas in *Native Son*, by the Joads in *Grapes of Wrath*, and by Frederick Henry in *A Farewell to Arms*, however, it appears favorable and promising.[3]

For the twentieth-century feminist novel, the flight stemming from despair is frequent. The majority of these novels end in flight and escape or death, literal or symbolic. Included among them are *Small Changes, Daughter of Earth, The Street, The Man Who Loved Children, Ripple from the Storm, Landlocked, The Golden Notebook, The Grass is Singing, The Women's Room, The Dollmaker, The Awakening, Daddy was a Number Runner, Up the Sandbox!, Looking for Mr. Goodbar, Woman on the Edge of Time,* and *Emmeline.* Through these endings the authors cry out a condemnation of racist, capitalist, sexist societies. In their attacks, though, they are not usually sustained by a conviction of victory. The flights and deaths reflect the belief evident in most of these novels that a change for the better in modern societies is highly unlikely. They support the observation that at this time mediation between the self and the world is impossible; one's choices lie only in surrender or recoil.[4] In flight, one recoils; in surrender, one finds death.

These endings further serve to complete the portraiture of the novels' heroines. The problems confronting the heroines always stem from their lives in patriarchal, capitalistic, modern societies; but the outcomes result from the heroines' interactions with these societies. Their characters do influence the conclusion given to the novels. Flight or escape for the heroine of the feminist novel does not suggest that in lighting out for new territory, she is a "fugitive" from the central concerns of modern life.[5] Instead, it signifies that dealing with society is impossible. To an extent, many of the heroines are not so much fleeing or escaping as being driven away. Feminist novels ending with the heroine's flight away from her society usually do not point out weaknesses in the heroine's character. Rather, they condemn the society which forces her to flee.

Although all the novels in the group ending in the flight of the central character condemn the society which has driven the heroine away, they do vary in tone. In its resolution *The Street* is probably the most desolate of the five novels included in this group. In her move to Chicago, Lutie Johnson is not so much fleeing or escaping as abandoning hope. She no longer believes that she or Bub can have any comfort or joy in their lives. Every opportunity for escape that presents itself depends upon her offering herself to some man who can give her an alternative; this she refuses to do.[6]

Although she is not really aware of it because of her acceptance of society's views of her, the novel clearly states that black women and children are not permitted the right to live or grow up in a racist, sexist society. It has been said that Huckleberry Finn's flight is partly an attempt to flee violence.[7] Lutie Johnson cannot escape it. Violence has become part of her, perhaps even a necessity for survival. In Chicago she is more likely to find death than escape.

There is a problematic aspect to this ending of *The Street* that can be found in some other feminist novels as well, including *A Proper Marriage* and *The Awakening*. It appears to result from the author's difficulty in portraying a woman leaving her children. Although it is quite fitting in many ways, this ending to *The Street* does present some distinct problems. After the sustained portrayal of Bub as the center of Lutie's life, it is scarcely possible to believe that she would leave him. Never in the novel is she concerned with her own appearance and reputation; she is solely concerned with how Bub's life is to be made better. It seems unlikely that at the end she would shift character so much that her utmost desire would be to prevent Bub from knowing what she had done. This is a possible response of love, of course, and it is true that she is not very enlightened politically. As a result, she could possibly still blame herself, even at the end. On the train, leaving for Chicago, she thinks:

Bub would never understand why she had disappeared. He was expecting to see her tomorrow. She had promised him she would come. He would never know why she had deserted him and he would be bewildered and lost without her.

Would he remember that she loved him? She hoped so, but she knew that for a long time he would have that half-frightened, worried look she had seen on his face the night he was waiting for her at the subway.

He would probably go to reform school. She looked out of the train window, not seeing the last-minute passengers hurrying down the ramp. The constricton [sic] of her throat increased. So he will go to reform school, she repeated. He'll be better off there. He'll be better off without you. That way he may have some kind of chance. He didn't have the ghost of a chance on that street. The best you could give him wasn't good enough.[8]

As her love for him was generally portrayed, however, her leaving him alone, abandoned and terrified in jail, not even knowing what had happened to her, is problematic. Although her societally imposed conscience could make her blame herself for everything, even it would struggle to convince her that life in jail, a result of life on the street, would be better for Bub than staying with her. It is likely that the problem for Petry with this ending was that in trying to find the most hopeless and wrenching of conclusions for her novel, she had to portray a scene most difficult for her, as a women novelist, to imagine: a mother very much in love with her child voluntarily leaving. Although the attempt to run from a violent and cruel society is a fitting ending for this novel, Lutie's desertion of Bub is questionable.

An ending nearly as despairing occurs in *Daughter of Earth*. For Marie Rogers/Agnes Smedley, there is also to be no life, no love in racist, sexist, capitalist society. For a woman who grew up in poverty and turned to Marxism, the only means of survival, of effective work, lies in escape to another country. This ending, like that in *The Street*, explicitly condemns society for driving away the heroine. In *The Street*, the society mutilates a person who merely wants a life for herself and her son. In *Daughter of Earth*, it defeats a person who works for a reasonable life for all people. Unlike *The Street*, *Daughter of Earth* does suggest some weaknesses in the heroine. It is possible to view Marie Rogers as a runaway, fleeing problems too complicated, too difficult, for her in the United States. As has been noted of Lilith, her flight might be one "of escape rather than an active rebellion."[9] Marie's terror of love is a direct result of her country's patriarchal sexism. The ugly marriages she saw as a child revealed to her the underpinnings of matrimony in a patriarchal society. For the male, marriage provides a servant and prostitute; for the female it results in servitude and the life of a brood-mare. There is also an intimation, though, that

Marie is at fault for her inability to overcome her fear of love and affection. For these reasons, Marie's only hope lies "out of this country."[10]

Interestingly, too, the end of *Daughter of Earth* is more thoroughly feminist than any other part of the novel. When Marie first begins subconsciously to think of leaving Anand, for example, she becomes ill. She says of Anand:

He called doctors. They could find nothing wrong. Hysterical, perhaps, one suggested; these modern women seemed to find nervous trouble most attractive.
 "I want a rest; I want peace," I said to Anand.
 "What do you mean?"
 "I wish to go away."
 "Without me—or with me?"
 "Without you. I have a friend... Listen, Anand... I have a friend in Denmark. She has often invited me to come to her. Maybe I will be better there."[11]

Anand insists on viewing her decision as a personal one involving him instead of a political one concerning society's direction of the relationship between men and women. Marie comes to realize that the choice she makes is political. She thinks:

When I made the final decision that would deprive me of the love I had longed for and fought for and lied for, that would perhaps even deprive me of all hope of work in the movement I loved, it seemed that I had decided to give up life itself. But then I fell into the first dreamless sleep for months.[12]

Later, when Anand tells Marie that Juan Diaz will use his rape of her to attack him, she openly states her thoughts:

"Well, Anand, he will not use it against you, for I will not give him the opportunity. I am going away. I can endure our life no longer. Men do not use such a weapon against a man—they use it only against a woman. Juan can hurt you only through me. He cannot hurt me—for I shall refuse to be hurt."[13]

This ending suggests that Marie's feminism starts to outweigh her Marxism. Perhaps it is because of its explicit feminism that at least one male critic has found the radicalism near the end of *Daughter of Earth* "hysterical."[14]

Martha Quest is yet another figure in the feminist novel constantly in flight. In *A Proper Marriage* and *Landlocked*, Martha most definitely attempts escape. In *A Proper Marriage*, her flight is from the traditional family and the female role in the family. In fleeing Doug, she actually flies from a living death, a life which holds security as its highest value. In doing so, she gives up her daughter, Caroline, as well. As in *The Street*, this ending involves a woman leaving her child. Martha, like Lutie, babbles certain idiocies to herself, including the one that she is setting Caroline free. Later, when she recalls thinking that, she wonders, "What on earth had she meant by it? How could she have said it, thought it, felt it?"[15] It seems more likely, given Martha's relationship with Caroline, that she would have insisted on taking Caroline with her, both of them fleeing the family. Once Martha has left Caroline, however, events in *A Ripple from the Storm* and *Landlocked* follow logically enough. Martha's flight again, in *Landlocked*, is singularly appropriate. In fleeing the aridity of male-female relationships and the society of Africa, the death of the good symbolized by Athen's murder and Thomas' death, and the loss of innocent belief in left-wing political struggle, Martha tries to escape the modern world. By returning to an island surrounded by the sea, Martha hopes to lave her dry and barren soul in fresh waters. In fleeing to England, though, one suspects that Martha will only find the modern world there, too. That, though, is for the final volume. For this volume, *Landlocked*, the ending is an inauspicious one for Martha.

In two other novels, *The Man Who Loved Children* and *Small Changes*, the escape endings are far more hopeful. In these, one can think, at least to some extent, that the escapees may truly elude their societies. Louie, in *The Man Who Loved Children*, is the only adolescent among the heroines of these novels ending in flight. It is largely for this reason that her running away is so much more joyous than the others. Her decisions and choices in leaving are not the final ones made by mature women in the other novels. She is starting her life. When Louie wonders "why everyone didn't run away,"[16] she reveals the viewpoint of her age; Lutie, Marie Rogers, and Martha cannot run away. Only the adolescent can. Of these heroines, it is only of Louie that one could say what Elizabeth Hardwick says of Thea in Hedda Gabler, that she was given "the courage to leave her husband and to set out, in the classical, illuminated, isolated way of a hero, to pursue her fate."[17] Louie is pursuing her fate; the others are being driven away. Louie leaves behind her many things, including the family in general symbolized by the Pollits in particular, patriarchy and modern imperialist society symbolized by Sam, and the concomitant destruction of woman symbolized by Henny. It seems likely that she will run into them again since the Pollits do represent their society. For this conclusion, however, what is more important is that Louie, like George Sand, has "gone for a walk round the world."[18]

Beth's escapes in *Small Changes* are purely pleasurable and successful. In her early escape from Jim, she flees being trapped by children and denied her own life. At that point, as an adolescent, she does truly "escape into adulthood"[19] by leaving Jim. She realizes that "staying together as they were meant that they would have children and buy a house and buy things to put in it. It meant never growing up. It meant never finding out what she wanted."[20]

She must escape the traditional life if she is to find maturity. Beth succeeds without qualification. When she escapes from the society that wants to deny her herself, she rises

...above the clouds. Up here the sun shone and the sky was a dark hard clear blue like the bathing suit sewn into the lining of her raincoat, stowed above her on the rack. She clasped her hands and joy pierced her. She was wiry with joy and tingling. How beautiful to be up here! How beautiful was flight and how free (even though it cost money). She was the only flying turtle under the sun.[21]

As an adolescent, like Louie, Beth's escape provides true freedom. At the end, when she escapes again with Wanda, she evades a society that wishes to punish her and her friends for not living as it demands they do. Once again, her escape is both rapturous and successful. Beth's excitement and almost child-like happiness are revealed as she establishes new identities for herself, Wanda, and Wanda's children and as she meets secretly with Louie. When Beth and Wanda and her family are reunited, they are delighted and quickly settled. Beth has two things as an adult, however, that none of the other heroines considered here have: her love for Wanda is true, lasting, and reciprocal, and she has a firm commitment to and understanding of herself as a woman connected to all other women. For her there is to be neither failure nor loneliness. Besides the jubilant tone with which the story of Beth ends, there is yet another aspect separating this novel from the other feminist novels ending in escape. Beth and Wanda at the same time both escape and fight. They make a positive, defiant move when they steal Wanda's children back from Joe's parents, and Beth states their choice clearly when Wanda asks her if she is scared. Beth answers, "Sure. Always. But now I know we can fight. And sometimes, sometimes, win."[22] Even Miriam's ending is not completely hopeless because she is shown occasionally viewing her relationship with Neil realistically and because she starts to develop a life of her own again so that her daughter will have a better model to follow. This novel of escape, unlike the others, ends hopefully because the characters are allowed to triumph over their society and situations and are given a belief in themselves and their ideals. As Wanda puts it, "The easiest way to protect ourselves is to do nothing political—and then whatever is the point!"[23]

There are several aspects to these novels ending in escapes that stand out from other novels with similar endings simply because these novels are political and feminist. Obviously, in escaping, the hero or heroine says "no" to his or her society. One can observe ordinarily in such novels that where the majority says "yes," it is the spirit of independence that is likeliest to say "no."[24] This observation, though important to other novels, is irrelevant to the feminist novel. None of the heroines in the feminist novels considered here, except for Louie in *The Man Who Loved Children*, is presented as especially extraordinary and enlightened. Rather, the emphasis here is placed on the connection between these women and the majority of

The Endings

other women; it is not placed on their being different from and elevated above the rest of the mass of female dullards. Additionally, it has been noted of other novels ending in escape that the heroines are taking the path of avoidance. That is not the case in these novels, except for a hint of it in *Daughter of Earth*. These characters are pictured primarily as being pushed away. Actually, from the viewpoint of these novels, Isabel Archer failed when she chose not to escape. Indeed, in refusing to escape from Osmond, she exhibits fear of Casper, of

> the chaos of his assertions, the hot wind of his sexuality, the "lightning" of his kiss, to flee down "a very straight path" to the moral security of Osmond's sacred, absolute devotion to form. She might instead flee the sterility of her marriage for the deepenings of love, rejecting society's restrictions in favor of personal needs.[25]

Paradoxically, escape means commitment, and staying in the marriage represents escape. She fears freedom and Casper more than entrapment with Osmond. In a real sense, her flight from Casper is an escape from freedom. In these feminist novels, staying put without fighting often means failure, the avoidance of life, and weakness. Flight is often a necessity.

Finally, in all of these feminist novels ending in flight except for *The Street*, and in many others ending differently as well, eschewal of the traditional family is essential. Some of the others include *The Awakening, Looking for Mr. Goodbar, Up the Sandbox!, The Dollmaker,* and *Fear of Flying*. For many of these heroines, for almost all of these novels, the traditional family epitomizes capitalist, patriarchal society. Indeed, in *The Man Who Loved Children*, the Pollit family symbolizes it. To be free, all the heroines must flee it. As in the case of *Villette*, "free is alone...."[26] This is why we find Beth early in *Small Changes*, after she has left Jim, renting a room to be alone in.[27] Simone de Beauvoir comments that in the past women shut up in their own immanence tried to have company by trapping men as well. For the heroines in the feminist novel, "today the combat takes a different shape; instead of wishing to put man in a prison, woman endeavors to escape from one...."[28] For the heroines to save themselves, they must fly from it. They respond like the male hero in Charlotte Brontë's *The Professor*, who "reacts to his perception of his 'female' powerlessness first with claustrophobic feelings of enclosure, burial, imprisonment, and then with a rebellious decision to escape."[29] The heroines must escape from their own powerlessness in a patriarchy.

Some heroines are not able to escape and so cannot save themselves. In this second group of novels, the outlook is generally quite hopeless. In three of the novels, *Up the Sandbox!*, *Daddy was a Number Runner*, and *The Women's Room*, the failure of flight leads to the figurative death of defeat. In four others, *The Awakening, Looking for Mr. Goodbar, The Grass is Singing*, and *Emmeline*, it leads to literal death. In two others, *The Dollmaker* and *The Golden Notebook*, there are some promising notes which tie them in with the third set of novels having more auspicious endings.

Up the Sandbox!, part of the first set, ends similarly, yet differently, from *Daddy was a Number Runner* and *The Women's Room*. Margaret Reynolds' failure to escape is partly her own fault as well as society's. Obviously, society has encouraged her to marry and have children; but she is the one who relegates thoughts of escape to the futility of daydreams. She refuses to think of flight as an actual possibility and denigrates these thoughts by consigning them to the level of childish dreams of fame and success. In some ways, the novel is really about an apolitical woman whose primary interest is herself and her family. She imagines herself famous, and she dreams of gargantuan funerals for herself. Even though she conceives of herself as a political radical and a great humanitarian, it often appears that her own egotism is the center of her dreams rather than any desire to help others. Her inability to escape is as much the fault of her own narcissism, passivity, and feeling of meaninglessness as it is the fault of society. She claims she does not believe in Paul's thesis that all revolutions are betrayed; but in reality, she does. She feels certain that her head will roll after the revolution. She is terrified of black people and shows her fears in the stories of the old man, of her political group shutting her out because she is white, and of her death at the hands of the Itwas.

In the other two novels of defeat, neither heroine is at all responsible for her failure. In *Daddy was a Number Runner*, for example, the only slim chance for escape lies in the community feeling that Francie discovers toward the end of the novel. That proves not to be enough, though. Without money, without power, there is no hope. At the end of this novel, death is the end result for nearly all the characters. Francie is not dead at the end of the novel, but she is only thirteen. In this novel, which focuses on the complete deprivation society visits onto black people, there can be no individual, personal error of any account when it is compared with the evil formed by the coalition of racist society.

Similarly, Mira in *The Women's Room* is banished by society to a rocky Maine coast. The difference is that Mira's pain is that of loneliness and separation. It is an aloneness made by society; one can either be alone in a marriage or alone by oneself. Francie's pain is also dictated by society, but she is denied fulfillment of even the most basic of material and spiritual needs. Although Mira is permitted the basic necessities, she finds that continued resistance to society, the ability to see it for what it is and to refuse to compromise with it, brings one exile and separation. As it was for Francie, the community Mira found with her friends was not enough to defeat society. The ending with Val dead and Mira banished, seems to indicate that Val's analysis is correct: the truth is death and exile.

In those novels ending with the heroine's death, she is always at least partly responsible. Of course, because these novels are political and feminist, society is the true murderer, but the heroine does have some character deficiencies which help society to rid itself of her. As Isadora Wing states in *Fear of Flying*, it is "easy enough to kill yourself...."[30] The ending of *The Awakening* was discussed in Chapter One. Edna actually serves society by committing suicide. Society does not want women like her, and she obligingly removes herself. The suicide itself reflects Edna's basic weakness, her inability to forego romance and her essential nineteenth-century romanticism. To a certain extent, Theresa in *Looking for Mr. Goodbar* also commits suicide. At the end, when she says, *"do it do it do it and get it over w—,"*[31] she is expressing her complete exhaustion with her life and her attempts to free her mind from the clutches of society. In a real sense, sex is suicide for her. She commits suicide every time she does not say "no" and, indeed, participates in her own rape. Her real weakness is her inability to think for herself. Having accepted society's sexism, there is no way for her to be free; death is the only escape as it is also for Edna. Gary White is not really her murderer. Like Theresa, he, too, has imbibed all of his society's twisted sexist views toward sexuality and women. Toward the end of his confession, after he has killed Theresa, he states, "*I think I was trying to warm her up. It was weird 'cause it was like...she was my friend.*"[32] He is right, of course. There is no reason why he and Theresa could not have been friends. By sending him to Viet Nam, by breathing a terror of homosexuality into him, and by repeatedly telling him that sex and women who like it are filthy, society makes Gary White a murderer. By convincing Theresa of many of the same things, it makes her a suicide.

In *The Grass is Singing*, Doris Lessing provides Mary with a similar set of circumstances. Society made her, too, into a certain kind of person, able to survive only in a particularly protected set of circumstances. When transplanted to Turner's farm where she must recognize and deal with society's and her own virulent racism and hatred of sexuality, she falls apart. When she recognizes Moses as a human being with whom she is strongly involved emotionally, she collapses. Tony, brought to care for the farm while Mary and Dick are gone, recognizes part of the problem:

...he [Tony] began to understand with a horrified pity, her [Mary's] utter indifference to Dick; she had shut out everything that conflicted with her actions, that would revive the code she had been brought up to follow.
    She said suddenly, "They said I was not like that, not like that, not like that." It was like a gramophone that had got stuck at one point.
    "Not like what?" he asked blankly.
    "Not like *that*." The phrase was furtive, sly, yet triumphant. God, the woman is mad as a hatter! he said to himself. And then he thought, but is she, is she? She can't be mad. She doesn't behave as if she were. She behaves simply as if she lives in a world of her own, where other people's standards don't count. She has forgotten what her own people

The Endings

are like. But then, what is madness, but a refuge, a retreating from the world?[33]

What Tony does not understand is that "like that" refers to Mary's sexual nature. Her friends, in the past, saw her as asexual; her sexuality was awakened by Moses. For Moses, too, the act of really seeing Mary as a person, of growing to hate her singly as a person, leads him to murder, something that would never have happened had he and the white people continued refusing to see one another and to simply act out a code. Society's racism kills Mary, but so does her own. In all three of these novels, the lesser or greater weaknesses of the characters contribute, though only in a small way, to their deaths. As a result, the endings of these three novels are not entirely desolate. The implication remains that one still has some control and some responsibility, that the evils of one's society can be overcome if one clears the mind of its propaganda, its distortions, its hatreds.

Emmeline is an entirely different matter. A thirteen-year-old seduced by her middle-aged employer bears no responsibility for her actions. Neither, in the twentieth century, does the same woman deserve scorn twenty years later for unknowingly falling in love with and marrying her own son. Contempt in this novel is reserved for the sexist society that destroys Emmeline's life. Matthew, her son, can escape because he is male. Just as Emmeline's brothers leave earlier in the novel to go west, so does Matthew. Women, of course, cannot flee from what they know, and so they remain, like Emmeline, with the results of horror. Special shame is reserved in this novel for the female characters, who support society rather than one of their own. The author comments, after Emmeline and Harriet talk, that "Emmeline lived in Fayette, in the house Matthew had built, until her death thirty-nine years later, but that was the last time she ever heard the sound of another woman's voice."[34] Her own sister and those women who should be her sisters never give her any assistance although some of the men do. At the end it develops that "the winter of 1899 was a particularly severe one." Everyone is absorbed because of this, and so Emmeline "died of cold and starvation during a period when, for six or seven weeks, no one happened to come by."³⁵ It is suitable that the fictional Emmeline should die in the year that *The Awakening* was published.

The last three novels ending in a figurative death have a much stronger note of hope. They are on a borderline with the third group of novels having much more positive endings. In *The Dollmaker*, for example, the ending is mitigated. Although Gertie destroys her block of wood, in effect destroying her life, she continues to have strong, committed ties to her neighbors and to the people she has come to know in Detroit. She has a community bond which promises some sustenance. Gertie, too, has some difficulties in overcoming societal propaganda. She blames herself ultimately for everything, accepting the dictum that the wife and mother is always responsible and guilty.³⁶ Reuben and Claude Jean are both furious with her for not fighting back.³⁷ Actually, since she sees herself as guilty and responsible, she cannot fight back. She does not perceive her problem as being one which can be fought against. Because she blames herself, she does not see her true enemy. Once again, society protects itself by blinding its victims to the truth and foisting a sense of guilt on them.

This is not the case for Connie Ramos in *Woman on the Edge of Time*. This novel does end with the heroine permanently locked into a state mental hospital, but it is not at all clear that her battle was a failure. In the terms set by this particular novel, Connie Ramos, a poor, supposedly insane, Hispanic woman may very well have saved the future of the planet by her actions, which culminate in the murder of four people. Her insight is that she turns away from guilt to anger, anger appropriately directed against the representatives of a hideous futuristic world. As Connie thinks to herself, she realizes that:

She hated Geraldo and it was right for her to hate him. Attacking him was different from turning her anger, her sorrow, her loss of Claude into self-hatred, into speed and downers, into booze, into wine, into seeing herself in Angelina and abusing that self born again into the dirty world. Yes, this time was different. She had struck out not at herself, not at herself in another, but at Geraldo, the enemy.³⁸

Later, she realizes that she, and others with her, are at war and not just with Geraldo. As she says near the end, "I'm a dead woman now too. I know it. But I did fight them. I'm not ashamed. I tried."[39] Connie may die, but her war is a victory.

In *The Golden Notebook*, the ending is mixed because there are two endings. "Free Women" ends with figurative suicide. Molly and Anna both give up; Molly makes a conventional marriage, and Anna takes a conventional job. "The Golden Notebook" ends with both Saul and Anna going back to writing. Not only do they not give up, they both have enough left in themselves to make another commitment. In effect, Anna describes them both when she says:

"There's a great black mountain. It's human stupidity. There are a group of people who push a boulder up the mountain. When they've got a few feet up, there's a war, or the wrong sort of revolution, and the boulder rolls down—not to the bottom, it always manages to end up a few inches higher than when it started. So the group of people put their shoulders to the boulder and start pushing again."[40]

That belief, that commitment, that not giving up, connects *The Golden Notebook* with the third set of novels. This small group of feminist novels, including *Fear of Flying*, *The Edible Woman*, *How She Died*, *Small Changes*, *Braided Lives*, *The Color Purple*, and *Meridian*, ends neither in evasion nor in death. Rather, the novels progress to a more hopeful denouement, with the heroine having worked through her problems, to some extent, and having reached an understanding of herself and her society. The novels end with the heroines not so much blazingly victorious as in control. They have some direction to their lives, an understanding of their situations, and a resolution to face what lies ahead of them with strength. Most of these figures must overcome problems in their own characters while they sort out their lives. These character weaknesses, besides having a bearing on the novels' outcomes, also have a direct relationship to the heroines' ages. Most of the central figures are mature women, not adolescents. Most have been married, have children, and have reached intellectual and emotional maturity. The attempts of the characters to deal with modern society and the resolutions of their struggles are the actions of mature adults. In presenting older, adult women as central characters, the feminist novel focuses on the figure of most interest to feminism. In so doing, it also dispenses, for the most part, with issues of youth, beauty, and narcissism. Avoiding the young, beautiful heroine, the feminist novel concentrates on the societal demands and political issues the mature woman faces. Of fundamental concern in these novels are the relationships of adults to one another and to their societies. Usually, they focus directly on such subjects and do not refer to them indirectly through the portrayal of adolescent struggles with family, authority, and self. The decisions the heroines make are final, not reflections of a stage through which they pass.

In such novels as *Fear of Flying*, *The Edible Woman*, *How She Died*, *Braided Lives*, *Small Changes*, *The Color Purple*, and *Meridian*, the endings reveal a heroine who whirls around and puts up a fight against the personal and societal demons pursuing her. Against the background of the other novels previously discussed, these end with a tone ranging from tentative hopefulness to positive joy. Some novels, like *Small Changes*, *The Four-Gated City*, *The Dollmaker*, *The Golden Notebook*, and even *How She Died* straddle two groups. *Small Changes* and *The Four-Gated City* are novels ending in escape and battle, while *How She Died* ends in death for one character and growth and commitment for the other. For the most part, the assertion of success that these novels make is low-key; the heroines do not expect a great deal from their victories, but that they are victorious is not to be doubted.

In *Fear of Flying* and *The Edible Woman*, the victory is over that part of the self which has been thoroughly indoctrinated by society. When these heroines want to break free from society, their societally imposed conscience incapacitates them. Ultimately, however, they defeat it. Despite the inane aspects of *Fear of Flying*, there is a story within this novel of a woman attempting to free herself from the handicaps society has placed on her. Isadora Wing knows a great deal about herself even at the beginning of the novel. Even then she is aware that she is invested with the same romanticism foisted upon all women in her society.[41] She knows, like the young, trapped, syphilitic wife in *Daughter of Earth*, that she tells her husband she loves

The Endings 117

him because she has nowhere else to go.[42] Although the realization is vastly understated, she does understand that leaving Bennett was her first independent action, and "even there it had been partly because of Adrian."[43] As the novel progresses, she learns even more. She discovers that she is not a person, that she does not feel whole without a man, even if that man can never remember her name.[44] She eventually understands that it is not a man she needs to find, but herself.[45] She realizes that she needs to learn how to mother herself.[46] At the end, Isadora succeeds. She states, "It was my fear that was missing" and "whatever happened, I knew I would survive it."[47] Unfortunately, there are problems with the ending. In an attempt to reach an open ending, one in which Isadora does not, like a nineteenth-century heroine, get divorced, Jong finishes instead with a lady or the tiger ending. Clearly, Isadora will do one or the other, either stay married or get divorced. For a novel in which the point is for the heroine to find herself, the ending, leaning so heavily on what she does with her marriages, is singularly inappropriate. It is certainly true that Isadora insists that the novel actually ends with her discovery of her own body and with her reliance on herself. Still, the novel might actually have ended there, and the issue of Isadora's marriage might have been dispensed with altogether. Even at the end, her last decision will center on her relationship with Bennett, with yet another man. Despite its evident flaws, however, this ending puts the novel into the category of those that terminate with a moderately successful heroine who faces her future with hope.

In *The Edible Woman*, the ending signals the completion of a similar quest. Marion, on the verge of marriage, suddenly sees the relationship between men and women, between modern human beings generally, as one of eat or be eaten, kill or be killed. In the shock of her discovery, she begins to imagine that everything she eats is alive. Eventually, she discovers that even tapioca pudding is full of eyes that are alive and glaring at her. She is well on her way to starving to death by the end of the novel. She saves herself by the test cake she bakes, the cake shaped like a woman and symbolizing herself. To her prospective husband, the cake is not at all amusing; it symbolizes the relationship he really wants which involves his consuming and subsuming Marion. Duncan, on the other hand, is not bothered by the cake at all; he enjoys every mouthful because he is not symbolically acting out his desires. He has no wish to devour Marion; his life is not based on the principle of defeating others before they defeat him. For Marion, the clarity of vision which comes from the results of the test saves her. She knows what her marriage would have been, and she knows that all life need not be so. Her novel does not end with her choosing a man but with her saving herself. It ends jubilantly with her first enjoyable meal in months and with her victory over the role into which she was pushed.

Meridian, *Braided Lives*, and *The Color Purple* also end with the successes of their heroines. Meridian understands "finally, that the respect she owed her life was to continue, against whatever obstacles, to live it, and not to give up any particle of it without a fight to the death, preferably *not* her own."[48] Truman thinks about Meridian at the end of the novel and realizes that "this part of her, new, sure and ready, even eager, for the world, he knew he must meet again and recognize for its true value at some future time."[49] Meridian goes on fighting for her people and her world, stronger at the end than at the beginning. Jill in *Braided Lives* continues her political struggles as well and is even able eventually to forge a relationship with her mother. Celie in *The Color Purple*, along with the other female heroines, saves and unites an entire family, a family that in many ways represents the entire human race.

Unlike figures in novels by Miller and Mailer, like Rojak, these characters do not will the self through violence. They find themselves through their experiences, through their thoughts, and they commit themselves to their resultant vision. Their adventures are the antithesis of violence, and their discoveries are not shouted out. Part of what they discover is that everyone is ultimately alone, a knowledge both frightening and exhilarating. For these figures, after their trials, it is usually more of the latter.

In *How She Died* and *Small Changes*, the victory culminates in definite and definitive action. Jean's growth in *How She Died* finalizes in her decision to make a move, to change her situation. For Jean this must be her finale. Her passivity and timidity, her inability to move beyond single, personal relationships are gone. She makes a commitment, not in Mary's way but in her own way, to make things better, to help. For Mary, that commitment was everything; for Matt, it was nothing. Jean manages haltingly to reconcile the two and move forward. In part of her argument with Matt near the end, Jean refers to one of Mary's friends, an old man, by saying:

> "Oh, poor Papa Shaeffer," I said.
> "Poor Papa Shaeffer!" he said. "He thinks he's terriffic [sic]. He thinks he did his part to change the world. That's poor Papa Shaeffer's version of the good life."
> "You're using him to keep yourself aloof. That's what I do. It's not true what we say, in the way we use it."[50]

Jean points out to Matt that he justifies himself by making other people's efforts seem selfish, too, or by being cynical about their deepest motives. Although it is true that Papa Shaeffer sees helping politically as the "good life," that fact is not important. The end of the novel is Jean's beginning of a new life, and the tone is one of success, modulated, to be sure, but still success. The import is that Jean's decision matters, that what she does with her life matters, that she matters. Her commitment to something outside of her own personal happiness matters.

In *Small Changes*, too, the end is one of victory. This is one of the novels that straddles two groups. It is both a novel of escape and of fighting back. Beth eludes Jim, but she is not truly free until she fights him. Similarly, at the end when the law attacks Wanda and Beth, they fight back and win. They still must flee by going into hiding and changing their names, but they are successful in getting the children back and in being able to live together. Their ending is a celebration. For Miriam, there are obviously going to be hard times; but even for her, there are indications that she will survive and surmount them. One is not given reason to think that Neil will steal her children. Rather, for Miriam, her analysis of herself is the end and it is accurate:

> She felt in herself Wanda's strength for her children; maybe not the greater strength it would take to put herself first, but the strength

to fight for them, by all means. So she was not alone, but connected to them, and connected still to Beth and Wanda, not only through the money she secreted from household expenses for them but in her daily thoughts, her sense of them as a counterexample to defeat. Connected to Dorine, connected still in a muted, never to be complete way to Phil. Connected to Sally, who wrote her halting but faithful one-page letters. Her students at the free school. Whoever she was preparing her access codes and information retrieval expertise for. Out of such connections she could weave no security, no protection against her worst fears. But of such connections were wrought an end to the slow relentless dying back she had known, and the slow, undramatic refounding, single thought by small decision by petty act, of a life: her life. That life shone too, dimly but with considerable heat, banked coals in the dark.[51]

Miriam's life has almost been snuffed out by the lack of air in it, but it promises to burst into flames and light once the doors are flung open on her marriage. Miriam, it is suggested, will find her own victory supported by the community of others.

The Four-Gated City also concludes with both the flight and fight of the entire human species. There is little doubt at the end as to which community of people will finally triumph. Martha's community, having escaped to an island after the atomic war, survives and, it is implied, goes back to what human beings once were and ahead to what they might become, ahead to something better. Martha comments "that we took heart and held on to our belief in the future for our race. And, from that time, we put aside thoughts of being rescued. We knew that there wasn't much prospect of it, but now we actively did not want it."[52] Then the "new children" arrive and are described as "our guardians. They guard us."[53] There is more than a small implication that these children will guard the world and the entire human race. Joseph, one of the children, predicts that he will eventually go to live with Francis Coldridge as indeed he does at the end of the novel. The reader suspects that the children's other clairvoyant observations are also accurate, including the one that "one day all the human race will be like them."[54] From the descriptions in this novel, the future looks far superior to the past.

In these last novels, the heroines go into combat. Their victories range from the starting point of freeing oneself from the grip of societal pressure and indoctrination to the maturity of taking positive action, of moving out to affect the world, in no matter how small a way. All these novels exhibit an enmity to the established order[55] in their conclusions. Some of them even assert, along with Beth, that sometimes the one who defies can win, and they show their heroines doing so. They support the statement that freedom consists of revolt, but the last of them do not agree that its price is always defeat.[56] In effect, the authors of these novels free women when they themselves disengage "from the traditional view that women who experiment with their lives are either damned or doomed...."[57]

As mentioned earlier, the endings of these novels not only make strong statements about society, but, often, they also reflect facets of the central heroine's character. The endings of these novels are particularly significant when viewed in relation to the heroine's age. Almost all of these novels focus centrally on a mature woman. Sometime she is beautiful; sometimes she is not; but she is always an adult. Even those novels which show the heroine growing up from childhood, for example, *Small Changes* and *The Women's Room*, center principally on her adult life. The decisions she makes and their results are conclusive. They are not the decisions of a youth or the ending which is a beginning. These heroines demand to be viewed as adults. Even in those two novels dealing with an adolescent heroine, *The Man Who Loved Children* and *Daddy was a Number Runner*, the circumstances slant the heroine away from childhood and youth. Henny counterbalances and interacts with Louie and takes the center stage as much as Louie does. Further, Sam is the actual child in the novel. In *Daddy was a Number Runner*, Francie at the end must be the world's oldest thirteen-year-old. What her society does is to eliminate childhood and adolescence. One is an old woman at thirteen. Maturity in these novels is defined as a way of looking at the world and a state of mind, not a function of age. Similarly, an adult in terms of years can be far more childish intellectually and emotionally than many children.

This focus on the mature woman is part of the tradition of realism. Virginia Woolf comments upon the disparity between

ficition and reality when she remarks, "She [woman] dominates the lives of kings and conquerors in fiction; in fact she was the slave of any boy whose parents forced a ring upon her finger."[58] The feminist novel insists on the reality. In *Daughter of Earth* we see Marie Rogers' mother making her stand when she refuses to tell her husband how she voted.[59] Given her husband's dispostion, such temerity in reality and in the novel could cost her her life. In *The Man Who Loved Children*, too, one is presented with the viewpoint and life of a mature woman. One reads: "What a dreary stodgy world of adults the children saw when they went out! And what a moral, high-minded world their father saw! But for Henny there was a wonderful particular world, and when they went with her they saw it."[60]

The point is made, too, that this view is not a unique, individual one because "it was not Henny alone who went through this inferno, but every woman, especially, for example, Mrs. Wilson, the woman who came to wash every Monday."[61] In these novels we do not see the "dreary stodgy world of adults" through the eyes of the adolescent. We do not see the "moral, high-minded world" of the complacent, white male in his patriarchal setting. Nor do we see the symbolic, young, beautiful woman of fiction. Instead we see the worlds of mature, adult women with their weaknesses, their flaws, their strengths. We see their place in society. And whether these women end by evading their societies, by being driven away, by dying, or by fighting back, they must be viewed as adults, not as children, or adolescents, or symbols.

Adulthood is a positive quality shared by almost all of the heroines of the feminist novel; it is not a repulsive feature of old age. However, there are several negative character traits that are prevalent in these novels and that, when attached to the central figure, are sure to spell her doom. These include passivity, guilt, and self-doubt. Such character weaknesses often have a direct impact on the ultimate end of the novel because it is the character's interaction with society that determines the fate of the character. It is made quite evident in almost all of these novels that these traits are specifically and intentionally instilled into women by their societies. By the society, they are viewed as positive attributes; by the feminist novel, they are not. Although not speaking specifically of women, Marie Rogers remarks of this situation, "Thus I learned that if you are sick or injured, people love you; if you are well they do not."[62] The task for most of the heroines in these novels is to overcome the sickness or injury society has given them and then deal with what follows. Some of the heroines cannot; surprisingly, many can and do.

The ascription of weaknesses to the heroines and their resultant deaths can give the impression in some of these novels of a certain conservatism on the parts of their authors. Killing off the heroine occasionally indicates an unwillingness on the author's part to face the radical restructuring her own vision requires. To impute some fault, no matter how small, to the heroine and then to dispatch her can provide an escape for the author from the implications and extrapolations of her novelistic statement. This seems particularly true of *The Awakening*.

Probably the most furiously attacked and most frequently presented character flaw in the feminist novels is the one of passivity, or, as it is sometimes labeled, "nostalgia." In floating on the overglorified joys of the past, one submits to the evils of the present. In focusing on this trait, these novels deal with a characteristic often identified as symptomatic of modern mass society's illness. Irving Howe describes this modern mass culture as one that is relatively comfortable materially but that exists basically as a half-welfare, half-garrison state. The primary characteristic of the population is passivity. People are indifferent and atomized, and their primary function is consumption. Their lives are adrift.[63] Of course the passive, modern character is common in most modern fiction, for example, in Farrell's Danny O'Neill novels, where one meets that ubiquitous figure to whom things always happen but who cannot himself make anything happen.[64] The difference in the feminist novel is that one is dealing with a character who is actively encouraged to be passive, not just as a member of mass society, but as a woman. The female's talents are either to be repressed or to be degraded into mere prettiness. She is not to venture forth or to act. Being a consumer reaches its epitome in her; she is not to act except in consuming. For Marion in *The Edible Woman*, her upcoming marriage brings what is expected of her as a wife and of everyone, to some extent, into sharp relief. Even her job for Seymour Surveys provides material to encourage more consumption. For the inert modern woman, even when having a child, supposedly her chief goal, she is not to deliver it but to be delivered of it. In love, she is the beloved, not the lover. This is fitting since the lover determines the value and quality of the love while the beloved has nothing to say about it.[65] The society undermines even the active woman with a supportive husband by suggesting that she has fallen into such a condition. She is "lucky" to have such a husband; one does not suggest that she might, in fact, have chosen him.[66] In investigating and stressing this submission, the feminist novel focuses on an important aspect of modern society and of feminism.

In most of the feminist novels in which the passivity of the main character is stressed, the heroine succeeds in overcoming it. In *Small Changes* and *How She Died*, she overcomes her inertia and moves into concrete action. Beth grows out of the passivity forced upon her early in *Small Changes*. Her first action is her flight from Jim; but she goes on to many more, including her daring kidnapping of Wanda's children. If anything, Beth is perhaps too successful in overcoming her earlier background to be quite believable. On the other hand, Miriam, if anything, grows too docile as the novel proceeds. She and Beth exchange places. Miriam does not have the strength to attack Wilhelm Graben; her reasons for having a child end with a ridiculous "why not?"[67]; and she works very hard at becoming the stereotypical, complete housewife and mother. Even she, at the end, though, looks as though she will overcome her problem. She begins to take a few personal actions which promise to become more meaningful and collective later.

In *How She Died*, too, Jean grows to the point of taking concrete action. Jean becomes very much aware during the novel of her own submissiveness and fear. She is unable to turn Bob down even though she is completely revolted by his masochism. In addition, she has managed, as Lessing's female characters have not, to separate the body and the mind so that she can enjoy sex with Bob while she loathes him mentally.[68] Eventually, she comes to realize also that she tries to please

The Endings

because she is afraid. She realizes, "I wasn't yielding and feminine and giving and all that crap with men because of my generous, womanly nature, but because I was scared to be straight with them. I was terrified of men's displeasure."[69] She believes that if she is passive, she will please men. Eventually, she even comes to realize that she is trying to fill the emptiness in herself with a man. Her growth and insight into herself enable her to risk angering Matt by telling him she will not leave her children for him, and ultimately, by deciding to go back to Pennsylvania and try to help women like herself. She can even face his scorn. In both of these novels, the main characters move out of their passivity into action.

Others, although having overcome their passivity, are less successful in moving beyond it. In *The Edible Woman*, Marion succeeds very well in coming out of her long submersion. However, her triumph seems primarily a personal one with little to indicate that her new vision will affect anything but her own life. In *The Women's Room*, Mira's activity is crushed after her separation from Ben and the death of Val. In some ways, she actually returns to the brooding that occupied so many years of her marriage. Val fights to the end; Mira becomes sluggish. In *Fear of Flying*, there is not enough indication of movement. Isadora does make a commitment to her own independence. Unfortunately, however, the ending mitigates this new-found freedom by its passivity. Isadora sits in the bathtub, surely the most vulnerable of all positions, waiting to see what will happen. It is true that in her new strength, Isadora may feel that she can handle anything. The effect is muted, however, by her return to dealing with the marriage as her first action and by her waiting. In all three of these novels, although the heroine is presented as overcoming her own docility, there remains a decided lack of action. If passivity is defined as the ability to observe without the ability to act,[70] then the heroines' successes in these three novels are muffled by their lack of action.

In the remaining novels dealing expressly with passivity, *Up the Sandbox!*, *The Company She Keeps*, and several of Doris Lessing's novels, the heroines fail. The failure in *Up the Sandbox!* is really a result of the heroine's refusal to try. There can be no question of success since her rebellion is confined to daydreaming. Further, her inertia is so closely connected to her fascination with herself that she cannot move beyond herself to others. Even the final event which eliminates her alter ego, her pregnancy, is not the result of a decision. Instead, it occurs because, as Margaret recalls, "I thought of saying something, of stopping us, and then decided, or perhaps more accurately gave up making a decision, and relaxed into a love that would last uninterrupted by other pressures for a short while."[71] The irony is explicit. For the sake of a brief moment, Margaret trebles the pressures that will ultimately close out her life.

The Company She Keeps provides a thorough investigation of the extremity of passivity. Margaret is so entirely yielding that she must adopt others to become a person. This novel does not present a possibility of Margaret's overcoming her problem. What it does present is her eventual realization of exactly what her problem is:

for the first time she saw her own extremity, saw that it was some failure in self-love that obliged her to snatch blindly at the love of others, hoping to love herself through them, borrowing their feelings, as the moon borrowed light. She herself was a dead planet. It was she who was the Nazi prisoner, the pseudo-Byron, the equivocal personality who was not truly protean but only appeared so.[72]

Her hopes for success at the end are quite limited. She prays that in her passivity, she can at least continue to observe accurately. The loss of that would mean death.

In Lessing's novels, also, the heroines' failures are marked. In her novels of Anna, Martha Quest, and Mary, Lessing suggests that the characters will survive if they decide to. As one critic has remarked, "the low vitality that characterizes Lessing's protagonists is the result of their great refusal to be."[73] In Anna in "Free Women," we see a woman unable to control anything. Things keep happening to her; she is not really living her life. Martha Quest has the same problem. At one point in *Landlocked*, she realizes that "she should have made up her mind finally weeks ago, and having made up her mind, told him. She had not, because of her tendency—getting worse—to let things slide, to let things happen."[74] This tendency, passivity, nostalgia, is the primary modern threat to the world and to women as Lessing presents it in these novels. The lack of belief in anything, the jesting at values, the inability to say anything positive without betraying it by a self-mocking smirk, are the parents of passivity, nostalgia, cynicism, and ultimately, the principle of joy in hate.

Another aspect of this passivity of importance in Lessing's novels is the heroine's refusal to accept responsibility for herself by her wrong-headed commitment to romantic love.[75] She wants a man to save her. She wants men to be real men but forgets they are experiencing the same fragmentation, the same nostalgia she is, and she does not realize that she cannot sit patiently waiting until they fight their way out. The inability to move, to act, because it seems that it will make no difference, affects both women and men. When Saul and Anna finally do succeed in "The Golden Notebook," it is because each forces the other to act. They both save each other. Once they both move and overcome their inertia, they can continue on their own. Unfortunately, even this success is short-lived because "The Golden Notebook" ends with a summary of Saul's novel that suggests that whatever attempts at freedom or brotherhood or sisterhood are made will be destroyed by the robots of the modern world. This ending also suggests that Saul's observations will be ignored by the world since the only comment made about his novel is the dry remark that it "did rather well."[76]

In focusing so frequently and intensely on passivity, the feminist novel singles out a problem that touches the modern world generally and women specifically. Assuredly, this problem is not dealt with by the feminist novel alone. Elizabeth Hardwick speaks of it, for example, when she comments, "Nostalgia is the emotion most deeply felt in Virginia Woolf's novels... Nostalgia is passive, the books are passive, requiems, unlike any other."[77] It surfaces again when she remarks that the F. Scott Fitzgeralds' "tone about themselves, their mood, is the fatal one of nostalgia—a passive, consuming, repetitive poetry."[78] In Lessing's novels, it is the failures and misfits upon whom one must depend for hope. The danger is that the boulder-pushers are the ones subject to being eviscerated by nostalgia. It is those who feel joy in hate who are full of energy. For the feminist novel generally, obedience and submission must be thrown off by the world and especially by women. Guilt is another characteristic imposed upon women which is frequently presented in these novels. Four in which this character flaw figures prominently include *The Street, Daughter of Earth, Small Changes,* and *Looking for Mr. Goodbar.* In *The Street,* guilt is the prime mover of the ending. Petry clearly shows that Lutie's feelings of guilt are intentionally infused into her by society. The ruin of her life and Bub's life is quite obviously the result of society's actions, not her own, and her self-defense is quite obviously that and not murder. However, it benefits society for her to think that she is the one at fault. When Lutie kills Boots, it is revealed that

she was striking at the white world which thrust black people into a walled enclosure from which there was no escape; and at the turn-of-events which had forced her to leave Bub alone while she was working so that he now faced reform school, now had a police record.
She saw the face and head of the man on the sofa through waves of anger in which he represented all these things and she was destroying them.[79]

Later, though, her societally induced conscience returns, and she convinces herself she is a violent murderer, not a person who began by defending herself against rape and assault. In that way, responsibility cannot be accurately assigned, and she and Bub will die, not attack.

In *Daughter of Earth,* Marie Rogers' sense of guilt is her most feminine feature. She feels guilty about her brothers and sisters, her chance for education, her mother, and, finally, even about Juan Diaz. Her feelings of guilt constantly plague her and do nothing to enhance her efforts in helping others. Despite her rhetoric, it is apparent that she still blames herself, the individual, rather than society, for her problems and the problems of her family. Although she sees more clearly than this intellectually, emotionally, in her conscience, she is still the indoctrinated, feminine woman. This, too, serves society because it interferes with her political efforts and clouds her vision.

In *Small Changes and Looking for Mr Goodbar*, one finds two women, Miriam and Theresa, whose lives are shaped by their feelings of guilt. Miriam is guilty because she is not as she should be, because she was not pretty as a child, because she displeases her family, because men, from their distorted viewpoint, distrust her. So she reaches for atonement by sacrificing herself in her marriage to Neil. Part of the reason she agrees to have children is to get rid of her guilt. She thinks that in "becoming a mother, she would contain her mother and no more miss her and no more carry that old guilt. She would prove them all wrong. She would prove that Neil was right to love her and marry her, to take a chance on her."[80] By having children, she will become a normal woman. She will validate her claim on a regular, customary life. She will exorcise Graben's assertion that she was born to be a courtesan, and she will vindicate Neil's choice of her as a housewife and mother. Her sense of guilt keeps her from doing the things she wants to do, the things she thinks important. By beginning to overcome her guilt at the end of *Small Changes*, there is hope that Miriam will grow.

It is far worse for Theresa. Her guilt, amazingly over similar things, her lack of prettiness, her sickliness, her family's displeasure with her, distorts her into several people. Her guilt is so overwhelming that she considers herself worthless. Unlike Miriam, she cannot even try to prove that she is good. She laughs at or becomes furious with James when he suggests that she is. It is right that she should be miserable, unhappy, alone. Of course, Theresa and Miriam both blame themselves. It would never occur to Theresa to hold society responsible for any of her problems because it has thoroughly convinced her that she herself is the culprit. Similarly, Miriam, though much more politicially astute than Theresa, is still sure that her personal problems are purely her own and that they will be solved if she works harder. For all these women afflicted by guilt, except possibly for Miriam, the ending is death or flight.

The final feminine trait attacked in these novels is self-doubt. Although almost all of the heroines are afflicted by self-distrust to some degree, this characteristic figures most strongly in Harriette Arnow's *The Dollmaker*. Gertie's first error occurs when she listens to her mother's dictum that she is a bad wife not to join her husband in Detroit. It is true that John, who also listens to Gertie's mother, takes back the deed he gave Gertie while he blathers on about duty as Gertie's mother had done. However, Gertie's fate had been sealed earlier because she had listened to her mother and had already been pulled along by her mother's will. Gertie's sin is in doing what others tell her to do. Others can make her feel guilt for not doing what they say is her duty. She is made to feel wrong about carving too beautiful a Christ figure for a poor woman when Clovis tells her they can make more money if she only produces mediocrities. She feels guilt about saving money so they can return to the land, for not liking Detroit even though it ruins her life and murders her children, and for letting Cassie remain imaginative and different from the other children. Like Huckleberry Finn, she thinks the voice of society must be right and distrusts herself. The difference is that where Huck's view is treated with irony, Gertie's is treated with profound pity and with anger as well. Marie Rogers in *Daughter of Earth* shudders when she hears the word "dooty," but Gertie listens and is culpable only because she does.

Her mother's voice is the voice of society. Clovis and the "adjusted" people in Detroit act on her only secondarily. Early in the novel it is clear that Gertie's father wants her and her children to buy the farm and stay close by, but Gertie does not do so. Although she loves him deeply, his wishes are not the wishes of society, the voice of duty. It is Gertie's mother and her insistence that one must do what is dislikeable that represent society in this novel. Society and Gertie's mother are those who would make Walt Whitman sick discussing their duty to God.

It is because she listens to them that Gertie's life is destroyed, Cassie killed, and the laughing Christ split apart. Most bitter of all are the reflections of this that face Gertie. When they arrive in Detroit, her children are more shocked at her weak ways than at the city. She is out of her element and cannot function. In a terrible scene, Clovis, realizing they have been

The Endings

destroyed by Detroit and all it symbolizes, says that if he had known Gertie had had all that money, he would have told her to buy the farm.[81] Strong and brave as she is, Gertie fails because she doubts herself, because she listens to society. In the feminist novel, the issue is not really over the heroine's individual will or personal desire. Those considerations are not paramount. What is focused upon is her reliance upon herself, her trust in her own ideas and feelings, and her concomitant ability to make commitments and to take action.

The main character in the feminist novel, then, generally does have some control over her destiny. In a large number of these novels, the heroine is partially responsible for the end of her novel. These novels predominantly terminate in escape or death, but there is a small group of them which provides an alternative ending. In those that end in escape, the heroine is usually being driven away. In both these and those ending in death, there is ordinarily no hope or optimism to be found with regard to either the heroine's or society's fate. In the third group, though, there is a definite tone of success and hope. Here the heroines neither flee nor die. Instead, they fight back, and they all enjoy some measure of success. The heroines return to their past, to their roots, and they battle their demons. Most importantly, they win. Those who are most thoroughly victorious are also able by the end of the novel to take action and to make commitments. This small group of novels provides an alternative to the usual despair and pessimism found at the end of many twentieth-century novels. Here the characters battle their own weaknesses and society's, and they emerge with some successes. In these ways, these novels provide their own particular viewpoint, the viewpoint of "The Other."

In the past, women were most often defined and categorized in terms of what they are not and have not, not in terms of what they are and have. They were usually seen and saw themselves in relationship to men, not alone. When they did draw together, it was said, perhaps justly, that women "are always compelled... to band together to establish a counter-universe, but they always set it up within the frame of the masculine universe."[82] Now this is changing. Anaïs Nin queries, for example, "I don't know why we have never had a word for the man who inspires the woman. We never had a Mr. Muse."[83] For some of these authors, it appears true that "the step from rebellion to revolution is a step beyond nostalgia (for what one has known and hated and enjoyed defacing) toward the creation of new alternate values."[84] These authors are presenting new ideational worlds; they have "come upon strange, unfathomable, repellent, delightful things: we shall take them, we shall comprehend them."[85]

NOTES

1. Irving Howe, *Politics and the Novel* (New York: Horizon Press, Inc., 1957), p. 227.
2. Sam Bluefarb, *The Escape Motif in the American Novel: Mark Twain to Richard Wright* (Columbus: Ohio State University Press, 1972), p. 3.
3. Ibid., pp. 3–11, 40–41.
4. Ihab Hassan, *Radical Innocence: Studies in the Contemporary American Novel* (Princeton, N.J.: Princeton University Press, 1961), p. 327.
5. Ibid., p. 257.
6. Thelma J. Shinn, "Women in the Novels of Ann Petry," *Contemporary Women Novelists: A Collection of Critical Essays*, ed. Patricia Meyer Spacks (Englewood Cliffs, N.J.: Prentice-Hall, Inc., 1977), p. 109.
7. Bluefarb, *The Escape Motif*, p. 13.
8. Ann Petry, *The Street* (Boston: Houghton Mifflin Co., 1946), pp. 434–35.
9. Sandra M. Gilbert and Susan Gubar, *The Madwoman in the Attic: The Woman Writer and the Nineteenth-Century Literary Imagination* (New Haven, Conn.: Yale University Press, 1979), p. 35.
10. Agnes Smedley, *Daughter of Earth* (1929; reprint, Old Westbury, N.Y.: The Feminist Press, 1973), p. 406.
11. Ibid., p. 401.
12. Ibid., p. 403.
13. Ibid., p. 404.
14. Walter B. Rideout, *The Radical Novel in the United States, 1900–1954: Some Interrelations of Literature and Society* (Cambridge, Mass.: Harvard University Press, 1956), p. 151.
15. Doris Lessing, *Landlocked* (New York: Simon and Schuster, Inc., 1966), p. 503.

16. Christina Stead, *The Man Who Loved Children* (1940; reprint, New York: Holt, Rinehart and Winston, 1966), p. 489.
17. Elizabeth Hardwick, *Seduction and Betrayal: Women and Literature* (New York: Random House, 1974), p. 71.
18. Stead, *The Man Who Loved Children*, p. 491.
19. Bluefarb, *The Escape Motif*, p. 45.
20. Marge Piercy, *Small Changes* (1972; reprint, Greenwich, Conn.: Fawcett Publications, Inc., 1974), p. 38.
21. Ibid., p. 46.
22. Ibid., p. 527.
23. Ibid., p. 532.
24. Hassan, *Radical Innocence*, p. 40.
25. Patricia Meyer Spacks, *The Female Imagination* (New York: Alfred A. Knopf, 1975), p. 252.
26. Kate Millett, *Sexual Politics* (Garden City, N.Y.: Doubleday and Co., Inc., 1970), p. 146.
27. Piercy, *Small Changes*, p. 47.
28. Simone de Beauvoir, *The Second Sex*, ed. and trans. H. M. Parshley (1953; reprint, New York: Random House, 1974), p. 798.
29. Gilbert and Gubar, *The Madwoman in the Attic*, pp. 319–20.
30. Erica Jong, *Fear of Flying* (New York: Holt, Rinehart and Winston, 1971), p. 315.
31. Judith Rossner, *Looking for Mr. Goodbar* (New York: Simon and Schuster, Inc., 1975), p. 284.
32. Ibid., p. 19.
33. Doris Lessing, *The Grass is Singing* (London: Michael Joseph, Ltd., 1950), p. 232.
34. Judith Rossner, *Emmeline* (New York: Simon and Schuster, Inc., 1980), p. 339.
35. Ibid., p. 340.
36. Harriette Arnow, *The Dollmaker* (New York: Macmillan Co., 1958), p. 318.
37. Ibid., p. 286.
38. Marge Piercy, *Woman on the Edge of Time* (New York: Alfred A. Knopf, 1976), pp. 19–20.
39. Ibid., p. 375.
40. Doris Lessing, *The Golden Notebook* (New York: Simon and Schuster, Inc., 1962), pp. 627–28.
41. Jong, *Fear of Flying*, p. 10.
42. Ibid., p. 123.
43. Ibid., p. 311.
44. Ibid., pp. 274–75.

45. Ibid., p. 296.
46. Ibid., p. 277.
47. Ibid., p. 339.
48. Alice Walker, *Meridian* (New York: Simon and Schuster, Inc., 1976), p. 200.
49. Ibid., p. 219.
50. Helen Yglesias, *How She Died* (Boston: Houghton Mifflin Co., 1972), p. 337.
51. Piercy, *Small Changes*, p. 538.
52. Doris Lessing, *The Four-Gated City* (New York: Alfred A. Knopf, 1969), p. 643.
53. Ibid., p. 647.
54. Ibid., p. 648.
55. Alfred Kazin, *On Native Grounds: An Interpretation of Modern American Prose Literature* (New York: Reynal and Hitchcock, 1942), p. 31.
56. Hassan, *Radical Innocence*, p. 29.
57. Annette Kolodny, "The Lady's Not for Spurning: Kate Millett and the Critics," *Women's Autobiography: Essays in Criticism*, ed. Estelle C. Jelinek (Bloomington: Indiana University Press, 1980), p. 255.
58. Virginia Woolf, *A Room of One's Own* (New York: Harcourt, Brace and Co., 1929), p. 45.
59. Smedley, *Daughter of Earth*, p. 86.
60. Stead, *The Man Who Loved Children*, p. 13.
61. Ibid.
62. Smedley, *Daughter of Earth*, p. 38.
63. Irving Howe, *A World More Attractive: A View of Modern Literature and Politics* (New York: Horizon Press, Inc., 1963), pp. 84–85.
64. Chester E. Eisinger, *Fiction of the Forties* (Chicago: University of Chicago Press, 1963), p. 66.
65. Hassan, *Radical Innocence*, p. 209.
66. Alice S. Rossi, "Women—Terms of Liberation." *The Seventies: Problems and Proposals*, eds. Irving Howe and Michael Harrington (New York: Harper and Row, Publishers, 1972), p. 254.
67. Piercy, *Small Changes*, p. 377.
68. Yglesias, *How She Died*, pp. 159–60.
69. Ibid., p. 190.
70. Rideout, *The Radical Novel*, p. 112.
71. Anne R. Roiphe, *Up the Sandbox!* (New York: Simon and Schuster, Inc., 1970), p. 23.
72. Mary McCarthy, *The Company She Keeps* (1942; reprint, New York: Harcourt, Brace and World, Inc., 1970), p. 303.

The Endings

73. Alice B. Markow, "The Pathology of Feminine Failure in the Fiction of Doris Lessing," *Critique* 16, no.1 (1974): 99.
74. Lessing, *Landlocked*, p. 276.
75. Markow, "The Pathology of Feminine Failure," p. 88.
76. Lessing, *The Golden Notebook*, p. 643.
77. Hardwick, *Seduction and Betrayal*, p. 142.
78. Ibid., p. 92.
79. Petry, *The Street*, p. 430.
80. Piercy, *Small Changes*, p. 377.
81. Arnow, *The Dollmaker*, pp. 389-90.
82. de Beauvoir, *The Second Sex*, p. 664.
83. Anaïs Nin, *A Woman Speaks*, ed. Evelyn J. Hinz (London: W. H. Allen and Co., Ltd., 1978), p. 96.
84. Kate Millett, *Sexual Politics*, p. 350.
85. Arthur Rimbaud, "Letter to Paul Demeny, May 15, 1871," *Lettres de la Vie Litteraire d'Arthur Rimbaud (1870-1875)*, ed. Jean-Marie Carre (Paris: Bibliophiles de la Nouvelle Revue Francaise, 1931), p. 66. Trans. in de Beauvoir, *The Second Sex*, p. 795.

5
Portrayals of Slavery and Freedom

The viewpoint of "The Other" is the subject and essence of the feminist novel. In the feminist novel "The Other," the perpetual object, becomes subject. The feminist novel fights off and turns on itself the man-made myth about women that Simone de Beauvoir describes in the following passage:

> Woman thus seems to be the inessential who never goes back to being the essential, to be the absolute Other, without reciprocity. This conviction is dear to the male, and every creation myth has expressed it, among others the legend of Genesis, which, through Christianity, has been kept alive in Western civilization. Eve was not fashioned at the same time as the man; she was not fabricated from a different substance, nor of the same clay as was used to model Adam: she was taken from the flank of the first male. Not even her birth was independent; God did not spontaneously choose to create her as an end in herself and in order to be worshipped directly by her in return for it. She was destined by Him for man; it was to rescue Adam from loneliness that He gave her to him, in her mate was her origin and her purpose; she was his complement on the order of the inessential.[1]

There is a sense of shock for many women as they see themselves portrayed for the first time as the subject in feminist novels.[2] Often, these novels cause female readers to discuss "them, finally, in such a way that they matter, not in literary history, but in our lives,"[3] much in the way that books affect Doris Lessing's heroines. This sudden collision with oneself also suggests immediately to the reader that the male vision one had so thoroughly accepted is not the universal vision.[4] In all its various aspects, the feminist viewpoint is very different from what has been viewed as a generic outlook. Certainly, it has its own truths as well. Germaine Bree has suggested of some very early feminist writers that:

> It was perhaps because of their very position as "outsiders," not admitted to institutions of learning, that, in a time of rapid social change they were able to some extent to detect more clearly than most of their male contemporaries some of the essential trends and social myths of the moment.[5]

The position of feminist writers as "outsiders" still holds true today. Germaine Bree also comments that although the status of French women has changed recently, "the *image* of woman, the manner of representing her, has not greatly evolved."[6] Fortunately, at least in the feminist novel, this no longer holds true. Now the image of woman, as it is presented in literature, is changing, and so, with it, is the image of man. The view of the female as desirable sexual object has long been accepted. Simone de Beauvoir has remarked, however, that, "The truth that for woman man is sex and carnality has never been proclaimed because there is no one to proclaim it."[7] Now these writers are pronouncing it.

As they do so, they proceed to use men occasionally as symbols and to present women always as themselves. Their use of other metaphors and symbols differs as well from what one is accustomed to when dealing with the "universal vision." Indeed, as the symbolic and generic is representative of the group,[8] then it is to be expected that a woman writer's use of symbols in a feminist novel should be markedly distinctive. As Simone de Beauvoir comments:

> The symbol does not seem to me to be an allegory elaborated by a mysterious unconscious; it is rather the perception of a certain sig-

nificance through the analogue of the significant object. Symbolic significance is manifested in the same way to numerous individuals, because of the identical existential situation connecting all the individual existents and the identical set of artifical conditions that all must confront.[9]

In the feminist novel, the use of symbols is additionally important because just as the political is often incarnated in supposedly non-political behaviors such as appetites, manners, and sex,[10] so is the political often presented in the symbolism of the feminist novel.

Not surprisingly, the metaphors and symbols used in the feminist novel cluster around images of entrapment and freedom. Entrapment is usually linked with men and marriage. Freedom, on the other hand, comes, strikingly, with the maturity of age and is represented both through the world of children and the world of work. In its symbolism, the feminist novel completes its portrayal of the world as it is seen by women. Along with the other stylistic elements expressing the ideology of the feminist novel, its symbolism provides an overview of its politics.

A wide variety of symbols represents slavery and entrapment in the feminist novel. Some of them are usually thought of as representing the domestic sphere, and the rest center specifically on men and women's relations to them. Male characters themselves most often represent society in general or the United States in particular, both monoliths of repression. One finds the general stated as the specific in *A Ripple from the Storm* when Martha Quest observes of her husband Douglas, and her acquaintance, William, that "then, for a few moments, she had seen the two men as one, and identical with the pompous, hypocritical, and essentially male fabric of society."[11] Several characteristics, attributed to both modern society and men in general, can be extracted from the equating of the two in the feminist novel. Most central is that both the society and its representatives suffer from a profound inability to feel and to love. In effect, men typify the technical, brave new world. They create and mirror a world of coldness, cynicism, and amused indifference. Marge Piercy's *Small Changes* provides some excellent examples. For instance, one is presented with Wilhelm Graben's facetious viewpoint on the preparation of missile software:

"Now, you are exploding, say, a five-megaton warhead to knock down a missile no bigger than a barn. Obviously, this does not require a warhead of five hundred million tons of TNT—Hiroshima was destroyed by twenty thousand tons' equivalent. Thus you can deduce that accuracy is simply not in it. They're figuring on exploding a five-megaton bomb to knock down a missile because they are not counting on being in the same state with it—states imagined to be lines superimposed upon the air..." His voice was calm and mocking. She grew colder and colder. He thought all this funny. He had learned to live with it. Perhaps she would too. Or perhaps it was better to be a high-class whore than a high-class scientist. She sipped brandy while the fumes crept up her nose and the room floated in the cold blackness of outer space and megadeaths.[12]

In addition to Graben, Jackson and Phil, for most of the novel, are presented as cold, dehumanized beings produced by the modern world. Partly to reveal Miriam's difficulties in seeing reality and partly to highlight Phil's and Jackson's inhumanity, Piercy juxtaposes Miriam's views of them with their private thoughts. Romantic Miriam, when she first meets Phil, thinks:

It was exactly like a daydream. It was a fantasy, so she knew just how to behave. She did not hesitate, she did not worry that she would not know what to say. She went with him laughing and gazing at him, looking and looking at him while the world changed colors. He was beautiful and that made her want to laugh and touch him.[13]

Contrasting with Miriam's innocence and joy is Phil's description to Jackson of his and Miriam's first meeting. Miriam's playfulness and her delight in discovering sexuality are matched against Phil's delight in finding someone to use. Phil tells Jackson:

"you know I picked her out right away, I mean you couldn't miss her sailing in like the Russian Navy. That is a woman that is built, I said to myself. She was wearing a shitty college girl outfit consisting of dirty laundry bags, but you just couldn't miss that body if she was wearing a barrel. Caught her eye right away and it didn't take thirty seconds to execute the mission."[14]

When Miriam talks or thinks about Phil, she uses his name. Phil never mentions Miriam's name when describing her to Jackson. Further, he views her as machinery rather than as a person and remarks to Jackson that there is "all that lovely equipment ready to function when you plug in."[15]

In general, Phil and Jackson are changed when their actions are filtered through Miriam's mind. When she talks about them, they are human beings. When Piercy presents them alone or with each other, they are cold, guarded, hard, machine-like. When considering Miriam's best friends, people who matter very much to her, Phil thinks, "Beth made him sore. He was sure she could open up and give a bit of sweetness. Then she'd gone and got Dorine to move into that dykey setup with that crazy hillbilly about to drop her kid."[16] Jackson is even more inhuman than Phil. When Phil tries to tell Jackson about the terrifying emotions he had had during a group rape he was involved in, Phil realizes that "there was something about the way Jackson was listening, saying with a laugh at one point that he had never raped anyone except his wife Sissy, and grinning, that made the story come out with him [Phil] being fastidious instead of scared shitless."[17]

Later, as Miriam, Phil, and Jackson's relationship becomes more complicated, Miriam very slowly and partially realizes its true nature. Phil and Jackson can discuss the relationship very coolly. In a scene that occurs when Miriam walks out on them, Phil argues with Jackson, asking:

"What's the big idea giving ultimatums?" Phil said softly to Jackson. "Enough with the melodrama."
"She's not going to push me around. This is my house and if she doesn't like it, she can pack and clear out."
"Yeah, and leave us fucking our hands? Come off it, you got her really mad now."[18]

Miriam does understand eventually that both Phil and Jackson are afraid of caring and loving, but she does not ever recognize the degree to which both are petrified. Ultimately, there is a tone of hopefulness because Phil does change, suggesting that both modern society and the men who mirror it can come back to life. Jackson never does, however.

In several other feminist novels as well, male characters epitomize modern society and its separation from human feelings, emotions, and love. In many of Lessing's novels the male characters' lesser ability to love, although saving them from romantic love and its concomitant platitudes, represents a severe liability.[19] In a gruesome scene from *The Golden Notebook*, Paul shoots pigeons in a leisurely, relaxed way, and the smell of blood mounts. Maryrose protests that she will be ill, and Paul responds:

> "Patience," said Paul. "Our quota is nearly reached."
> "Six will be enough," said Jimmy. "Because none of us will eat this pie. Mr. Boothby can have the lot."
> "I shall certainly eat of it," said Paul. "And so will you. Do you really imagine that when that toothsome pie, filled with gravy and brown savoury meat, is set before you, that you will remember the tender songs of these birds so brutally cut short by the crack of doom?"
> "Yes," said Maryrose.
> "Yes," I said.
> "Willi?" asked Paul, making an issue of it.
> "Probably not," said Willi, reading.
> "Women are tender," said Paul.[20]

Paul thinks it humorous, but the real issue is that the men in Lessing's novel have struggled hard to eliminate warmth and emotion and have succeeded.

In *Up the Sandbox!* Paul, Margaret's husband, represents male society in its rejection of feeling and elevation of hard rationality, but it is revealed at the same time that he himself is changed by society into something less than he might have been. He is at the same time society's representative and its victim. The comments are made about Paul that:

> Such a short while ago, just yesterday, it seems, he was an ordinary bright student, a young man with a passionate conviction that our society was immoral and in need of change.... he found himself my

husband, an instructor of history in the School of General Studies, and a doctoral candidate, with a working wife, an apartment, a hi-fi set, dishes that matched from my mother, carpeting of sorts, a modern sofa— a gift from my aunt—and there he was, the owner of objects, of books. All he lacked now, he grumbled, was the life insurance policy that his father with all his Yankee caution was forever pressing him about.[21]

In many ways, Margaret and Paul's dreams were the same and as hers are destroyed by marriage and by her own weaknesses, so are his. One major distinction between them, though, is that her emotions and feelings and personal attachments remain while Paul's are being killed off. In a devastatingly accurate observation, Margaret thinks of saying to her husband:

Paul, my darling, I know that things are not at a high pitch of romance. You do not feel you would die without me—in fact, certain exciting possibilities occur to you in the event of my suddenly having a heart attack while carrying home the groceries, or my being murdered by some drug addict, who only wanted to steal your typewriter which I foolishly defended with my life.[22]

Margaret's third pregnancy entombs her, and the marriage, according to society's rules, finishes the destruction of Paul's ability to feel and to love.

In *Fear of Flying*, men in general represent the same inability to experience emotion, to respond and relate to another human being. At one point in the novel, Isadora and her friend, Pia, describe their experiences with various men they meet while touring Europe. Most of the men seem to be looking for someone with whom they can act out various sexual encounters they had read about in books. Isadora comments that:

The best part of these adventures seemed to be the way we went into hysterics describing them to each other. Otherwise, they were mostly joyless. We were attracted to men, but when it came to understanding and good talk, we needed each other. Gradually, the men were reduced to sex objects.
There is something very sad about this. Eventually we came to accept the lying and the role-playing and the compromises so completely that they were invisible—even to ourselves.[23]

Isadora and Pia become completely like the men. People in modern society become iron men and women. They march about, interacting with other people only by acting out roles.

Many other female characters observe that the men who people their novels are only partly human because of their elimination of their own feelings. Jill, in *Braided Lives*, comments on Gerrit, "When I cry in front of him, he thinks there's something wrong with my eyes. He can only view expression of emotion as aberration or sickness."[24] Similarly, Connie in *Woman on the Edge of Time* notes:

> she thought that these men believed feeling itself a disease, something to be cut out like a rotten appendix. Cold, calculating, ambitious, believing themselves rational and superior, they chased the crouching female animal through the brain with a scalpel. From an early age she had been told that what she felt was unreal and didn't matter. Now they were about to place in her something that would rule her feelings like a thermostat.[25]

Dolores in *The Bleeding Heart* believes that men have already implanted in their own bodies what they attempt to place in Connie's. She thinks, "What was it with men, that they could switch feelings off and on? As if they had separate selves, pieces not essentially connected to each other except by the fact that they inhabited the same body.[26] For both these heroines and for many female critics, this annihilation of feeling is the ultimate horror of the twentieth century. Anaïs Nin observes that "the way we have learned to protect ourselves is *not to feel*, which is a terrible danger because then we really become sub-human or non-human and are as far away from our real connection with human beings as we possibly can be."[27] The outrages committed by modern society occur most easily when human beings disconnect themselves from their emotions. In the feminist novel, "far from being a sign of irrationality, women's emotionality and personal involvement is a positive, life-affirming value."[28]

In all of the novels in which men represent society, the male characters also become the embodiment of its attitude toward women. Perhaps one novel illustrates this best. In Agnes Smedley's *Daughter of Earth*, near the end, Marie Rogers marries Anand, an Indian revolutionary with whom she has been working. Anand is presented as an exceptional person, especially in his thoughts and ideas about women. Marie listens "to the things he said about women—his revolution extended to women—without the freedom of women the world could never advance...."[29] He is not a hypocrite, and Smedley presents him as one of the most gentle and compassionate people, male or female, in the novel. Yet, when it becomes apparent to him that Marie has had physical relationships with other men before him, he cannot accept it. Marie describes:

a night when I awoke to find him bending over me, watching. I stared, speechless, at his strange, drawn face.
"Tell me what men said to you," he asked.
"What—what men?"
"The men you lived with!"[30]

At another point, while Marie listens to Anand, she thinks to herself, "Even as he spoke so well, so reasonably, I watched him and doubted. I did not believe that race had anything to do with man's primitive attitude toward woman as a purely physical being."[31] She is right, of course, and eventually she must leave him. The teachings of a patriarchal society are incorporated into the male characters. Even when they know their attitudes are wrong and wish to rid themselves of them, they cannot. In many of the other novels as well, such as *Small Changes*, *The Golden Notebook*, *A Proper Marriage*, and *The Women's Room*, male characters serve as vehicles to portray societal hatred, disdain, and abuse of women. Female characters risk permanent entrapment, living death, when they become involved with these men.

For a final glance at the "pompous, hypocritical and essentially male fabric of society," one can turn to the boring visages of Mr. Pontellier in *The Awakening*, Paul in *Up the Sandbox!*, or Norm, Mira's husband, in *The Women's Room*. Or one can reflect on the comment about Margaret in *The Company She Keeps* when the narrator states that "her [Margaret's] only dull moments were the evenings she spent alone with the Young

Man."[32] For hypocrisy unmasked, one must observe Anton in *The Children of Violence* series, Sam in *The Man Who Loved Children*, and Ben in *The Women's Room*. In *The Dollmaker*, society's hypocritical insistence that men are strong and its corollary that women are weak is attacked throughout the novel. The attack starts at the beginning when Gertie saves the life of her son, Amos, by performing an emergency tracheotomy. She cannot even tell her husband, Clovis, about it because he cannot bear to hear it.

In many feminist novels, then, male characters represent the insidious, threatening aspects of modern societies. In others, they function more specifically to exemplify the United States. In effect, the authors employ certain personal characteristics of their male characters to represent aspects of the United States. The picture which emerges is of a country marked by innocence and ignorance. In the view of the United States, all its actions stem from worthy motives; its own innocence is boundless. Wanting to know, it then tries to possess; fearful of the unknown, it produces racism, sexism, and hatred of diversity. The ultimate result is violence. A few novels that illustrate this equating of the male with the United States particularly well include *The Man Who Loved Children*, *The Women's Room*, *The Company She Keeps*, *Looking for Mr. Goodbar*, and *How She Died*. Doris Lessing often uses male characters to represent various countries, but they function differently from the male character who represents the United States. In *Landlocked*, for example, each man represents a country and quality. Athen means Greece and goodness; Anton Hesse is a hypocritical, emotionally dead Germany; Thomas is a fevered Israel. In the other novels, though, one sees not so much a portrayal of the effects of nationalism as an intense look at various facets of the American psyche in particular. Taken together, these novels provide a feminist look at the similarities between the American male and America itself.

Christina Stead's portrayal of Sam, the father in *The Man Who Loved Children*, is a fully developed picture of what appears in sections in the other novels. At the beginning, Sam is a bureaucrat stationed in Washington. He is proud of his governmental associations and is given to mouthings of Jefferson.

One of Sam's outstanding characteristics is his ignorance and simultaneous elevation of himself. His lack of knowledge and understanding is revealed consistently throughout the novel but is best encapsulated when he tries to understand his growing children. In thinking of Louie in particular:

> his palpitating heart could not bear to think of her coming to shipwreck on the hidden reefs of youth: and, for her sake, he went through all the literature on adolescence, becoming more horrified every day as Satan's invisible world was revealed to him, who had been a bloodless youth living on greens and tap water.[33]

He is completely unable to comprehend the children and their thoughts, so he begins to follow them around and sneak up on them, hoping to surprise them at something that will make things clear to him. As it is described, "He sensed that there was something going on, like an incantation perhaps, about which he knew nothing. He tried to think back to his youth, but could remember very little but quickly repressed shames and moral thoughts."[34] This is the sort of ignorance with which Sam is beset, and to combat it, like twentieth-century America, "he pried and pried, hoping to discover, in the love of science and youth, the mysteries about him."[35]

At the same time Sam's arrogance matches his ignorance. He never listens to anyone and automatically assumes that no one else can have as much to say as he. So, when he thinks of Louie, who not only knows in adolescence much more than he does in adulthood, but who also has far more promise, he decides, "Certainly Louie would grow up to be like her own sweet, womanly mother, a blessing to some man. Thus he dismissed Louie...."[36] At another point in the novel, Sam compares himself with God, thinking that if he had many wives, it would be "godlike." Later, he asks his servant, Naden, if he thinks that he, Sam, has "feet of clay."[37] He even elevates himself above God when Naden remarks:

> "You are good, sah: you are as a god."
> "No, Naden: just a man looking for the right and for the happiness of others."
> "Sah, you are as the gods."

"I do not believe in gods, only in good," said Sam. "Gods demand sacrifices: good gives to all."[38]

Sam, in effect, is kinder than God.

Linked with this ignorant pride in himself is Sam's desire to know everything. As Virginia Woolf comments in *A Room of One's Own*, one of the advantages of being a woman is not having the need to possess everything one sees.[39] In a parallel with the United States, Sam simply must dominate in all circumstances and situations. Rather late in the novel, for instance, Louie suggests that she should leave home. She is in the process of breaking off from Sam and the family, but he will not hear of it. He comments "It must never be, Louie—a woman must not leave her father's home till she goes to her husband: that is what I am here for, to look after you."[40] In actuality, for Sam, the family is the best of places for him to exercise all his authority and control. He keeps wanting to expand it, to add more people to it. When Lady Modore tells him he has too many children, he says, " 'I could never have too many,' he cried earnestly and began to tell her how he would like to have a Malay wife, a beauty like he had seen with her baby this day, a Chinese wife, and an Indian wife...."[41] He and his family are a microcosm of the United States' relations with other countries. Interestingly, too, when Sam leaves, the children break free and start to think their own thoughts and make their own plans. It happens that:

In all the wild, vacant months that had passed, like a stupid, shouting, windy holiday, they had never given one thought to their father's schemes and ideas. It had been nothing but Little-Sam's and Saul's and Ernie's ideas, a great savanna of opportunity in which they stumbled, ranged, hallooed, occasionally catching sight of each other, at intervals dreaming about a personage, genie of the swamp, who called himself Sam-the-Bold, their father, and was away, his wand broken.[42]

Sam, of course, in his monumental pride, never recognizes any of this and even prates that:

"We must never think about money or of owning things," said Sam kindly, bending a rather dewy eye on her. "Greed, the desire to possess, money, the currency of greed, is the root of all evil, it is the means of devouring others, and the lives of others: you know how I feel about that."[43]

Sam does not realize that the devouring of other peoples' lives is the center of his own.

In other novels as well, this need to control and dominate everything is highlighted in the male characters. The near rape of Mira in *The Women's Room*, for example, results solely from her desire to be free. When she goes dancing and is then left alone by her date, she is fair game. Her simply being there is enough to initiate the wish to possess. At the end of the novel, it is revealed that even Ben is not free from the compulsion to command. Eventually, he must marry Mira and have her go where he goes even if it means the destruction of her career; and she must have children even though she does not want any. Almost all of the other male characters in the novel have a similar problem; and their problems bear a resemblance to American difficulties in Viet Nam and elsewhere, which are referred to in the setting of the novel. Harley, Norm, and all the husbands in Beau Reve feel compelled to possess, to command, to dominate. They must always be the subject and the center. Jill in *Braided Lives* recognizes the male desire to dominate when she speaks to Donna of Mike and says, "But what I've fought for, waited for and finally got now is a little freedom." Donna replies, "You think he's going to put you in a cage?" and Jill answers, "Love says, mine. Love says, I could eat you up. Love says, stay as you are, be my own private thing, don't you dare have ideas I don't share."[44] In effect, the father or the male character is portrayed as an authoritarian figure representing the authoritarian state. Slavery or annexation is the lot of the female who associates too closely with these figures.

Another quality frequently attached to the United States and investigated in great detail in some of these novels is innocence. Sam possesses an abundance of this characteristic. Late in the novel, it seems to Henny that "she saw her husband for the first time: she had married a child whose only talent was an air of engaging helplessness by which he got the protection of certain goodhearted people."[45] Henny comes to realize that Sam is an incorrigible innocent, that he wishes to live as a child. When Sam is attacked at his job and scandal is hinted at, the narrator observes that "all the children, though, believed the [sic] Sam was utterly innocent, which in fact he was, innocent too, of all knowledge of men, business, and politics, a confiding and sheltered child strayed into public affairs."⁴⁶ Unfortunately, Sam's total innocence has some disagreeable facets. A certain hypocrisy is involved in keeping his innocence because he cannot allow unpleasant truths to reach his consciousness. As a result, when Louie tells him that she poisoned Henny, Sam simply refuses to believe it. He answers, "I have got to take you away from school and keep you at home with me until you recover. You are not yourself." To this, Louie replies, "You don't notice anything. Everything has to be what you say."⁴⁷ She is completely right, of course. To maintain his innocence and goodness, certain things must go unnoticed.

Additionally, Sam must always give himself nothing but the best of motives. Consequently, when he finds himself lecherously considering a number of women, he discards possible explanations for his thoughts until he comes up with a suitable one which is that "it is love coming to claim me: I have been so long without love, hated at home, living in terror of my children's lives: it is pure, tender, normal love."⁴⁸ Always, Sam sees himself as innocent and good. As a result, it is obviously other people who cause evil. He does not realize that evil comes from his own innocence. For example, at one point, as he babbles on, he comes up with a system for creating the super-race which involves weeding out misfits and degenerates. There is no malice in his idea as he sees it; he is simply delighted with the idea of producing a new improvement. He even assures the children that people would ask to be euthanized because they "would be taught, and would be anxious to produce the new man and with him the new state of man's social perfection."⁴⁹ This is not a theory likely to gain wide acceptance in the United States or anywhere else, one would hope. It is a representative instance, though, of how Sam's strong belief in his own righteousness and innocence can lead him into dabblings that could destroy other people. Because of his naivete, innocence, and blindness, and because of his pattern of jollying people along,

Sam raises wrath and fury all around him. He does not see this anger as justifiable or recognize his own contribution to it but assumes that those who are attacking him are evil.

In *The Company She Keeps*, on the other hand, Jim is made to see his own hypocrisy and, eventually, even that the hypocrisy comes from his need to protect his innocence. Jim, like Sam, assumes that his motives and thoughts are pure. Like Sam, he thinks over his own troublesome actions and thoughts until he comes up with the most flattering explanations. At one point, when arguing with Mr. Wendell, Jim finds out something about himself that he would rather not know, so he searches until it appears different. The narrator observes:

He [Jim] did not believe in war, either; at least he said he didn't, not in imperialist war anyway; but the words he had just spoken seemed to show that he did, that he believed in it more than anything else, more than free speech, more than the right to agitate against the government. He was so deeply chagrined by this discovery that the thread of the debate slipped from his hands, and it did not occur to him until he lay in bed that night that the old man had not answered the question but only parried it, and in such a way as to assert his moral superiority, to remind Jim of his long and heroic career as a fighter for peace. Jim laughed to himself, and turned over, contentedly.[50]

Later, at the end of the chapter, Jim realizes why he hates Margaret so. He thinks:

If he had it to do over again, he would make the same decision. What he yearned for perhaps was the possibility of decision, the instant of choice, when a man stands at a crossroads and knows he is free. Still, even that had been illusory. He had never been free, but until he had tried to love the girl, he had not known he was bound. It was self-knowledge she had taught him; she had showed him the cage of his own nature. He had accommodated himself to it, but he could never forgive her. Through her he had lost his primeval innocence, and he would hate her forever as Adam hates Eve.[51]

Jim loses his innocence; Sam never does; but in both instances, their personal innocence brings ugliness and evil, not goodness and joy.

All of these characteristics, the ignorance and innocence and the need to possess and control, lead to racism, sexism, and eventually, to violence. The racism is revealed most clearly, again, in *The Man Who Loved Children*. Sam talks to Naden, his servant in Malaysia, in the same way he talks to his children. He lectures him and explains his own ideas to him and rarely listens to Naden's responses. If he does hear Naden, he usually misunderstands him. Most telling of all is Sam's answer to Naden's description of how the races came to be. Sam tells Naden that white men feel superior to other races and asked him how he feels about that. Naden responds:

"He [the white man] thinks what he thinks because he is young in the world, as a child, as my child will feel when he is a two-year-old and will be butting me with his head. That cannot last very long. The Kings of Egypt were dark; all the world was dark until a very little while ago. Then the white man came from some little crack in the earth. He does not know about the times before he came. This is how we feel, sah; he is an accident."

This surprising answer quieted Sam for a space; at length he answered (they were walking through a garden, planted with old trees, and beside high white walls),

"This is a wrong idea you have."[52]

Sam in his arrogance and ignorance and need to dominate cannot allow Naden even the right to his idea, let alone the possibility that it might be accurate.

Other novels portray American patriarchy very well through the male characters' hatred of women and sex. *The Women's Room* is filled with minor male figures who despise women. Harley is an excellent representative of this type, especially in his contempt for Iso and her gay relationships. Also, in *The Company She Keeps*, one can find male examples of the fear of sexuality. Jim, for example, considers that:

In the socialist millennium, of course, everything would be different: love would be free and light as air. Actually, this aspect of the socialist millennium filled Jim with alarm; he hoped that in America they would not have to go so far as to break up the family; it would be enough if every man could have the rock-bottom, durable, practical things, the things Nancy cared about so very, very much.[53]

In Gary White in *Looking for Mr. Goodbar*, one can find the epitome of hatred of women and sex. He absorbs, indeed encapsulates, the traditional American male role and its values: blondes are the best women; gays are the offal of society; sexually active women cannot be teachers; and, most important, anger and violence are the best aphrodisiacs. He and Theresa Dunn are Mr. and Miss America, and it is logical that their relationship should end in murder and suicide.

The Women's Room is riddled with violence stemming from the characters' hatred of women and sex. The minor figures' physical abuse of their wives and Val's violent end are most representative. However, *The Man Who Loved Children* best portrays the source of the American pastime of violence. Sam's recurrent sadism comes from his need to control. Sam's joy in cruelty is particularly evident in the scene involving Ernie's beloved lead collection and in another focusing on Little-Sam and the marlin remains. Sam attempts to steal Ernie's collection and throws the remains of the fish on his other son to force his will upon them. Sam's own ignorance forces him on in these acts of cruelty toward his children because if he cannot understand them, he must at least dominate. In an interesting passage that helps to illuminate Sam's problems, he explains in his tiresome, twisted language, while talking to Louie, that:

"Now wimmin is prone to murder," said Sam. "In wicked old Europe still, you get the village witch planning to murder husbings for them wives what is a bit tired of making coffee for the old man."
"Do they?" asked Louie entranced.
"Yiss, and fum what I know of some wimminfolk what I know," continued Sam chuckling, "they would very much like to get to know them there witches. En some husbings too would like to know such witches." Louie giggled. "We could get rid of our old wives which is always mad at us and we could get sweet little beauts what is seventeen years old," said Sam. Louie giggled.

Louie and Sam chattered for a while on this interesting subject of countenanced murder, and then Sam told Louie that they must be serious, for murder was really a serious thing, because it meant hate, and hate produced all the wickedness of the world.[54]

What actually produces Henny's simultaneous murder and suicide and Henny's and Louie's hatred is Sam. In effect, it is Sam's brand of love and goodness that produces the wickedness of the world.

In these feminist novels, then, the male figures are very often used to dramatize aspects of modern society in general and of the United States in particular, both of which seek to enslave women. Similarly, sexual relationships come to typify women's political power struggles. Sexual interactions and sexuality itself serve as the main backdrop for almost all feminist novels. This scenario is an excellent choice because the authors' treatment of power, domination, and control can be exemplified in the characters' sexual encounters.

In *Braided Lives*, for example, Peter's attempts to subordinate Jill are symbolized by their physical relationship. Jill relates, "If he would touch me before he came in, if he would eat me, I would come better, but he says wanting that shows I am sexually immature and stuck in the clitoral phase of development. If I was a real woman, he says, I would not need stimulation."[55] Sex and sexuality itself are consistently presented as elements of entrapment because the women characters can expect only attempts at enslavement from the men with whom they become involved. The men who represent modern society and the United States expect patriarchal sex. As Jill decides in *Braided Lives*, "if sex is a war I am a conscientious objector: I will not play."[56]

Several important statements made in these novels about sexual relationships help to explain the centrality of sex. Often, in male-authored novels, sex, and women especially, are presented as puzzling secrets, deep mysteries. In feminist novels, a key aspect of the characters' sexual encounters is their clarity. Often, the heroines first come to grips with their real emotions and feelings during sex. It is impossible for them to lie to themselves then. In Erica Jong's *Fear of Flying*, for example, Isadora first addresses her problems in her marriage when she realizes she pretends Bennett is someone else while they make love. She asks herself: "At what point had I started pretending Bennett was somebody else. Somewhere around the end of the third year of our marriage. And why? Nobody had been able to tell me that."[57]

Later, she explains it to herself: "You are what you dream.

You are what you daydream. Masters and Johnson's charts and numbers and flashing lights and plastic pricks tell us everything about sex and nothing about it. Because sex is all in the head."[58] Isadora starts to imagine Bennett is someone else when she can no longer hide the realities about her marriage from herself.

Similarly, Beth in *Small Changes* recognizes many of her problems with Jim during their sexual nightmares. Jim always asks without interest if she enjoys their sex and Beth "was embarrassed to say anything, but she started wondering if that wasn't a form of lying to him. Finally she told him one night that it wasn't good for her. He called her frigid."[59] Later, it is noted that "Jim stayed mad at her until she began making noises like the movie actresses did. Then he loved her again."[60] The stupidity and deadliness of Jim and Beth's marriage roles are found in their sexual relationship as well. Just before Beth leaves, Jim becomes suspicious of her and tries to figure out what is happening. Sexually,

he tried being gentle. He caressed her with his finger tips. He tried kissing her vagina. Through all the experiments he watched. Because he watched she tightened. She was aware of him waiting and she could not respond. Her body felt like a watch ticking. She wished that he had tried some of his experiments earlier, but now with those suspicious eyes and his anger banked and gathering interest, she could not breathe in bed with him. Her body mistrusted. She had to resume making the passionate moans she had learned.[61]

Jim's gentleness is not real and their marriage is a role, too. Like those of Doris Lessing's heroines, Beth's physical feelings cannot be stimulated against her emotions.

For all of the heroines, mechanical, disinterested sex is impossible. Sofia in *The Color Purple* makes a representative statement on dissociated sex when she says of Harpo and sex with him, "Heartfeeling don't even seem to enter into it. She snort. The fact he can do it like that make me want to kill him."[62] Isadora Wing, on the other hand, initially thinks of this sort of physical relationship as something to be sought. She finds that once she knows a man as a person, she is no longer interested in him because of his tedious problems and tiny concerns. So she reasons that strictly anonymous sex must be preferable. As she grows and learns throughout the novel, though, she comes to a new conclusion. When she realizes that she is no longer interested in mechanical sex, she thinks, "maybe my psyche had begun to change in a way I hadn't anticipated. There was no longer anything romantic about strangers on trains."[63] What has happened is that Isadora has found herself and thinks of herself as a person. Once she does that, she no longer has any interest in anonymous people or in relationships that are not real.

Of great interest in these novels is the statement they make about the supposed radicalism of sex and sexuality. Male critics and authors have a great deal to say and suggest about the ties between political freedom and spontaneous, free sex. Irving Howe points out, for example, that the totalitarian state is the enemy of erotic freedom and that the unplanned is subversive.[64] He also discussed sexuality as a threat to traditional modes of life and institutions even in democratic states.[65] Generally, sex and sexuality are presented by most male critics as radical attacks on society. Obviously, "treating male sexual concerns and feelings from a male point of view is... legitimate, but the fact needs to be made clear that the view is male and not global."[66]

As the feminist novel points out, the revolutionary potential of sexual attacks on society for the female is far more complicated and fraught with difficulties. In *Daddy was a Number Runner*, sex for Francie is a white man pursuing a twelve-year-old black girl. The rape in Piercy's *Small Changes* may have been liberating for Phil's friends; it was something quite different for the girl. As Piercy points out, Miriam's florid body makes her both more visible than other women and, as a result, more vulnerable.[67] Miriam is not allowed to feel free in her body. When she does, as in the dance scene in her home, her husband attacks her. Similarly, when Mira does the same in *The Women's Room*, she is almost raped. Carolyn Heilbrun observes of Dido, a woman who succumbs to her own sexual desires, that "seized with unrequited love for a man who must follow *his* destiny undeterred by casual affairs in caves, she forgets everything but passion as she throws herself upon her sword."[68] The female character who intends to enjoy her erotic feelings is often used, not liberated.

The real radicalism of sex rests in female sexuality, and the obstacles to its release are almost innumerable. Perhaps worst, the sex act itself is viewed almost universally as degrading for women and has rarely been portrayed in literature from the woman's point of view. Simone de Beauvoir remarks "a woman must have a considerable amount of cynicism, indifference, or pride to regard physical relations as an exchange of pleasure by which each partner benefits equally."[69] The reason, of course, is the arrangement of the world as it is mirrored in sex. As Kate Millett remarks, one must consider the possibility that frigidity is a political statement.[70] The appearance of what is commonly labeled "frigidity" may be something quite different. One can observe in *Princess of Cleves*, for example, "a woman denying herself a love affair even when all obstacles to it are removed, perhaps out of a sense of her own self as discoverable in the control of sexual passion."[71]

For all these reasons the feminist novel almost universally views sex and sexuality as fraught with traps. For Beth in *Small Changes*, her escape involves releasing her sexuality with women. With them, she need not fear power struggles, indifference to her pleasure, or entrapment. Mira in *The Women's Room*, who stays with men, finds that there is a large price to pay if she is to continue to enjoy herself sexually with Ben. That price is getting married, giving up her career, and having babies. It is too high a price to pay. Female sexual freedom, it is suggested in these novels, is chimerical until it is tied to real political freedom for women. The two are inextricably connected.

There is an undercurrent in some feminist novels, however, that suggests that female sexuality and its corresponding passions and feelings may be freed as romanticized illusion dies. There are many reasons why "female sexuality bugs people,"[72] but one is certainly the modern confrontation between reality and the "conventional belief about female sexuality in general: that women prefer love and romance to physical consummation."[73] A representative portraiture of genuine female sexuality released from the fog of romantic polemics and cliches is that of Shug in *The Color Purple.* She comments of men at one point, "I would never be fool enough to take any of them seriously... but some mens can be a lots of fun."⁷⁴ Another time, Celie, referring to Albert, asks, "You still love him?" and Shug answers, "I got what you call a passion for him."⁷⁵ Shug uses the appropriate names for what she feels. She develops enormous passions as well for a nineteen-year-old boy and for Celie, whom she also loves deeply, but these feelings never destroy her. She understands her own emotions. Toward the end, the other women in the novel and Shug become very close and can communicate with each other without speaking. Grady comments that women should be careful about their behavior because "a woman can't git a man if peoples talk."⁷⁶ All the women laugh because they are not interested in "getting a man." They free themselves in the course of the novel and interwined in the process is the release of their authentic sexual natures. For a sexist society, such female sexuality represents the "wild zone."⁷⁷ Henry Adams surmises that "America's folly" in its "abandonment or misunderstanding of its women" might be "the result of thinking they knew only too well what women are and thus dared not to let loose her particular force."⁷⁸ One can also speculate that "The symbolism of Hester Prynne's dark hair is frightening in its implications; no wonder society made her confine it under a neat Puritan cap."⁷⁹ The female authors of the feminist novel are neither frightened by nor ignorant of female sexuality and provide remarkable and accurate portrayals of its present, multifaceted nature.

These positive images of female sexuality do not obscure the recognition, however, that the final and most dreaded trap sprung by men and sexuality is marriage. Marriage is the worst of all confinements in the feminist novel. It is universally condemned in every novel except two of the novels by black women, Petry's *The Street* and Meriwether's *Daddy was a Number Runner.* Marriage is presented as a microcosm of patriarchy and capitalism because it is the one institution absolutely necessary for the functioning of both. The emphasis of marriage, as it is described in these novels, is on possession and rule and order. Of course, the wife is the one to be possessed, ruled, and ordered; she is the one who is to be made weak and subservient. It is the domination and exploitation of her that is necessary for patriarchy; it is familial privacy, possession, and rule that is necessary for capitalism.

In all these novels, but most emphatically in *The Women's Room*, there is not a worthwhile marriage to be found. When the novels consider marriage in general, the verdict is that presented in Woolf's *Orlando*: to see everyone as a couple is repugnant. Marriage generally is repugnant, and many of the novels point out that it is not only the woman who is destroyed by it. As Joe and Clara's marriage is described in Atwood's *The Edible Woman*, it destroys the core of both their beings. Marie Rogers in *Daughter of Earth* shouts out the most emphatic statement of all when she asserts, "I would never marry... I would never have children... I would never be so weak as to love!"[80] The crux is that she does marry. The need for love, for a sexual release, for closeness, leads almost inevitably to the prison of marriage.

The most heavily emphasized and despised aspect of marriage in these novels is its demand that the woman become chattel. In *Daughter of Earth* the representative marriage is one in which the wife is made to stop working immediately. When she becomes pregnant and is no longer able to work, the representative statement of marriage is made. Her husband, during a quarrel, shouts at her:

"Give me back the clothes I bought you!" he bellowed at her one day.
"Damn it, kid, you know I love you!" she begged through her tears—for now she could not go back to work even if she wished.[81]

She must pretend that she loves him and be docile because she can no longer take care of herself. As Marie Rogers comments, the life of a prostitute is better than the life of a wife because the prostitute is paid and has the authority to throw the man out of her house.[82] Marie Rogers could have spoken the very words of the writer Gloria Anzaldúa who states, "The concepts 'passive' and 'dutiful' raked my skin like spurs and 'marriage' and 'children' set me to bucking faster than rattlesnakes or coyotes."[83]

Often, it is demonstrated that the individual worth, goodness, or generosity of the male character in a relationship has no bearing on the catastrophe of marriage. As has been observed of *Jane Eyre*, "even the equality of love between true minds leads to the inequalities and minor despotisms of marriage."[84] In *The Four-Gated City*, one notes, for example, that "Jimmy wished to marry Iris, but she did not want to marry again. Once was enough, she said. Meanwhile they lived together and proposed to continue to live together."[85] One finds, too, that Lynda Coldridge is "in a very expensive mental hospital because she could not stand being Mark's wife, and Francis's mother."[86] Mark and Francis are not monsters, but marriage is a monstrosity. Without thinking of any man in particular, Jill observes early in *Braided Lives*, while contemplating possible stories for her adult life, "Marriage does not figure in the tales I tell myself. I see it daily and it looks like a doom rather than a prize. Mother is always saying Riva was a dancer, but then she got married; Charlotte was a buyer for Crowley's, but then she got married."[87] It has been noted of the modern male writer that he "averted his eyes from married life as from the grave: perhaps he suspected a resemblance between them."[88] This joint aversion toward marriage evinced by many modern male writers and nearly all the female authors of feminist novels originates from far different vantage points. These authors may very well share a similar belief, though, that marriage represents "the end of experience."[89]

In Piercy's *Small Changes*, almost all male and female relationships, whether the individuals are married or not, are characterized by the male desire to possess. Jackson, in explaining his guarded attitude toward Miriam, states:

"I stole you from Phil. How can I not expect that Phil will steal you back? Or somebody else."

"You didn't 'steal' me from Phil, because Phil didn't 'have' me in the sense you mean. I'm sick of this having."[90]

In marriage, though, things are far worse. Jim rapes Beth when they are married, not when they are single or divorced. Jackson rapes Sissy, his wife, not Miriam, his lover. When

Miriam marries, Beth cannot find her because Miriam has changed her last name. As Beth comments, "Miriam Stone, Mrs. Neil Stone, was her name. She had to find out that strange name before she could find her. Miriam Berg was no more. Women must often lose a friend that way, and never be able to find each other again."[91] The loss of name is symbolic of the loss of self that marriage demands of the woman.

For Sam in *The Man Who Loved Children*, it is not just owning Henny but owning his children that he needs. For him a woman disobeying her husband is the same as a man not contributing to the gods. His children are his playthings, and the entire family structure suits his wish to see himself as a god. The Pollit family and Sam especially serve as representatives of patriarchal structure, "And the freedom that Henny screams and bites and kicks for is a positive goal."[92] Particularly appropriate for this novel is Simone de Beauvoir's observation that "Marriage incites man to a capricious imperialism: the temptation to dominate is the most truly universal, the most irresistible one there is; to surrender the child to its mother, the wife to her husband, is to promote tyranny in the world."[93]

A final symbol of domestic entrapment that is closely connected with those discussed earlier involves food. The appetite for food is symbolic of the appetite for sex, and the handling of the two is similar. If frigidity may be a political statement, so too, may anorexia nervosa. As Simone de Beauvoir notes, one way a young girl has to flout or attack society is to develop whimsical food habits.[94] In some of these novels, too, the attitudes toward food suggest a return to Emerson and Thoreau, to self-reliance and away from the fat, satiated, secure and ordered lives that those in the modern world are supposed to want.

In several feminist novels, a marked distinction is made between the way food and eating are handled in marriage and outside of it. Like sexuality, food can be connected with the trap of marriage. In *Small Changes*, Beth and Jim encounter this fact even while they are planning to marry. Jim

liked chocolate cake the best and so did she, but the baker said nobody ever has chocolate wedding cake and her mother acted as if there was something dirty-minded in wanting it. So they had what the baker called Lady's Cake. It had pink rosebuds and green leaves and a chubby bride and groom holding hands under an archway.[95]

Jim and Beth's desires are no longer important. There is a ritual to be honored in the ceremony and the cake selection, and there is a ritual in the marriage. Jim will play the male part in it and Beth the female. The marriage is partly represented for Beth by the heavy, time-consuming meals she must continually prepare for Jim. The narrator comments that "these meals" seemed designed to rob her of the precious bit of energy left after eight hours standing behind the counter, the energy to suppress her aching feet and aching back, to steal a little of something sweet from the fading day."[96] She is nauseated by the flesh of dead animals that Jim calls meat. After she leaves Jim, she changes the food she eats along with her life:

She ate brown rice and whole-grain breads and granola and muesli and cracked wheat and lentils and navy, lima, mung, marrow, kidney, and turtle beans.... Always she had liked breakfast, cereals and breads and eggs, so now she would eat breakfasts all day long, instead of the fuss her dad had called dinner and Jim supper.[97]

Beth's meals become, like her life, spare and lean, but nourishing. Similarly, Dolores in *The Bleeding Heart*, a person very different from Beth, thinks of her lover that if they were married, "I'd resent cooking dinner every night, and he wouldn't be happy with a cheese sandwich, as I am."[98]

A contrast between married meals and single meals is made by comparing Miriam's and Beth's eating patterns. As a child, Miriam was overweight; she grew slimmer after she left home. Once she marries, however, she begins cooking large meals. She likes cooking which Beth does not, but she worries as well. She tells Beth, "I'm gaining weight. You don't know, but I used to be fat." When Beth asks why she does not eat less, Miriam replies, "How can I cook a gorgeous supper and not eat?"[99] Miriam's problem with fat is due to her marriage. She must cook large meals because Neil wants them and because she is the servant. Miriam does not admit the reality and continues to view her problem as an individual tendency toward overweight. Beth turns from sex with men and the meals of marriage to sex and love with Wanda and grows stronger. Miriam settles for poor sex with Neil and compensating rich meals and grows heavy.

In *The Awakening*, a similar meal ritual is attached to marriage. Although the ritual is enjoyable when performed for Robert because passion is included, it still represents the pattern of marriage. Simple, enjoyable parts of single life, like eating, turn into time-consuming, complicated occasions for argument in marriage. As the Pontelliers argue over meals, so, too, do the Pollits. Sam asks Henny several times over one meal, "Have we salad, Henrietta?"[100] Henny is humiliated and outraged because Louie's teacher is present for dinner and because Henny has just been forced to sell all her belongings to keep the family financially alive. They cannot afford salad, but as the master, Sam assumes that Henny, the slave, is responsible.

In two other novels, food and eating are connected to sex and the modern world through violence. For Marian in *The Edible Woman*, all food is alive and eating it represents the violence that men do to women and that people generally in modern society do to one another. Early in the novel, Len and Peter laugh over the remains of a slaughtered rabbit. Marian, still human, is ill at the sight. Everything becomes alive to Marian; the petals and flowers on Clara's dress are alive and move in Marian's eyes. Everywhere she sees predators consuming and eating. Eventually, she can eat nothing at all. In this novel, the violence of marriage is represented by the consuming of women. The violence of modern life shows through the eating and butchering of living things in *The Edible Woman* as it does also in the pigeon-killing scene in *The Golden Notebook*.

Like Marian, every heroine in the feminist novel would agree with Anaïs Nin "that my struggle was against every trap, every entrapment of experience, every limitation, every restriction."[101] It may very well be true that "The major claim made on behalf of American women between the two world wars was, not surprisingly, that of freedom,"[102] but it is also noteworthy that many years earlier "What Martineau and Brontë were creating and responding to in their respective works, what many women then and since have identified with, is an archetypal female success story, a passage from imprisonment to freedom."[103] Consequently, as this passage takes place in the feminist novel, those images representing slavery, entrapment, and living death, are contrasted against opposing representations of freedom. Maturity is the first of these, and it must be attained before liberty can become a reality. The youth and the adolescent cannot really be free, these novels seem to suggest. Age in itself is not to be directly equated with maturity, but the chances of reaching psychological adulthood in youth are slim. This is not to say, of course, that the attainment of adulthood brings freedom for all the heroines in the feminist novel. Quite the contrary, for many it brings death or the necessity of flight. Even so, some of these novels exhibit disinterest in the blindness, the struggles of adolescence. In those novels that do portray the heroine during her early years, that period is generally passed over quickly in favor of the years of her twenties, thirties, forties, and even fifties, when the heroine is reaching whatever emotional and mental maturity she is to attain. Those authors focusing on a revolutionary heroine do not often picture an adolescent but a mature woman. For most of these novels, the statement that "the task of the adolescent is to put adolescence behind her"[104] is quite appropriate. These novels align themselves against the observation that "next to failure, age has come to be considered the most reprehensible condition in our society."[105] It might be in the future that changing demographic patterns and an aging America could lead generally to older women heroines, but for now, this emphasis on maturity in the feminist novel stems from something else. The authors' interest in women is in their intellectual, emotional, and psychic growth, awakening, or stultification, not in their youth, beauty, charm, or symbolic sexual potential.

Most representative of this characteristic of the feminist novel are *The Awakening*, *The Dollmaker*, *Small Changes*, *How She Died*, and *Fear of Flying*. The heroines in *The Awakening* and *The Dollmaker* are not completely able to free themselves either from society or from their adolescence. Edna's continued clinging to adolescent romanticism has already been discussed. The problem for Gertie in *The Dollmaker* is somewhat different. Her strength, emotional and physical, are lauded throughout the novel. As it develops, though, Gertie is never able to grow away from her childhood fear of her mother. Gertie's mother can still force her to do what she does not want, even if it means bowing to the foolish daydreams of her boy-husband and, in effect, losing her life and her children's lives. Gertie cannot quite reach the maturity of depending upon her own conscience as well as her own strength.

In the other three novels, the heroines achieve their freedom with their maturity. Wanda in *Small Changes* is an excellent example of the freedom that comes with full adulthood. In her youth, Wanda is unable to resist Joe, marries him, and becomes a wife:

Wanda arrived at suppertime with Luis by the hand and the baby on her back—a small chunky woman with dark wiry hair and intense black eyes—burning, worried, overworked, desperate, and strong as a mule.... Joe went with her. A simple division of labor, Miriam thought wryly, watching them depart: she loves and he permits himself to be loved.[106]

At that point, Wanda has youth and beauty but not maturity. Much later, Beth thinks:

She could not imagine Wanda younger or with unlined skin or with her hair all black or her waist tiny as she said it had been before she bore her children. She felt jealous sometimes when she met someone, man or woman, who had known Wanda before. But she fought that. All that living had gone to cure this salty woman to just the right taste for her. Wanda did not close her off from others, did not hold her in a box-shaped intimacy, and she fought herself not to clutch. It was a sureness.[107]

The sureness comes from Wanda's adulthood. Wanda is sure— of herself, her ideals, her values, her life. The loss of youth and beauty does not matter because Wanda has become a person in her own right.

Jean in *How She Died* and Isadora in *Fear of Flying* achieve maturity by the end of their novels also. Jean surmounts her own passivity and takes positive steps toward doing something she considers meaningful. Isadora surmounts her fear when she gains adulthood by accepting herself as the director of her own life. Of particular interest in connection with these portrayals are Leslie Fiedler's comments upon American novels, in particular that they seem "innocent, unfallen in a disturbing way, almost juvenile"[108] and that their authors "shy away from ...any full-fledged, mature women."[109] In moving away from the traditional emphasis on the adolescent and on the physical development of women and their youth and beauty, the feminist novel, like its heroines, moves toward its own adulthood.

Associated with the mature woman in these novels are her children. Perhaps surprisingly, children are more often linked in the feminist novel to liberty than to entrapment. Frequently, too, the woman is presented alone with her children. If the father is present, he is likely to be insignificant and merely provide background. Of consequence to this portrayal is Joelynn Snyder-Ott's comment regarding the contrasting male and female paintings of the mother and child relationship. She notes that:

> If we examine the three versions and numerous drawings of Renoir's wife Aline nursing his son Pierre, we can make an interesting observation. In each painting, Renoir focuses on his wife's exposed breast and upon the little boy's naked lower half. Aline gazes at the painter. She is not depicted as emotionally involved with little Pierre. Cassatt's mother and child, on the other hand, are depicted as actively involved with each other.[110]

In the feminist novel, too, the mother is usually actively engaged with and emotionally connected to her children. Even more important, children come to exemplify some of what the modern world desperately needs.

Children provide, first of all, a link to sanity for many of the women in the feminist novel, They provide a connection to humanity and to reality. They are that thing that, without question, one must stay sane for. When Milt tells Anna in *The Golden Notebook* that she is lucky to have her daughter, Janet, Anna replies, "I know it. That's why I'm sane and you're nuts."[111] Lutie's final defeat in *The Street* is portrayed by her giving up her son, Bub. As long as she has her son to work and live for, she can continue. When she and he are separated and she leaves him, she is finished. For Jean in *How She Died*, her children help her in pulling through to a new maturity. When her son, Terry, says they must be a lot of trouble to her, she replies, "Terry, don't be crazy. You're the best thing in my life, you three."[112] She is not mouthing reassurances; she is being accurate. Her children are also part of what makes her start to think of changing her life, and it is Matt's suggestion that she leave them that helps her separate from him.

In Harriette Arnow's *The Dollmaker*, children play an even larger role. Gertie and her children come to represent the human family and humanity generally. Their desire to work the land, to live in their own rough home, and to be the part of nature that the human being should be is set off against the mechanized, modern world symbolized by Detroit. In the rural setting, Reuben grows strong and healthy, Cassie's imagination flowers, and Gertie can save Amos' life from diphtheria. Transplanted to the city, Cassie dies because Gertie cannot save her. To Detroit and the people who run it, the train that kills Cassie is more important and more valuable than the child. Gertie would like to kill the train but cannot because it is not human. Gertie with Cassie dying in her arms evokes the image of Mary holding Christ's battered body. The child comes to represent the Savior, and it is ultimately only the children's laughter and the chain of communion that links Gertie to her neighbors that can save her.

Children are further presented in the feminist novel as possessors of goodness and idealism. In their way, they strengthen and support their mothers. Fortunately, one does not find in these novels the ridiculous idealizations of children mouthed by Sam in *The Man Who Loved Children*. His idiocies over the birth of a child and his strong need to have children as his legacy are not mimicked by the heroines. Their experience with children is real, not imagined; so they can see the joy in the child without building power structures around it. The mother and child relationship is never set up for adoration. As a result, the true beauty of the child is evident.

The child is the ultimate representation of true innocence

and joy. An excellent example occurs in *How She Died* when Mary's son, Mark, asks her what happens to people after they die. Mary says that people grow into something else then, and Mark questions:

> "But after you're in the ground, do you come out again a little baby?" I said no, that you would come out again as grass and trees and leaves. He said that he would rather come out as a little baby boy again. I didn't say anything. After a while I got up, covered the baby and was about to go out of the room, when he said, "After I'm dead, you know what Mommie? My penis is going to grow into a flower."[113]

Mary leaves the room and tell the other guests what Mark said to her. Then she "thought of him awake, staring at the ceiling, listening to me repeat what he had said and hearing the exclamations and the laughter." The adults defile the child's innocence and betray his trust.

Many times, too, the children in the novels, with a clear-sightedness unclouded by relativism, state the obvious for the adults. Terry in *How She Died* points out to Jean what she is doing by letting Mary go to Bellevue. Jean bears part of the responsiblity for Mary's incarceration because she concurs in sending Mary there. She tries to escape her accountability by refusing to be there when Mary is taken away. In *The Dollmaker* Cassie acts out Gertie's feelings when she cuts a new dress off a new doll so that the old doll can have something nice to wear. Like Gertie, she instinctively recognizes that new is not often better. In a touching scene, Wheateye, the neighbor child, keeps Cassie's memory alive by continuing to play with Callie Lou, Cassie's friend of the imagination. The children do not have their visions befuddled by confusion, fear, or sentimentality. Children instinctively know what is right because they have not learned the cynicism of the adult or adult ways of covering up the truth. Children are not piteous in these novels. They have qualities that the adults in their maturity must retain. Those qualities can be seen in Beth's joy in *Small Changes* and in Mrs. Van and Johnny in *A Ripple from the Storm* when together they "gave such an impression of warmth and of trust that more that [sic] one member of the group involuntarily sighed and envied them."[114] It is the task of the adult to retain the idealism and the goodness of the child.

In those novels where the children are linked to madness and despair, it is because of the adults' distortion of the world. Inevitably, in these novels, the mother is trapped in a traditional marriage, as in *Up The Sandbox!*, *A Proper Marriage*, *The Awakening*, *The Man Who Loved Children*, and *The Women's Room*. In *Small Changes*, the children take on different characteristics as the adult relationships differ. Wanda and Beth's children are a joy and a delight; they participate in the adults' freedom. In Miriam and Neil's marriage, the joy Miriam finds in Ariane and Jeffrey is muted by the trap her relationship with Neil has become. It is, in fact, the traditional marriage that entombs the woman, not the children. Edna Pontellier, supremely unfitted, had children because one is supposed to get married and have children. A child's world is sane; many adult worlds are not. An exquisite small example occurs in *Small Changes* when the commune family of Dorine, Laura, Connie, and Beth argue over whether the children should be allowed to play with a doll house Dorine has brought from her home. The argument flies back and forth as one side argues that it teaches consumerism and heterosexual, traditional marriage while Dorine argues that it is only a play house with which one can do anything. In the end, the outcome is settled by the children because "by the time they finished the debate Fern and David had found the dollhouse and were playing with it."[115] Once again, the adults need to regain some of the children's qualities.

Further, the terror of children that some of the characters feel is usually a sign of a problem. Marie Rogers' fear in *Daughter of Earth* of both love and children is a rational recognition of what love, sex, and children usually mean for a woman in this society. On the other hand, Marie's terror is so profound that it destroys any chance for joy in her personal relationships. In *Looking for Mr. Goodbar* as well, Theresa's attitude toward children of her own mirrors her self-hatred and her schizophrenia. She can love the children she teaches as Miss Dunn. As the sexual Terry, she must avoid children and the sick child she once was. It is not ultimately the children who are burdens but the society and its ideas of marriage for women. For the most part, the symbolic overtones surrounding the portrayal of children in the feminist novel are positive ones. The child, in fact, can save the parent.

In moving away from the personal and domestic qualities of age and motherhood into the public world of money and work, one finds that the material world in general and money in particular are necessary elements of freedom. There exists an interesting dichotomy in the feminist novel with regard to finances and the material realm. In the very recent feminist novel of the last twenty years, economics and money are not central issues. They are brought forward for consideration, of course, usually in connection with the heroine's need for privacy and independence to pursue her work. In the feminist novel authored by black women, however, and in earlier feminist novels by white women, money is a primary focus in the novel.

In Meriwether's *Daddy was a Number Runner* and Petry's *The Street*, for example, poverty is the center of both heroines' problems. Francie, only twelve, is forced to let Mr. Morristein, the white butcher, and Max, the white baker, run their hands all over her to get two extra soup bones and some extra rolls.[116] In effect, the jobs open for black women are those of whore, laundry worker, or house cleaner. Other than that, one can run poker games or have a baby every year.[117] These are the reasons Sukie, Francie's friend, is always mean, and they are the reasons that Francie, later, is also always mean. It is when they have some money that Francie's mother and father are soft and loving. One must have some comfort to have peace; so after they hit the number, Francie notices about her parents that:

There was something different about them tonight, some soft way they looked at each other with their eyes and smiled.
  I went to bed and didn't even bother to pull the couch away from the wall, I was that happy. Let the bedbugs bite. Everybody, even those blood-sucking bugs, had to have something sometime.
  We were eating high off the hog and it sure was good to get away from that callie ham which you had to soak all night to kill the salt

and then save the juice and skin to flavor beans and greens for weeks later. Nobody had to coax me now to eat those delicious pork chops and gravy and roast turkey which Daddy stuffed with his Guchie recipe. Daddy was a real mean cook when he had something to work with. That's what he was during the war, a cook with the navy.

It was nice, just like old times again. James Junior and Sterling came home every evening for dinner and we all ate around the diningroom table and then played checkers afterward or sang around the piano with Daddy or caught a cool breeze up on the roof and Daddy had stopped slamming doors or cursing so much.[118]

Francie also gets some new clothes and takes music lessons, but then the money is gone, and the family is back where it was. The black men share this poverty with the black women, and the distance between them is not very great.

A marked contrast is evident here between the white -and black-authored feminist novel. Virginia Woolf, for example, in *A Room of One's Own*, points out the same connection made in Meriwether's novel between money and meals. Woolf's distinction focuses on the different meals men and women are served and on the effect the meals have on their dispositions and attitudes. The difference between the two portrayals is that for Francie's family, the meals are a reflection of individual and family survival while for Woolf's characters they are a reflection of the possibility for achievement. Here food, usually a symbol of entrapment, is a secondary result of money, which does indeed buy freedom.

For Lutie in *The Street*, money could give her and her son, Bub, a life also, but she is never permitted to have it. Because she and her husband have no money, her marriage falls apart. When she works, she does not make enough money to have someone care for Bub after school, and he eventually ends up in jail. She does not have enough money to free him, and, finally, both their lives are ended.

In *Meridian* and *The Color Purple*, the reader is confronted as well by abysmal material poverty. The different economic realities presented in these feminist novels by authors of color are mirrored in the critical literature. Gloria Anzaldúa advises, for example, "Forget the room of one's own—write in the kitchen, lock yourself up in the bathroom."[119] One cannot evade the probability that the black or Hispanic reader must often feel when reading a white-authored feminist novel as women often feel when reading a male-authored work, that is, that she is reading literature "by and about" people "who are fantastically privileged."[120] Cherríe Moraga makes a similar observation when she turns to India and notes "the kind of poverty that even poor Americans could not begin to conceive. India. India was the unraveling. How insignificant our troubles seem in the United States... How ridiculously small my own struggles."[121]

There is yet another strong distinction to be made between the black- and white-authored feminist novel. It lies in the respective portrayals of the male. The black male does not stand as a symbol of modern society or the United States. No matter what the heroine's frustration and anger may be in relation to the black men in her life, there still exists a banding together against another enemy, a white and racist society. A significant example occurs in *The Color Purple* when all the black people, male and female, join together to help Sofia. When they find that Sofia, the invincible, the strong one, is playing Celie's role, "Mr. _____ suck in his breath. Harpo groan. Miss Shug cuss."[122] The men and women have the same response. They must forge a union against the whites who threaten Sofia, so "us all sit round the table after supper. Me, Shug, Mr. _____, Squeak, the prizefighter, Odessa, and two more of Sofia sisters."[123] Society's primary weapon against the black is poverty, and so money is an important symbol and reality in these novels. It is quite difficult at times not to feel that the black-authored novel is more committed to political freedom and equality than the white since the issues it confronts are so very basic to human survival. One senses that the white author can ignore these issues since they are not a problem for her. On the other hand, the money provides for all, black and white, a desired base for the same ultimately desired things—self-love, an independent moral life, and freedom.

Only two of the white-authored novels deal with proverty as the black-authored novels do. One is Smedley's *Daughter of Earth* in which the effects of having no money are visited upon Marie's family. In Arnow's *The Dollmaker*, too, it is the farm and independence that Gertie's money could buy and the desire for material things that sends Clovis off in search of a factory job. The results of poverty and the freedom money can bring are clearly presented in both novels.

In most of the other white-authored novels, however, money is usually ignored because the heroine has enough of it. If it is developed as an issue, money is usually presented within the framework Virginia Woolf's thoughts provide. For Miriam in *Small Changes*, for example, not earning money herself means that her time and work are no longer important. She can no longer value her time. On the other hand:

It was acceptable for Neil to be selfish about his time and his energies and his desires, to withdraw and preserve himself. It was all right for him to emerge demanding love and comfort and amusement. Because he was the breadwinner.

But by virtue of ceasing to earn, Miriam ceased to be able to be selfish.[124]

There is also a marked anger in *Small Changes* and in *The Man Who Loved Children* that anyone should be able to shunt the practical things of life off onto someone else. Because he brings home money, because he is the ruler, Neil does not need to worry about practical things, like meals. Wanda takes care of the practical things for Joe, like his children and his food. Miriam's Jackson does not want to worry about the practicality of birth control and accuses women who do of having "little minds."[125] Similarly, Henny in *The Man Who Loved Children* must steal money from her son and sell all the things she loves so the family can survive while Sam leans back and demands salad they cannot afford. Even the money that brings freedom does not validate the enslavement of others.

The final mark of freedom is work, work that is freely undertaken for a good reason and that is purposeful.[126] When Simone de Beauvoir comments upon this kind of work, she states, "To paint, to write, to engage in politics—these are not merely 'sublimations;' here we have aims that are willed for their own sakes."[127] This is work, not a job. The work brings freedom in taking one outside of oneself, in giving a meaningful purpose because the work itself matters. The kind of work that the heroines in the feminist novel undertake varies, but the work is always similar in one respect. It matters in itself to the heroine performing it. For some, their work is political, like Miriam's, Martha Quest's, Marie Rogers', and Mary's in *How She Died*. Others have an artistic leaning, like Lutie Johnson, Edna Pontellier, and Isadora Wing. Mary's work in *The Grass is Singing* would seem stultifying to many but not to her because she loves the work she does. Her loving it makes the work important. The loving of it is the reason it is chosen. Because she does not love the work she selects, Anna's choice at the end of *The Golden Notebook* is a failure. A marriage welfare center, the Labour Party, and classes for delinquent children might be meaningful in an objective sense. They are not for Anna because she does not want them. She loves writing and uses the other jobs to escape her work of writing, so she fails. The meaning comes from the joy of the work and the effort put into it, not from the conscious willing of the work to be meaningful.

Finally, some of the heroines are great at what they do; some are not. There is no failure in not being great, though, as Terry asserts in *How She Died*. The greatness demanded in one's work is parallel to the self-interest demanded in capitalism. The amount of talent the heroines in the feminist novel exhibit is not as important as the joy and fulfillment they get from their work. Miriam is brilliant and exceptional; Edna is not; both care very much about their work. Work cannot save the heroine, but it is always connected with her freedom.

That freedom, as Jill in *Braided Lives* describes it, "is a daily necessity like water, and we love most loyally and longest those who allow us at least occasionally to vanish and wander the curious night. To them we always return from the eight deaths before the last."[128] The freedom that emerges for some of these heroines is not, of course, free license. This is one of the reasons that work is so strongly connected with this liberty. It is the opposite of that described by de Beauvoir when she comments, "Montherlant has chosen a liberty *without object*, that is to say, he prefers an illusion of autonomy to the authentic liberty that takes action in the world; it is this detachment and freedom from responsibility that he means to defend."[129] In throwing off their old prescribed roles, the heroines of the feminist novel move into a new world. It is a world their creators describe and fill with new images and new values. To understand this world, one must recognize the change in viewpoint and the resultant change in construction. It is a vision called into being in part by a modern world that needs it. The insights and portrayals of the feminist novel fight against the Machine and Nuclear Age, well described in *The Dollmaker* by the symbol of Oak Ridge: "A strange place it was ... where people worked without knowing what they did, and never asked."[130] The feminist novel not only asks; it suggests alternatives, alternatives generated from the world of "The Other."

NOTES

1. Simone de Beauvoir, *The Second Sex*, ed. and trans. H. M. Parshley (1953; reprint, New York: Random House, 1974), p. 159.

2. Nancy B. Evans, "The Value and Peril for Women of Reading Women Writers," *Images of Women in Fiction: Feminist Perspectives*, ed. Susan Koppelman Cornillon (Bowling Green, Ohio: Bowling Green University Popular Press, 1972), p. 313.

3. Barbara Currier Bell and Carol Ohmann, "Virginia Woolf's Criticism: A Polemical Preface." *Feminist Literary Criticism: Explorations in Theory*, ed. Josephine Donovan (Lexington: University Press of Kentucky, 1975), p. 57.

4. Joelynn Snyder-Ott, "The Female Experience and Artistic Creativity," *Art Education* 27 (September 1974): 18.

5. Germaine Bree, *Women Writers in France: Variations on a Theme* (New Brunswick, N.J.: Rutgers University Press, 1973), p. 30.

6. Ibid., p. 8.

7. de Beauvoir, *The Second Sex*, p. 161.

8. Nathan Irvin Huggins, *Harlem Renaissance* (1971; reprint, New York: Oxford University Press, Inc., 1974), p. 171.

9. de Beauvoir, *The Second Sex*, p. 52.

10. Irving Howe, *Politics and the Novel* (New York: The New American Library, Inc., 1955), p. 36.

11. Doris Lessing, *A Ripple from the Storm* (New York: Simon and Schuster, Inc., 1966), p. 29.

12. Marge Piercy, *Small Changes* (1972; reprint, Greenwich Conn.: Fawcett Publications, Inc., 1974), p. 373.

13. Ibid., p. 100.

14. Ibid., p. 101.
15. Ibid., p. 102.
16. Ibid., p. 284.
17. Ibid., p. 288.
18. Ibid., p. 298.
19. Alice B. Markow, "The Pathology of Feminine Failure in the Fiction of Doris Lessing," *Critique* 16, no. 1 (1974): 92.
20. Doris Lessing, *The Golden Notebook* (New York: Simon and Schuster, Inc., 1962), p. 429.
21. Anne Richardson Roiphe, *Up the Sandbox!* (New York: Simon and Schuster, Inc., 1970), pp. 80–81.
22. Ibid., p. 83.
23. Erica Jong, *Fear of Flying* (New York: Holt, Rinehart and Winston, 1971), pp. 108–9.
24. Marge Piercy, *Braided Lives* (New York: Random House, 1982), pp. 441–42.
25. Marge Piercy, *Woman on the Edge of Time* (New York: Alfred A. Knopf, 1976), p. 282.
26. Marilyn French, *The Bleeding Heart* (New York: Random House, 1980), p. 45.
27. Anaïs Nin, *A Woman Speaks*, ed. Evelyn J. Hinz (London: W. H. Allen and Co., Ltd., 1978), p. 13.
28. Carol P. Christ, *Diving Deep and Surfacing: Women Writers on Spiritual Quest* (Boston: Beacon Press, 1980), p. xiv.
29. Agnes Smedley, *Daughter of Earth* (1929; reprint, Old Westbury, N.Y.: The Feminist Press, 1973), p. 369.
30. Ibid., p. 379.
31. Ibid., p. 378.
32. Mary McCarthy, *The Company She Keeps* (1942; reprint, New York: Harcourt, Brace and World, Inc., 1970), p. 15.
33. Christina Stead, *The Man Who Loved Children* (1940; reprint, New York: Holt, Rinehart and Winston, 1966), p. 309–10.
34. Ibid., p. 310.
35. Ibid.
36. Ibid., p. 219.
37. Ibid., p. 205.
38. Ibid., p. 206.
39. Virginia Woolf, *A Room of One's Own* (New York: Harcourt, Brace and Co., 1929), p. 52.
40. Stead, *The Man Who Loved Children*, p. 342.
41. Ibid., p. 219.
42. Ibid., p. 239.

43. Ibid., p. 103.
44. Piercy, *Braided Lives*, p. 103.
45. Stead, *The Man Who Loved Children*, p. 305.
46. Ibid., p. 314.
47. Ibid., p. 487.
48. Ibid., p. 218.
49. Ibid., p. 51.
50. McCarthy, *The Company She Keeps*, p. 180.
51. Ibid., p. 246.
52. Stead, *The Man Who Loved Children*, p. 207.
53. McCarthy, *The Company She Keeps*, pp. 186–87.
54. Stead, *The Man Who Loved Children*, p. 128.
55. Piercy, *Braided Lives*, p. 283.
56. Ibid., p. 79.
57. Jong, *Fear of Flying*, p. 36.
58. Ibid., p. 37.
59. Piercy, *Small Changes*, p. 30.
60. Ibid., p. 31.
61. Ibid., pp. 38–39.
62. Alice Walker, *The Color Purple* (New York: Simon and Schuster, Inc., 1982), p. 68.
63. Jong, *Fear of Flying*, p. 332.
64. Howe, *Politics and the Novel*, p. 246.
65. Ibid., p. 171.
66. Marcia Holly, "Consciousness and Authenticity: Toward a Feminist Aesthetic," *Feminist Literary Criticism: Explorations in Theory*, ed. Josephine Donovan (Lexington: University Press of Kentucky, 1975), p. 44.
67. Piercy, *Small Changes*, p. 68.
68. Carolyn G. Heilbrun, *Toward a Recognition of Androgyny* (New York: Alfred A. Knopf, 1973), p. 52.
69. de Beauvoir, *The Second Sex*, p. 719.
70. Kate Millett, *Sexual Politics* (Garden City, N.Y.: Doubleday and Co., Inc., 1970), p. 116.
71. Heilbrun, *Toward a Recognition of Androgyny*, p. 87.
72. Piercy, *Braided Lives*, p. 302.
73. Catharine R. Stimpson, "Zero Degree Deviancy: The Lesbian Novel in English," *Critical Inquiry: Writing and Sexual Difference* 8 (Winter 1981): 371.
74. Walker, *The Color Purple*, p. 220.
75. Ibid., p. 78.
76. Ibid., p. 182.

77. Elaine Showalter, "Feminist Criticism in the Wilderness," *Critical Inquiry: Writing and Sexual Difference* 8 (Winter 1981): 179–205.

78. Martha Banta, "They Shall Have Faces, Minds, and (One Day) Flesh: Women in Late Nineteenth-Century and Early Twentieth-Century American Literature," *What Manner of Woman: Essays on English and American Life and Literature*, ed. Marlene Springer (New York: New York University Press, 1977), p. 241.

79. Ibid.

80. Smedley, *Daughter of Earth*, p. 168.

81. Ibid., p. 73.

82. Ibid., p. 142.

83. Gloria Anzaldúa, "La Prieta," *This Bridge Called My Back: Writings by Radical Women of Color*, eds. Cherríe Moraga and Gloria Anzaldúa (Watertown, Mass.: Persephone Press, Inc., 1981), p. 202.

84. Sandra M. Gilbert and Susan Gubar, *The Madwoman in the Attic: The Woman Writer and the Nineteenth-Century Literary Imagination* (New Haven, Conn.: Yale University Press, 1979), p. 356.

85. Doris Lessing, *The Four-Gated City* (New York: Alfred A. Knopf, 1969), p. 3.

86. Ibid., p. 114.

87. Piercy, *Braided Lives*, p. 22.

88. Carolyn G. Heilbrun, "Marriage Perceived: English Literature 1873–1941," *What Manner of Woman: Essays on English and American Life and Literature*, ed. Marlene Springer (New York: New York University Press, 1977), p. 160.

89. Ibid.

90. Piercy, *Small Changes*, p. 212.

91. Ibid., p. 329.

92. Marilou B. McLaughlin, "Sexual Politics in *The Man Who Loved Children*," *Ball State University Forum* 21 (Autumn 1980): 37.

93. de Beauvoir, *The Second Sex*, p. 519.

94. Ibid., p. 395.

95. Piercy, *Small Changes*, p. 22.

96. Ibid., p. 32.

97. Ibid., p. 48.

98. French, *The Bleeding Heart*, p. 145.

99. Piercy, *Small Changes*, p. 339.

100. Stead, *The Man Who Loved Children*, p. 393.

101. Nin, *A Woman Speaks*, p. 223.

102. James W. Tuttleton, " 'Combat in the Erogenous Zone': Women in the American Novel Between the Two World Wars," *What Manner*

of Woman: Essays on English and American Life and Literature, ed. Marlene Springer (New York: New York University Press, 1977), p. 271.

103. Mitzi Myers, "Harriet Martineau's Autobiography: The Making of a Female Philosopher," *Women's Autobiography: Essays in Criticism*, ed. Estelle C. Jelinek (Bloomington: Indiana University Press, 1980), p. 59.

104. Patricia Meyer Spacks, *The Female Imagination* (New York : Alfred A. Knopf, 1975), p. 115.

105. Ihab Hassan, "The Idea of Adolescence in American Fiction," *American Quarterly* 10 (Fall 1958): 315.

106. Piercy, *Small Changes*, pp. 230–31.

107. Ibid., p. 484.

108. Leslie A. Fiedler, *Love and Death in the American Novel* (New York: Criterion Books, 1960), p. xviii.

109. Ibid., p. xix.

110. Snyder-Ott, "The Female Experience," p. 18.

111. Lessing, *The Golden Notebook*, p. 661.

112. Helen Yglesias, *How She Died* (Boston: Houghton Mifflin Co., 1972), p. 49.

113. Ibid., p. 94.

114. Lessing, *A Ripple from the Storm*, pp. 176–77.

115. Piercy, *Small Changes*, p. 346.

116. Louise Meriwether, *Daddy was a Number Runner* (New York: Prentice-Hall, Inc., 1971), pp. 41–42.

117. Ibid., p. 187.

118. Ibid., p. 67.

119. Moraga and Anzaldúa, *This Bridge Called My Back*, p. 170.

120. Patsy Schweickart, "Reading Ourselves," p. 8 of paper submitted to Florence Howe Essay Contest to appear in *Reader, Texts, Contexts: Essays on Gender and Reading*, eds. Flynn and Schweickart (Baltimore: Johns Hopkins University Press, to be published Dec., 1985).

121. Moraga and Anzaldúa, *This Bridge Called My Back*, p. 154.

122. Walker, *The Color Purple*, p. 88.

123. Ibid., p. 90.

124. Piercy, *Small Changes*, p. 460.

125. Ibid., p. 194.

126. Erazim V. Kohak, "Being Young in a Postindustrial Society," *The Seventies: Problems and Proposals*, eds. Irving Howe and Michael Harrington (New York: Harper and Row, Publishers, 1972), pp. 159–62.

127. de Beauvoir, *The Second Sex*, p. 57.
128. Piercy, *Braided Lives*, p. 551.
129. de Beauvoir, *The Second Sex*, pp. 226–27.
130. Harriette Arnow, *The Dollmaker* (New York: Macmillan Co., 1958), p. 105.

6
Conclusion

Although each of the novels discussed in the previous chapters has been reviewed as a feminist novel, all also have their parts to play in other traditions. Smedley's *Daughter of Earth*, for example, cannot be overlooked in a review of the proletarian novel. *The Dollmaker* and *The Street* are as representative of naturalism as they are of feminism. In addition, the modernist elements of many of the recent novels are of marked importance. Investigations of how these novels fit into various categories and how they might differ from similar male-authored novels could be of great interest. Further, the interplay or disjunction between the novels' feminism and their other qualities could reveal a great deal about them. Such studies will help to incorporate more female-authored literature into the literary and critical canons because they will elucidate how such material melds with and differs from male-oriented traditions. Work must simultaneously be invested in delineating female literary history and female literary genres; literature can benefit substantially from such descriptive criticism.

Worthy of study, too, are more specific and less historically focused subjects, such as the many different uses to which women novelists put modern forms. Most of the authors studied here believe that the structures of fiction should help to make art understandable.¹ Since women so often live in that part of life which has no order,² the ability to shape and form and create—to give meaning to the world anew in one's work—brings a special satisfaction. Just as "[man] began to express himself through the shape he imposed upon the world, to think of the world and of himself,"³ so, too, are women now forming their world and their vision of it. The statement that "this world, always belonging to men, still retains the form they have given it"⁴ must now be subjected to qualification. Perhaps it is merely a coincidence that so many feminist novels have been written in the last eighty years. It is also possible, however, that modern form and experimentation are especially well suited and easily shaped to women's issues and feminist ideology. Certainly, the uses that women authors make of modern stylistic devices are keys to the meanings of their novels. There are many more novels to consider than have been mentioned here and many more areas to investigate. In the area of symbolism alone, one might look at the woman author's use of nature and natural features. The portrayal of landscape and of birds in novels by women has been brought up briefly in critical works by Elizabeth Hardwick, Ellen Moers, and Simone de Beauvoir, but there is surely more to be learned. Virginia Woolf suggests that the presentation of female friendships in the female-authored novel will be of great importance, but little study has yet been given to this feature. In addition, the ways in which women authors perceive words and language generally are of central concern, especially in the political novel. An analysis of the presentation of states of madness and violence in the feminist novel or the female-authored novel would also prove useful to an understanding of the individual novels. Finally, serious attention must be given to the meaning of the movement in both feminism and the feminist novel away from the rational and toward the mystical, the clairvoyant, and the telepathic. All these areas can provide fertile beginnings for investigation.

This study deals with individual feminist novels and with the genre. When all the novels are considered together, they comprise a massive attack on the modern world. There are several characteristics of this world that the novels present as

Conclusion   183

significant. First, this modern world is characterized by totalitarianism, defeated radicalism, and disabled liberalism.[5] Second, these novels show a world in which the "modern," in both history and literature, is the equivalent of extreme situations and radical solutions.[6] The main tendencies at work on the earth are an unremitting organization of society and an unending creation of new, vast destructive energies against civilization.[7] Third, in the new world, one confronts massism and the mass society.[8] Finally, and perhaps most important, the people inhabiting this world are the victims of uncertainty, insecurity, doubt, chaos, passivity, and nihilism. Their own characteristics are those most contributory to the continuation and solidification of the trends at work in the twentieth century.

Of import to an understanding of the feminist novel is the inherent dichotomy which exists between Orwell's *1984* and Huxley's *Brave New World*. In general, *1984* is more applicable to Russia than the United States, and its world calls forth the rebel. On the other hand, *Brave New World*, in general is more applicable to the United States than to some other countries, and its world calls forth the passive victim. It is Huxley's portrayal, minus his reactionary attitudes, that most fully describes the modern world as the feminist novel sees it. This is partly so because the feminist novels discussed here are written by Western, English-speaking women. The world they picture is epitomized by the sedated human mannequin seated in front of the wall screen in *Fahrenheit 451*. It is a brave new world focused beyond freedom and dignity, a world that will not end with a bang but with a muted whimper. The terror of this world is that it produces a need on the part of its people for mindlessness, unthinking peace and security, and complete dependence. In effect, it produces the most prominent psychosis of the twentieth century—the need to escape from freedom.[9] Huxley's brand of primitivism is not an adequate alternative to this world.

To the extent that an ideology is partly a response to a fear, the feminist canon as it is presented in these novels is partly a response to this vision of the modern world. Because of the sophistication of this viewpoint, an important part of the feminist canon resides paradoxically in its suspicion of ideology.

This feminist hostility toward ideology includes two basic assumptions that must be understood. First, since the modern period is epitomized by ideology, everyone feels pushed toward aligning with one even though no ideology can encompass all of an individual's ideals and values. Anna provides a perfect example in *The Golden Notebook* when she explains why she joined the Communist Party. She states "the left people were the only people in the town with any kind of moral energy."[10] She can, of course, possess moral energy of her own; but she feels compelled to make a stand with a group and with an ideology. Later, too, when reading a newspaper attack on the Soviet Union, she writes, "What they said about it seemed to me true enough, but the tone—malicious, gloating, triumphant, sickened me, and I felt glad I had joined the Party."[11] The newspaper takes the recent failures of the Soviet Union as a sign that those Communist values Anna admires are also false, and Anna feels obliged to resist what she opposes by aligning with what she does not believe in. This aspect is similar to George Orwell's observation that fascism drives one to join any group it persecutes.

Second, this need to connect oneself with an ideology is part of what feminism attacks in the twentieth century. One can seek the comfort of an ideology because of one's need to be dependent. An ideology can provide the "consolation and protective monism of a system."[12] An ideology is also essential if a modern ruler is to hold his/her followers, and it also gives those rulers psychological and moral assurance.[13] As Irving Howe states in *Politics and the Novel*, the methods of new dictatorships demand the establishment of an ideology and the concomitant arousal of mass support.[14] He further asserts that "In our time ideology cannot be avoided, ... But ideology is also a great sickness of our time—and this is true despite one's suspicion of most of the people who say so."[15] At the same time that the feminist novel forms an ideology, it attempts to avoid ideology altogether. In effect, it urges one to be alert enough to follow justice as it changes sides. One cannot adhere to a set of rules set down by an ideology because the problems of the modern world are insidious and in flux. There are no practical

Conclusion 185

guides in these novels. A lock-step approach will not permit one to deal with the problems of the twentieth century.

This is also part of the reason that feminism, as it develops in these novels, is individualistic. This is not the brand of individualism that holds the individual of more importance than the mass but one that demands that the individual must not perish in the twentieth century. The individual is not to be separated from other people, but neither is s/he to be subsumed by the group. Individualism is effectively redefined away from isolation and into a combination of the personal and political, the self and the group. The same novels that put stress on the individual also look forward to a collective sharing. As Agnes Smedley puts it, "Everyone seemed to hover close to some tantalizing, communal racial memory."[16]

The emphasis that the feminist novel puts on individualism also includes a deep respect for personal emotions and feelings. The feminist novel demands that a person be evaluated quite apart from her/his ideology or political views. In its elevation of feeling over ideology, the feminist novel supports Bertrand Russell's view that "kindliness and tolerance are worth all the creeds in the world."[17] Maryrose in *The Golden Notebook*, separated from ideology, provides an excellent example of the importance of feeling and emotion. Maryrose is so intertwined with and closely connected to the center of her feelings that she is never led astray. Whatever runs counter to decency and kindness she instantly rejects because she does not rely on jargon or try to reason away the differences between wrong and right. As Anna says of Maryrose, "she had a capacity for silencing us all."[18]

In most instances, the individual is evaluated in the feminist novel as an individual, not as a member of a group or as a supporter of an ideology. In general, Anna's classification of some of her friends as good people and some as not, despite their supposedly similar beliefs and goals, would be instantly supported by the outlook of the other novels.[19] In these novels, the only acceptable reason for supporting an ideology is that it meshes with one's best emotions and one's sense of humanity. As Anna remarks of Ted Brown, "He was the only genuine socialist of the three—I mean socialist in his instincts, in his nature."[20] If one supports an ideology because the head is convinced while the heart remains untouched, one is left open to accepting all sorts of logical horrors.

Being in touch with the heart, the emotions, the senses, remains, then, an essential part of the feminist canon. Good and evil exist; they are personal as well as world-wide; they are represented by what people are and do and feel and think. Mary McCarthy presents one very important aspect of this insistence on the reality of good and evil in *The Company She Keeps*. When the heroine thinks over her visits to her psychiatrist, she notes of her husband:

That was what he had sent her to the doctor for—a perfectly simple little operation. First comes the anesthetic, the sweet, optimistic laughing-gas of science (you are not bad, you are merely unhappy, the bathtub murderer is "sick," the Dead End kid is a problem child, poor Hitler is a paranoiac, and that dirty fornication in a hotel room, why, that, dear Miss Sargent, is a "relationship"). After consciousness has been put to sleep, it is a very easy matter (just look the other way please; it isn't going to hurt, but the sight of the instruments seems to disturb excitable people like yourself), it is a very easy matter to cut out the festering conscience, which was of no use to you at all, and was only making you suffer. Then the patient takes a short rest and emerges as a cured neurotic; the personality has vanished, but otherwise he is perfectly normal.... He has returned to the Garden of Eden, the apple is back on the tree, the snake is a sportive phallus.
...

Already, in her own case, the effects of treatment were noticeable. "You have lost those unnatural high spirits," her friends told her. "You are not so tense as you used to be. You don't get so excited about causes." It was true, she was more subdued; she did not assert herself in company; she let her husband talk on his own subjects in his own vein; she told white lies, where before she had only told black ones. She learned to suppress the unpleasant, unnecessary truths....

And under the pressure of this, her own sense of truth was weakening.[21]

If one attempts to deny the existence of evil, one succeeds only in denying the good as well and replacing them both with nothing, the epitome of evil in the modern world.

It is this final symptom of nihilism to which the other problems of the modern world lead. In its attack on passivity and roles, the feminist novel attacks the central essence of the brave new world of the twentieth century. To become active and to refuse roles conveniently provided for one requires positive values and goals of one's own. Having neither, passivity and role assumption are nearly foreordained. Politically, one is useless at best. As Irving Howe comments, it is a characteristic of the modern age that people who believe in nothing call themselves liberals.[22] In this world there is no black and white, good and bad, right and wrong. There is only a state of gray formed of relativism, repetitive processes, cyclical occurrences, amoral technology, and behaviorism. While the feminist novel stresses the importance of changing our ways of looking at men and women, at our values, at ourselves, it also emphasizes new goals and a new world view. It seconds Simone de Beauvoir's observation that "aims that transcend individual love and personal happiness can take shape only in a world that recognizes the value both of love and of happiness."[23]

The feminist novel, like most political novels, would welcome the demise of politics. It does not assert that political struggle is the ultimate goal of human life. It does recognize, however, that one cannot really escape politics in our time without also escaping our time altogether. It is true that "to make freedom a fact is the central effort of all political struggle."[24] Yet, the freedom the feminist novel fights for is not denied by visible, concrete bars and prisons. It is denied by the intangible bars and prisons of the modern world. In this world, or any world, "where freedom is absent, politics is fate."[25]

NOTES

1. Erica Jong, *Fear of Flying* (New York: Holt, Rinehart and Winston, 1971), p. 113.
2. Herbert Marder, *Feminism and Art: A Study of Virginia Woolf* (Chicago: University of Chicago Press, 1968), p. 33.
3. Simone de Beauvoir, *The Second Sex*, ed. and trans. H. M. Parshley (1953; reprint, New York: Random House, 1974), p. 74.
4. Ibid., p. 756.

5. Irving Howe, *Politics and the Novel* (New York: Horizon Press, Inc., 1957), p. 199.

6. Irving Howe, *A World More Attractive: A View of Modern Literature and Politics* (New York: Horizon Press, Inc., 1963), p. ix.

7. Ihab Hassan, *Radical Innocence: Studies in the Contemporary American Novel* (Princeton, N.J.: Princeton University Press, 1961), p. 14.

8. Howe, *A World More Attractive*, p. 84.

9. Susan Koppelman Cornillon, ed., "The Fiction of Fiction," *Images of Women in Fiction: Feminist Perspectives* (Bowling Green, Ohio: Bowling Green University Popular Press, 1972), p. 122.

10. Doris Lessing, *The Golden Notebook* (New York: Simon and Schuster, Inc., 1962), p. 69.

11. Ibid., p. 156.

12. Alfred Kazin, *On Native Grounds: An Interpretation of Modern American Prose Literature* (New York: Reynal and Hitchcock, 1942), p. 377.

13. Howe, *Politics and the Novel*, p. 249.

14. Ibid., p. 102.

15. Ibid., p. 71.

16. Agnes Smedley, *Daughter of Earth* (1929; reprint, Old Westbury, N.Y.: The Feminist Press, 1973), p. 26.

17. Daniel Aaron, *Writers on the Left: Episodes in American Literary Communism* (New York: Harcourt, Brace and World, Inc., 1961), p. 59. From Bertrand Russell, "Soviet Russia—1920," *The Nation* 111 (July 31, 1920): 121–26.

18. Lessing, *The Golden Notebook*, p. 90.

19. Ibid., p. 109.

20. Ibid., p. 79.

21. Mary McCarthy, *The Company She Keeps* (1942; reprint, New York: Harcourt, Brace, and World, Inc., 1970), pp. 276–80.

22. Howe, *Politics and the Novel*, p. 111.

23. de Beauvoir, *The Second Sex*, p. 240.

24. Patricia Meyer Spacks, *The Female Imagination* (New York: Alfred A. Knopf, 1975), p. 309.

25. Howe, *Politics and the Novel*, p. 87.

Appendix: Critical Literature on the Political Novel

The words "politics" and "feminist" are capable of arousing an almost endless number of definitions and interpretations. They are also capable of arousing highly emotional responses. As a result, most authors of criticism on the political novel have tried to be very specific about what they think it is. Reviewing and examining this criticism can help to clarify what one means when speaking of the political and feminist novel. The variety of interpretations is itself instructive. Joseph Blotner describes the political novel in terms of its effect on the reader. He views the novel as a political instrument if it attempts to gain the reader's support for a cause, arouses his or her distaste for a course of action, or produces a re-evaluation of previously accepted political beliefs.[1] Like all definitions based on the reader's response, this one has some limits to its usefulness. One can only surmise how most readers might respond to a novel, and, consequently, one can only arbitrarily decide whether or not a novel is political. This definition has the further disadvantage of limiting political novels to those having quantitative, utilitarian functions and effects.

Another critic, Gordon Milne, classifies the American political novel as a genre beginning in the early nineteenth century and marked by "the presence of political ideas and of the political milieu."[2] This definition is quite broad, so Milne qualifies it by adding that he "generally steers clear of the economic, social protest, proletarian, and utopian ideas."[3] He describes the nineteenth-century political novel as being relatively free of ideological discussion, focusing instead on the political scene and its actors and revealing the corruption, dishonesty, and ugliness found there. Both the political machinery and its officials are charged with corruption.[4] Describing these novels as essentially reformist, Milne states that in the early history of the political novel, the reforms are mild and that later, in Bellamy's *Looking Backward*, for example, they become more sweeping.[5] Although it seems odd indeed to label *Looking Backward* "reformist," most of the novels Milne considers are just that. Ihab Hassan states that political novels are not often successful in pushing through from local politics to the wider spheres of motive and idea,[6] but the novels examined by Milne do not even attempt it. Generally, if one narrows the definition of "political novel" to novels dealing with the formal structures of governments, with the machinations of Congress, or with party politics, one often restricts oneself to discussing novels written by very pragmatic authors who are somewhat less interested than most in ideas or in literature. Frequently, too, these novels are flawed by unaccomplished artistry. Milne found that many of the novels he discussed were marred by conventional plots, interspersed sentimental romances, and superficial characterizations.[7] The frequency with which these characteristics appear in the novels Milne considers is likely the result of Milne's selective definition rather than the unavoidable result of a novel's being political.

Morris Speare's definition of the political novel leans even more toward the realm of practical politics than does Milne's, and so has similar difficulties connected with it. Speare also includes the novel's effect on the reader in his definition. He suggests that the political novel is

a work of prose fiction which leans rather to "ideas" than to "emotions"; which deals rather with the machinery of law-making or with a theory about public conduct than with the merits of any given piece of legislation; and where the main purpose of the writer is party propaganda, public reform, or exposition of the lives of the personages who maintain government, or of the forces which constitute government.[8]

Irving Howe's description of the political novel is both more general and more inclusive than most critics'. His is the definition that Milne relies on most heavily. Indeed, their definitions are almost identical as Howe states that a political novel is one "in which political ideas play a dominant role or in which the political milieu is the dominant setting."[9] The primary difference between the two is that Howe does not "steer clear" of the economic, social protest, proletarian, and utopian areas. As a result, though his definition is quite general, it does allow him to discuss much more exciting and thought-provoking novels than Milne.

Another difficulty encountered in defining the political novel involves its separation from novels which are only clothed in the trappings of politics. For instance, Walter Rideout, in distinguishing between the radical and bourgeois novel, describes the bourgeois novel as exhibiting an animus against the surface manifestations of the acquisitive society. In other words, it rails against the coarseness and stupidity of society without actually attacking its economic injustice.[10] This type of novel seems to Rideout more representative of social criticism than of political statement. Perhaps such a novel springs from what Daniel Aaron calls the writer's sensitivity to the disparity between society's ideals and its practices and from hostility to a world that slights the artist's needs and values.[11]

There is a sense in which all art is political or propagandistic because it reflects some vision of the world.[12] All novels are not political to the same degree, however. Authors who avoid propaganda may be castigated by others who adhere strongly to a fixed dogma. As Edmund Wilson states, though, a first-rate book by an agonizing bourgeois may have more human value and revolutionary power than the statements of the second-rate Marxists who attack it.[13] Even novels that on the surface appear to have nothing to do with politics may carry a strong message. Doris Lessing's Anna says of such novels, "If Marxism means anything, it means that a little novel about the emotions should reflect 'what's real' since the emotions are a function and a product of a society."[14] Such statements reflect an awareness that novels can be political without being propagandistic and without losing artistic merit.

Yet other novels may be political only in that they reflect the author's unconscious acceptance of existing values and institutions.[15] Kenneth and Patricia Dolbeare argue that denying either capability or concern for changing the future is a political statement. Such helplessness or unconcern effectively celebrates whatever ideology is currently orthodox and allows acquiescence in the management of one's future by others.[16] In this view all literature is political. Even art presumably dealing solely with the individual psyche has political ramifications and makes a silent statement about the relative importance of the individual versus class or social reality. One can reason that the individual is affected strongly by his or her culture and by social change. Consequently, each author's societal and class position and time period produce different viewpoints.

In looking at all literature as political, one can even find that "a pastoral poem might very well by implication undermine chain stores."[17] This view of literature is of obvious import generally. Its insights are especially helpful critically when one is dealing with a work definitely and substantively political. Conceivably, a critic could discover something meaningful by investigating the politics of literature which disavows politics; but too often, one ends up railing against the supposedly non-political works rather than finding anything of interest in them. In so doing, the reader misses some of the most important aspects of such literature. An author's sensitivity, compassion, and concern for the human being can do a great deal to counter-balance the absence of political direction in his or her work or the absolute silliness of his or her political beliefs. Paradoxically, an author in his or her own life can be politically incoherent and even vicious and yet can write sensitive literature which impels readers toward a concerned, humanistic politics—one much more sympathetic and perceptive than the author possesses. One can agree that "any problem, any human trouble, has its attachments to institutions and issues, attachments which ought to be visible to the reader even when the writer has ignored them."[18] One can agree, but one must also add that the writer ought not to be condemned for having ignored them, and the reader ought not to be condemned to viewing such attachments in any one single way. It is critical that one be able to sympathize with the aggravation of a black critic who states, "It is as if it were defined, in the eternal constitution of things, that to be a Negro artist in America one must, in some way, be a race-conscious artist."[19]

Such concerns are tangential to the feminist novel, however, because political ideas are its dominant force. The intellectual theories and premises underlying such novels are of prime importance and all suggest a need for basic change and restructuring in Western government, culture, and society, rather than simply reform or modification. These novels are not pragmatic strategy maps nor are they centered on the practical workings of government. They support Irving Howe's statement that Henry Adams' *Democracy* is not a political novel in the sense that *The Possessed* and *Felix Holt* are. That is, the former concerns itself basically with the procedures of government and with practical politics while the latter two focus on "classes in combat, voices threatening from the social depths, intellectuals yearning to reach 'the people.' "[20] The feminist novel is much more like these last two than like Adams' *Democracy*. Similarly, the definition of the feminist novel used in the preceding study aligns itself more closely with Howe's appraisal of the political novel than with the perspectives of the more pragmatically oriented critics. Literature need not be apolitical to be "good" or even "great." It is often only our definitions that make it seem so.

NOTES

1. Joseph Blotner, *The Political Novel* (Garden City, N.Y.: Doubleday and Co., Inc., 1955), p. 10.
2. Gordon Milne, *The American Political Novel* (Norman: University of Oklahoma Press, 1966), p. 5.
3. Ibid., p. 6.
4. Ibid., p. 32.
5. Ibid., pp. 36–37.
6. Ihab Hassan, *Radical Innocence: Studies in the Contemporary American Novel* (Princeton, N.J.: Princeton University Press, 1961), p. 109.
7. Milne, *The American Political Novel*, pp. 38–39.
8. Morris Edmund Speare, *The Political Novel: Its Development in England and in America* (New York: Oxford University Press, 1924), p. ix.
9. Irving Howe, *Politics and the Novel* (New York: Horizon Press, Inc., 1957), p. 17.
10. Walter B. Rideout, *The Radical Novel in the United States, 1900–1954: Some Interrelations of Literature and Society* (Cambridge, Mass.: Harvard University Press, 1956), p. 115.
11. Daniel Aaron, *Writers on the Left: Episodes in American Literary Communism* (New York: Harcourt, Brace and World, Inc., 1961), p. 1.
12. Henry Hazlitt, "Literature versus Opinion," *The Writer and His Craft*, ed. Robert Morss Lovett (Ann Arbor: The University of Michigan Press, 1954), pp. 50–52.
13. Edmund Wilson, "The Literary Class War: I," *The New Republic* 70 (May 4, 1932): 323.
14. Doris Lessing, *The Golden Notebook* (New York: Simon and Schuster, Inc., 1962), p. 42.
15. Hazlitt, "Literature versus Opinion," pp. 50–52.
16. Kenneth M. and Patricia Dolbeare, *American Ideologies: The Competing Political Beliefs of the 1970's* (Chicago: Rand McNally College Publishing Co., 1976), pp. 220–21.
17. Aaron, *Writers on the Left*, p. 288.
18. Richard Mitchell, "An Age of Issues and a Literature of Troubles," *Western Humanities Review* 17 (Autumn 1963): 350.
19. Nathan Irvin Huggins, *Harlem Renaissance* (1971; reprint, New York: Oxford University Press, Inc., 1974), p. 195.
20. Howe, *Politics and the Novel*, p. 176.

Bibliography

Aaron, Daniel. *Writers on the Left: Episodes in American Literary Communism.* New York: Harcourt, Brace and World, Inc., 1961.
Abel, Elizabeth. "(E)Merging Identities: The Dynamics of Female Friendship in Contemporary Fiction by Women." *Signs: Journal of Women in Culture and Society* 6 (Spring 1981): 413–35.
Abel, Elizabeth, ed. *Critical Inquiry: Writing and Sexual Difference* 8 (Winter 1981): 173–402.
Arnow, Harriette. *The Dollmaker.* New York: Macmillan Co., 1958.
Atherton, Gertrude. *The Conqueror.* No place, no publisher, no date.
Atwood, Margaret. *The Edible Woman.* Boston: Little, Brown, and Co., 1969.
Atwood, Margaret. *Surfacing.* New York: Simon and Schuster, Inc., 1972.
Baym, Nina. "Melodramas of Beset Manhood: How Theories of American Fiction Exclude Women Authors." *American Quarterly* 33 (Summer 1981): 123–39.
Blotner, Joseph. *The Modern American Political Novel 1900–1960.* Austin: University of Texas Press, 1966.
Blotner, Joseph. *The Political Novel.* Garden City, N.Y.: Doubleday and Co., Inc., 1955.
Bluefarb, Sam. *The Escape Motif in the American Novel: Mark Twain to Richard Wright.* Columbus: Ohio State University Press, 1972.

Bree, Germaine. *Women Writers in France: Variations on a Theme.* New Brunswick, N.J.: Rutgers University Press, 1973.

Brophy, Brigid. *Don't Never Forget: Collected Views and Reviews.* London: The Trinity Press, 1966.

Burkom, Selma R. " 'Only Connect': Form and Content in the Works of Doris Lessing." *Critique: Studies in Modern Fiction* 11, no.1 (1963): 51–68.

Chase, Richard. "Radicalism in the American Novel." *Commentary* 23 (January 1957): 65–71.

Chopin, Kate. *The Awakening.* 1899; reprint, New York: W. W. Norton and Co., Inc., 1976.

Christ, Carol P. *Diving Deep and Surfacing: Women Writers on Spiritual Quest.* Boston: Beacon Press, 1980.

Clark, A.F.B. "Purity and Propaganda in Art." *University of Toronto Quarterly* 5 (July 1936): 567–82.

Commager, Henry Steele. *The American Mind: An Interpretation of American Thought and Character Since the 1880's.* New Haven, Conn.: Yale University Press, 1950.

Compton-Burnett, Ivy. *"A Family and a Fortune"* and *"More Women than Men."* New York: Simon and Schuster, Inc., 1965.

Conrad, Joseph. "Author's Note," *Chance.* Garden City, N.Y.: Doubleday, Page and Co., 1925.

Cornillon, Susan Koppelman, ed. *Images of Women in Fiction: Feminist Perspectives.* Bowling Green, Ohio: Bowling Green University Popular Press, 1972.

Critical Inquiry: Writing and Sexual Difference 8 (Winter 1981).

Culley, Margaret. "The Context of *The Awakening.*" *The Awakening,* by Kate Chopin. 1899; reprint, New York: W. W. Norton and Co., Inc., 1976.

de Beauvoir, Simone. *The Second Sex.* Ed. and trans. H. M. Parshley. 1953; reprint, New York: Random House, 1974.

De Man, Paul. "Georg Lukac's *Theory of the Novel.*" *Modern Language Notes* 81 (December 1966): 527–41.

DeVoto, Bernard. *The Literary Fallacy.* Boston: Little, Brown and Co., 1944.

Diamond, Arlyn, and Lee R. Edwards, eds. *The Authority of Experience: Essays in Feminist Criticism.* Amherst: University of Massachusetts Press, 1977.

Doherty, Thomas P. "American Autobiography and Ideology." *The American Autobiography.* Ed. Albert E. Stone. Englewood Cliffs, N.J.: Prentice-Hall, Inc., 1981. 95–108.

Dolbeare, Kenneth M., and Patricia Dolbeare. *American Ideologies:*

Bibliography

The Competing Political Beliefs of the 1970's. Chicago: Rand McNally College Publishing Co., 1976.
Donovan, Josephine, ed. *Feminist Literary Criticism: Explorations in Theory.* Lexington: University Press of Kentucky, 1975.
Drabble, Margaret. *The Waterfall.* New York: Alfred A. Knopf, 1969.
Durham, Marilyn. *The Man Who Loved Cat Dancing.* New York: Harcourt, Brace, Jovanovich, 1972.
Eble, Kenneth. "Introduction." *The Awakening,* by Kate Chopin. 1899; reprint, New York: G. P. Putnam and Sons, 1964. v-xiv.
Eisinger, Chester E. *Fiction of the Forties.* Chicago: University of Chicago Press, 1963.
Fiedler, Leslie A. *Love and Death in the American Novel.* New York: Criterion Books, 1960.
French, Marilyn. *The Bleeding Heart.* New York: Random House, 1980.
French, Marilyn. *The Women's Room.* New York: Harcourt, Brace, Jovanovich, 1977.
Friedman, Alan Warren. *Multivalence: The Moral Quality of Form in the Modern Novel.* Baton Rouge: Louisiana State University Press, 1978.
Gilbert, Sandra M., and Susan Gubar. *The Madwoman in the Attic: The Woman Writer and the Nineteenth-Century Literary Imagination.* New Haven, Conn.: Yale University Press, 1979.
Glasgow, Ellen. *Barren Ground.* New York: The Modern Library, 1936.
Hardwick, Elizabeth. *Seduction and Betrayal: Women and Literature.* New York: Random House, 1974.
Hassan, Ihab. *Radical Innocence: Studies in the Contemporary American Novel.* Princeton, N.J.: Princeton University Press, 1961.
Hassan, Ihab. "The Idea of Adolescence in American Fiction." *American Quarterly* 10 (Fall 1958): 312-24.
Hazlitt, Henry. "Literature versus Opinion." *The Writer and His Craft,* ed. Robert Morss Lovett. Ann Arbor: The University of Michigan Press, 1954. 39-54.
Heilbrun, Carolyn G. *Toward a Recognition of Androgyny.* New York: Alfred A. Knopf, 1973.
Hinz, Evelyn J., ed. *A Woman Speaks: The Lectures, Seminars and Interviews of Anaïs Nin.* London: W. H. Allen and Co., Ltd., 1978.
Hobbs, Glenda. "A Portrait of the Artist as Mother: Harriette Arnow and *The Dollmaker.*" *The Georgia Review* 33 (Winter 1979): 851-66.
Howe, Irving. "Arts and Letters: Literary Criticism and Literary Radicals." *American Scholar* 41 (Winter 1971): 113-20.

Howe, Irving. *Politics and the Novel*. New York: Horizon Press, Inc., 1957.

Howe, Irving, ed. *The Radical Imagination*. New York: The New American Library, Inc., 1955.

Howe, Irving. *A World More Attractive: A View of Modern Literature and Politics*. New York: Horizon Press, 1963.

Howe, Irving, and Michael Harrington, eds. *The Seventies: Problems and Proposals*. New York: Harper and Row, Publishers, 1972.

Huggins, Nathan Irvin. *Harlem Renaissance*. 1971; reprint, New York: Oxford University Press, Inc., 1974.

Jelinek, Estelle C., ed. *Women's Autobiography: Essays in Criticism*. Bloomington: Indiana University Press, 1980.

Jong, Erica. *Fear of Flying*. New York: Holt, Rinehart and Winston, 1971.

Kazin, Alfred. *On Native Grounds: An Interpretation of Modern American Prose Literature*. New York: Reynal and Hitchcock, 1942.

Lauter, Paul. "Afterword." *Daughter of Earth*, by Agnes Smedley. 1929; reprint, Old Westbury, N.Y.: The Feminist Press, 1973. 409–28.

Lessing, Doris. *The Four-Gated City*. New York: Alfred A. Knopf, Inc., 1969.

Lessing, Doris. *The Golden Notebook*. New York: Simon and Schuster, Inc., 1962.

Lessing, Doris. *The Grass is Singing*. London: Michael Joseph, Ltd., 1950.

Lessing, Doris. "Introduction." *The Golden Notebook*. New York: Simon and Schuster, Inc., 1962. vii-xxii.

Lessing, Doris. *Landlocked*. New York: Simon and Schuster, Inc., 1966.

Lessing, Doris. *Martha Quest*. New York: Simon and Schuster, Inc., 1952.

Lessing, Doris. *A Proper Marriage*. New York: The New American Library, Inc., 1954.

Lessing, Doris. *A Ripple from the Storm*. New York: Simon and Schuster, Inc., 1966.

McCarthy, Mary. *The Company She Keeps*. 1942; reprint, New York: Harcourt, Brace and World Inc., 1970.

McCarthy, Mary. *The Group*. New York: The New American Library, Inc., 1954.

McConnell-Ginet, Sally. "Linguistics and the Feminist Challenge." *Women and Language in Literature and Society*. Eds. Sally McConnell-Ginet, Ruth Borkar and Nelly Furman. New York: Praeger Publishers, 1980. 1–25.

McLaughlin, Marilou B. "Sexual Politics in *The Man Who Loved Children*." *Ball State University Forum* 21 (Autumn 1980): 30–37.

Malinowitz, Harriet. "The Limits of Imagination in Doris Lessing's *The Grass is Singing*." *Massachusetts Studies in English* 6, nos. 1 and 2 (1977): 103–10.

Marder, Herbert. *Feminism and Art: A Study of Virginia Woolf*. Chicago: The University of Chicago Press, 1968.

Markow, Alice B. "The Pathology of Feminine Failure in the Fiction of Doris Lessing." *Critique* 16 no. 1 (1974): 88–100.

Meriwether, Louise. *Daddy was a Number Runner*. New York: Prentice-Hall, Inc., 1971.

Miles, David H. "Portrait of the Marxist as a Young Hegelian: Lukacs' *Theory of the Novel*." *PMLA* 94 (January 1979): 22–33.

Millett, Kate. *Sexual Politics*. Garden City, N.Y.: Doubleday and Co., Inc., 1970.

Milne, Gordon. *The American Political Novel*. Norman: University of Oklahoma Press, 1966.

Mitchell, Richard. "An Age of Issues and a Literature of Troubles." *Western Humanities Review* 17 (Autumn 1963): 349–60.

Moers, Ellen. "The Angry Young Women." *Harper's* 227 (December 1963): 88–95.

Moers, Ellen. *Literary Women*. Garden City, N.Y.: Doubleday and Co., Inc., 1976.

Moraga, Cherríe, and Gloria Anzaldúa, eds. *This Bridge Called My Back: Writings by Radical Women of Color*. Watertown, Mass.: Persephone Press, Inc., 1981.

Morrison, Toni. *Sula*. New York: Alfred A. Knopf, 1973.

Morrison, Toni. *Tar Baby*. New York: Alfred A. Knopf, 1981.

Murdock, Iris. *The Red and the Green*. New York: Viking Press, 1965.

Oates, Joyce Carol. *them*. New York: The Vanguard Press, 1969.

Olsen, Tillie. *Yonnondio: From the Thirties*. New York: Delacorte Press, 1974.

Petry, Ann. *The Street*. Boston: Houghton Mifflin Co., 1946.

Piercy, Marge. *Braided Lives*. New York: Random House, 1982.

Piercy, Marge. *Dance the Eagle to Sleep*. New York: Simon and Schuster, Inc., 1971.

Piercy, Marge. *Going Down Fast*. New York: Simon and Schuster, Inc., 1969.

Piercy, Marge. *Small Changes*. 1972; reprint, Greenwich, Conn.: Fawcett Publications, Inc., 1974.

Piercy, Marge. *Woman on the Edge of Time*. New York: Alfred A. Knopf, 1976.

Porter, Katherine Anne. *Ship of Fools*. Boston: Little, Brown and Co., 1945.
Pratt, Annis. "Archetypal Approaches to the New Feminist Criticism." *Bucknell Review* 21 (Spring 1973): 3–14.
Rand, Ayn. *Atlas Shrugged*. New York: Random House, 1957.
Rideout, Walter B. *The Radical Novel in the United States, 1900–1954: Some Interrelations of Literature and Society*. Cambridge, Mass.: Harvard University Press, 1956.
Roiphe, Anne Richardson. *Up the Sandbox!* New York: Simon and Schuster, Inc., 1970.
Rossner, Judith. *Attachments*. New York: Simon and Schuster, Inc., 1977.
Rossner, Judith. *Emmeline*. New York: Simon and Schuster, Inc., 1980.
Rossner, Judith. *Looking for Mr. Goodbar*. New York: Simon and Schuster, Inc., 1975.
Samuelson, Ralph. "Virginia Woolf, *Orlando*, and the Feminist Spirit." *Western Humanities Review* (Winter 1961): 51–58.
Schweickart, Patsy. "Reading Ourselves." *Readers, Texts, Contexts: Essays on Gender and Reading*. Eds. Flynn and Schweickart. Baltimore, Md.: Johns Hopkins University Press, to be published December 1985.
Showalter, Elaine. *A Literature of Their Own: British Women Novelists from Brontë to Lessing*. Princeton, N.J.: Princeton University Press, 1977.
Smedley, Agnes. *Daughter of Earth*. 1929; reprint, Old Westbury, N.Y.: The Feminist Press, 1973.
Smith, Barbara. *Toward a Black Feminist Criticism*. Brooklyn, N.Y.: Out and Out Books, 1977.
Smith, Lillian. *Strange Fruit*. New York: Reynal and Hitchcock, 1944.
Snyder-Ott, Joelynn. "The Female Experience and Artistic Creativity." *Art Education* 27 (September 1974): 15–18.
Spacks, Patricia Meyer, ed. *Contemporary Women Novelists: A Collection of Critical Essays*. Englewood Cliffs, N.J.: Prentice-Hall, Inc., 1977.
Spacks, Patricia Meyer. *The Female Imagination*. New York: Alfred A. Knopf, 1975.
Spangler, George M. "Kate Chopin's *The Awakening*: A Partial Dissent." *Novel* 3 (Spring 1970): 249–55.
Speare, Morris Edmund. *The Political Novel: Its Development in England and America*. New York: Oxford University Press, 1924.
Spender, Stephen. "Writers and Politics." *Partisan Review* 34 (Summer 1967): 359–81.

Springer, Marlene, ed. *What Manner of Woman: Essays on English and American Life and Literature.* New York: New York University Press, 1977.

Stead, Christina. *The Man Who Loved Children.* 1940; reprint, New York: Holt, Rinehart and Winston, 1966.

Stone, Albert E. "Autobiography in American Culture: Looking Back at the Seventies." *American Studies International* 19 (Spring/Summer 1981): 3–14.

Trilling, Lionel. "Contemporary American Literature in Its Relation to Ideas." *American Quarterly* 1 (Fall 1949): 195–208.

Utter, Robert Palfrey, and Gwendolyn Bridges Needham. *Pamela's Daughters.* New York: Macmillan Co., 1936.

Walker, Alice. *The Color Purple.* New York: Simon and Schuster, Inc., 1982.

Walker, Alice. *Meridian.* New York: Simon and Schuster, Inc., 1976.

Wilson, Edmund. "The Literary Class War: I." *New Republic* 70 (May 4, 1932): 319–23.

Wilson, Edmund. "Marxism and Literature." *Atlantic Monthly* 160 (December 1937): 741–50.

Wilson, Edmund. *Patriotic Gore: Studies in the Literature of the American Civil War.* New York: Oxford University Press, 1962. 587–93.

Wimsatt, W. K., Jr., and M. C. Beardsley. "The Affective Fallacy." *Sewanee Review* 57 (Winter 1949): 31–55.

Woolf, Virginia. *Orlando, A Biography.* New York: Harcourt, Brace and Co., 1928.

Woolf, Virginia. *A Room of One's Own.* New York: Harcourt, Brace and Co., 1929.

Yglesias, Helen. *How She Died.* Boston: Houghton Mifflin Co., 1972.

Index

androgyny, 93
anger, 114
anti-authoritarianism, 12, 37–40
Arnow, Harriette. See *Dollmaker, The*
Atwood, Margaret. See *Edible Woman, The*
authorial stance, 33–36
authority, 34, 45–51
autobiography, 35–41, 72
Awakening, The (Chopin): authorial stance, 9; children, 18–20, 169; conclusion of novel, 17–18; maturity, 20–21; prototype, 8–9; roles, 12–14, 53–54; success, 174; symbolism, 23–26; talent, 16–17, 21–22; work, 174

black-authored and white-authored feminist novels, 158, 171–173
Bleeding Heart, The (French), 144

Braided Lives (Piercy), 118, 144, 149, 154, 160

children, 18–20, 166–170
Chopin, Kate. See *Awakening, The*
Color Purple, The (Walker): authority, 46; ending, 118; individualism, 54–55; money, 171, 172; multiple narrators, 72–73; sex, 155, 157–158
community, sense of, 58–60
Company She Keeps, The (McCarthy), 186; authorial stance, 38, 39–40; authority, 47–48; fragmented form, 76; men, 151; passivity, 126; point of view, 73; roles, 90–91

Daddy was a Number Runner (Meriwether), 58–59, 111, 170–171
Daughter of Earth (Smedley), 94; authorial stance, 40–41;

authority, 49–50, 52; children, 169; ending, 104–106; group, 57–58; guilt, 128–129; marriage, 159; Marxism, 49–50; men, 144–145; money, 172; naturalism, 181; unity, 85; work, 174
Dollmaker, The (Arnow): authority, 48; children, 167, 168; community, 58; ending, 114; individualism, 56; maturity, 164–165; money, 172–173; self-doubt, 130–131; work, 175

Edible Woman, The (Atwood), 84, 116–118, 163
Emmeline (Rossner), 113–114
emotion, 44, 144, 186
endings: death, 17–18, 102, 111–115; escape, 101–111; victory, 115–121
entrapment, 139

Fear of Flying (Jong): authority, 46; ending, 116–117; fragmented character, 71; maturity, 165–66; men, 143–144; sex, 154–155; work, 174
female friendships, 182
feminism, 27–28, 105
feminist authors, 138
feminist novel, definition of, 4–7
food, 23–24, 161–163
form, literary, 181–182
form of the novel, 7–8
Four-Gated City, The (Lessing), 120
fragmentation, 67–68, 71, 95
fragmented characters, 70–71
fragmented novel, 68, 73–77
freedom, 163–164, 174–175, 183, 187
French, Marilyn. See *Bleeding Heart, The*; *Women's Room, The*
frigidity, 157, 161

Golden Notebook, The (Lessing), 34–35; authorial stance, 38; children, 166; ending, 115, 127; fragmentation, 71–72, 73–75, 78–83; ideology, 44–45, 184; individualism, 185–186; men, 142; reportage, 61–62; roles, 91–93; work, 174
Grass is Singing, The (Lessing), 112–113, 174
guilt, 114, 128–129

homosexuality, 89–90, 112, 152
How She Died (Yglesias): children, 165–166, 167, 168; community, 60; ending, 118–119; ideology, 43; passivity, 124–125; point of view, 69–70, 77; success, 174; work, 174

ideology, 41–45, 48–49, 183–185
individualism, 52–53, 54–56, 185
insanity, 5–6, 182

Jong, Erica. See *Fear of Flying*

Landlocked (Lessing), 106, 126–127, 146
Lessing, Doris, 82, 126–127. See also *Four-Gated City, The; Golden Notebook, The; Grass is Singing, The; Landlocked; Proper Marriage, A; Ripple from the Storm, A*
Looking for Mr. Goodbar (Rossner): authority, 48–49; children, 169–170; community, 59–60; ending, 111–112; guilt,

129; individualism, 55–56; roles, 86–90

McCarthy, Mary. See *Company She Keeps, The*
Man Who Loved Children, The (Stead): authority, 47; children, 169; ending, 106–107; food, 163; men, 146–151; money, 173; racism, 152; roles, 54; violence, 153–154
marriage, 23, 27, 85–86, 109–110, 158–161
Marxism, 42, 49–50, 74, 106
mass, importance of the, 56–58
maturity, 115–116, 121–122, 164–165
men, 80–81, 83–84, 139–154
Meridian (Walker), 118, 171
Meriwether, Louise. See *Daddy was a Number Runner*
modern novel, 181
modern world, 102, 182–187
money, 170–172
mysticism, 182

narrators, multiple, 69–73
nationality, 4
naturalism, 181
nature, symbolic use of, 182
nihilism, 82–83
nineteenth century, the, 27–28, 62, 67, 95

objectivity, 38–40
Orlando (Woolf), 86

passivity, 75, 83, 91, 123–128, 187
patriarchy, 48, 102, 109–110, 152, 158, 161
personal and political views, 45, 58–60, 93–94

Petry, Ann. See *Street, The*
Piercy, Marge. See *Braided Lives; Small Changes; Woman on the Edge of Time*
point of view, multiple, 68–69, 72–73
political novel, 7, 8, 187
political revolt, 25
politics, 187
pornography, 93
possessiveness, 148, 149–151, 160, 161
proletarian novel, 181
Proper Marriage, A (Lessing): children, 169; ending, 106; roles, 92–93; unity, 83; work, 174

racism, 103, 110, 112, 113, 152
rape, 105, 156, 160
realism, 16
reality, 16
relationships, male and female, 5, 105
reportage, 60–62
Ripple from the Storm, A (Lessing), 139, 168–169
Roiphe, Anne. See *Up the Sandbox!*
roles, 53–56, 67–68, 85–93, 187
romanticism, 14–16
Room of One's Own, A (Woolf), 171
Rossner, Judith. See *Emmeline; Looking for Mr. Goodbar*

self-doubt, 129–131
self-limitation, 83–85
sex, 89, 112, 143, 154–158
sexism, 112, 113
sexuality, 24–26, 80, 113, 152, 154–158
Small Changes (Piercy): author-

ity, 46, 47, 48, 50–51; children, 169; ending, 106–108, 118–120; food, 161–163; fragmented form, 75; group, 56–57; guilt, 129; marriage, 160–161; maturity, 165; men, 139–142; money, 173; passivity, 124; point-of-view, 72; roles, 90; sex, 155; success, 174; work, 174
Smedley, Agnes. See *Daughter of Earth*
socialism, 42
Stead, Christina. See *Man Who Loved Children, The*
Street, The (Petry): authority, 48, 51–52; children, 166–167; ending, 102–104; guilt, 128; money, 170, 171; naturalism, 181; work, 174
subjectivity, 38–40, 44
success, 22, 174
suicide, 18, 111–112, 153
symbolism, 182

talent, exceptional, 16–17, 108–109

twentieth century, the, 28, 42, 45–46, 62, 82–83, 95, 101–102, 184–185

unity, 67–68, 77–82, 83–85, 95
Up the Sandbox! (Roiphe): children, 169; ending, 110; fragmented character, 70–71, 76–77; men, 142–143; passivity, 125–126

violence, 83–84, 152, 153

Walker, Alice. See *Color Purple, The*; *Meridian*
war, 83–84
Woman on the Edge of Time (Piercy), 114–115, 144
Women's Room, The (French), 55, 84–85, 111, 169
women's writing, 33
Woolf, Virginia. See *Orlando; Room of One's Own, A*
work, 22–23, 173–174

Yglesias, Helen. See *How She Died*

About the Author

JUDI M. ROLLER, a specialist in women writers and contemporary American literature, is Associate Registrar and Adjunct Assistant Professor of English at Wright State University, Dayton, Ohio. She has contributed to *College and University*.